Evaluating Educational Environments

Robert M. Smith
Pennsylvania State University

John T. Neisworth
Pennsylvania State University

John G. Greer
Memphis State University

With contributions by
Sara J. Forsberg, Pennsylvania State University
Richard M. Titus, U.S. Department of Justice

Charles E. Merrill Publishing Company
A Bell & Howell Company

Columbus   Toronto   London   Sydney

W

Published by Charles E. Merrill Publishing Company
A Bell and Howell Company
Columbus, Ohio 43216

This book was set in Times Roman, Helvetica, and Gothica.
The production editor was Jan Hall.
The cover was prepared by Will Chenoweth.

Cover photograph by Tom Hutchinson.
Chapter photographs: 1, 4, and 7—*Values and Teaching*, Merrill, 1977; 2, 3, and
6—*Resource Teaching*, Merrill, 1978; 5—George Smith.
(1925)

Library of Congress Catalog Card Number: 77–93480

International Standard Book Number: 0–675–08388–5

1 2 3 4 5 6 7 8 9 10—85 84 83 82 81 80 79 78

Printed in the United States of America

Preface

Astute diagnosticians are presently well beyond the point of focusing their assessment efforts exclusively on the child. For decades evaluation of the child was the sole orientation of the testing movement. Multiple forays were made into the psycho-educational domains of school children, to characterize, analyze, and discern cause-and-effect relationships in order to understand behavior. What makes this child's behavior or performance undesirable? And moreover, what can we do about it? All familiar cries of teachers. Sadly, this vigorous and expensive testing movement yielded minimal results in helping educators teach better or children learn better. Tests became fancier and the evaluators grew more attentive to administrative procedures and norms, but the actual usefulness of the information gathered was disappointing. In fact, the devilish question remains whether flipping a coin or tossing dice might not have been more help in determining which teaching method or instructional device should be used for a given child or group of children.

Indeed, at present we cannot say with assurance that such frivolous and random selection of an educational program would harm or help a child's educational progress more than the most sophisticated paraphernalia used today in many individual diagnostic efforts. However, we know if those in medicine, law, and pharmacy would support the untried and untested approaches we have used in education, they would be candidates for malpractice litigation. All around us are increasing number of students who wish to enter college and yet who have significant reading problems or difficulty in balancing a checkbook. These students are in severe need of remedial courses in the basic skills. Recently, a more aware public has begun to insist that school districts do a better job in helping children acquire higher levels of these basic skills.

While the tests grew popular, research on the nature of human learning established that the character of our experiences influences profoundly the quantity and quality of our learning. A quality environment will foster quality learning—an impoverished environment will lead to impoverished learning.

It was somewhat paradoxical that the testing movement emphasized the assessment of individuals at the same time the psychological and educational research strongly documented the powerful influence of the environment on learning. Yet, very little attention was given to assessing the characteristics of the environment. Strange, isn't it, that colleges have not provided formal instruction and supervised clinical experiences to help preservice teachers assess the instructional environment? Almost never is the inhibiting influence of an environment explored by questions such as these:

1. Does a teacher tend to give more negative reactions than positive rewards?

2. Does the physical environment of the classroom hinder easy communication among children when an objective of the lesson is to stimulate spontaneity in communication?

3. Are the proper instructional materials being used for a given lesson?

4. Is the instructional program sequenced throughout the day to capitalize on high-preference activities of the children, in order to enlist their full participation in low-preference activities?

5. Are there peculiarities in the social environment within the classroom that cause certain children to be cross or uncooperative?

Teacher Diagnosis of Educational Difficulties (1969) was written to assist teachers in assessing the daily progress of students in their classrooms; it looked specifically at the behavior and performance of the child. *Evaluating Educational Environments* is designed to help teachers become evaluators of the environment. It proposes that teachers are environmental manipulators; they are responsible for arranging each child's instructional environment to increase the likelihood that the child will learn in certain ways. To decide how the environment should be manipulated and structured, teachers must first be able to make accurate and reliable assessments of the pertinent characteristics of the instructional setting. In other words, *if we can't define it and assess it, it's difficult to know how to manipulate it.*

This book may be used as a supplementary text in any course on evaluation in education or any course on designing educational programs for children. We also believe that practicing teachers will find much of immediate value in these pages. To aid teachers and others in evaluating educational environments, two assessment instruments have been included for each major environmental area: a self-assessment checklist and an environmental profile. These tools are not designed to provide detailed evaluations; however, they will help evaluators gather, summarize, and interpret information about important environmental influences. A comprehensive profile at the end of the book summarizes the evaluation of all environmental areas. Perhaps, then, with the help of these tools, teachers can begin to develop as much skill in evaluating the strengths and weaknesses of the environment as they have in evaluating the strengths and weaknesses of children's performances. When this happens, the effectiveness of educational programs for children will be enhanced immeasurably.

Special thanks to Dr. Sara J. Forsberg, assistant professor of special education at Pennsylvania State University for contributing Chapter 3. Also thanks to Dr. Richard M. Titus, program manager of environmental design for the U.S. Department of Justice, for Chapter 5 and assistance with Chapter 7.

We express our particular appreciation to Mrs. JoAnn Dreibelbis and Mrs. Rebecca Young for their skillful assistance in typing this manuscript.

Contents

5 Evaluating the Physical Environment 127

6 Evaluating Community Services 157

7 Building an Effective Child and Environmental Evaluation Program 173

1

The Importance of Environmental Evaluation

The ability to make appropriate and pertinent judgments is a necessary personal quality for effective teaching and is a highly valued attribute in teachers. Decisions must constantly be made by every teacher about every child within a classroom. All decisions result in the teacher's taking some course of action, and it is a fundamental assumption that the process of decision making and the resulting action will directly benefit the child. For example, on the basis of their own perceptions, teachers make certain judgments about a child which, in turn, are converted into an instructional program that is presumed to increase certain reading skills. Teachers are also responsible for deciding how to deal effectively with socially inappropriate behavior, or assist youngsters in developing a positive attitude towards school. In short, teachers are in the "behavior business," that is, virtually all of their efforts are directed toward helping children develop more functionally adequate and complex behaviors in academic subject areas, motor skills, communication, and personal and social areas. This summarizes the whole focus of the school program—to help children develop a repertoire of behaviors that are applied in an appropriate and consistent manner.

Teachers are well aware that children differ among themselves in many areas of functioning, often to an extreme degree. In addition, a given child will usually show wide differences in performance among areas of functioning. Charlie is better in arithmetic computation than in arithmetic reasoning, is relatively stronger in spelling than in oral reading, and is able to express himself better in a written mode than orally. Such intra-individual strengths and weaknesses occur in each child's profile. Mabel can sound consonants and vowels but has difficulty remembering a sequence of written symbols, whereas Rebecca is very fast in silent reading but much slower in speaking. Teachers are taught that these types of within-child differences have some potential significance and a wisely conceived educational program will reflect such individual instructional needs. The key question we should ask is, "On what basis does a teacher make judgments about that instructional program which is considered best for a given child?" We must decide which variables are pertinent in judging the structure of an appropriate educational program for a given child.

Judgments about how an educational program should be structured and presented have traditionally been based on information about a child or a classroom of children who are relatively homogeneous. Such information has come from various sources, including observations by former teachers of the child, test data, reports by the child's parents, class performances by the youngster, a school nurse or a physician, and perhaps even observations made by other children. Some of the information gathered about children in school is frequently unclear or is of dubious accuracy because the data are the subjective and oftentimes biased perceptions of observers. In fact, even data from formal testing procedures can be inaccurate or unreliable because the evaluative devices selected by the testing psychologist or educational diagnostician were basically inappropriate for the child. The testing situation itself could be so poor that the child's performance is not an accurate representation of the youngster's typical overall performance. These kinds of possible errors can result in grossly inaccurate conclusions being made about a child's characteristics and, therefore, faulty judgments about the youngster's educational needs. These problems defy expedient resolution because:

1.   It is difficult to know *when errors* have been made in the process of collecting information about a child.

2.   The *magnitude of the errors* is impossible to determine.

3.   The *source of errors* is usually most unclear.

4.   The *reasons for errors* in information are difficult to identify, and

5.   The *interpretation of the information* for purposes of designing an appropriate educational program for a child can be completely foreign to the real educational needs of the youngster because interpretations were given to data which in and of themselves are faulty. Moreover, not only are there problems in interpretations because of faulty data; the interpretations themselves can easily be faulty, overextended, poorly conceived, and/or misapplied.

The thrust of educational evaluation for many decades has been oriented toward securing a reliably accurate description of a child's traits, aptitudes, abilities, and idiosyncrasies. In addition, a great deal of effort has been given to increasing the accuracy and reliability of these observations through the use of increasingly more sophisticated testing instruments, the training of educational diagnosticians, and the use of multiple procedures of observation to increase reliability. Being able to accurately and reliably describe a child's characteristics in meticulous detail is an important consideration in designing an educational program; however, its utility has limitations. Profiling a child's strengths and weaknesses does help to identify in which skill areas various components of the curriculum should be given especial attention. Educational assessment *of the child* does provide a means to determine appropriate behavioral or curricular objectives for each youngster.

But that is not enough. It cannot be assumed that the most well-defined, appropriate, and comprehensive curriculum will result in good learning. Good learning is the result of good teaching. There is no better measure of the quality of a child's educational environment than the changes which have occurred in that child following the teaching act. The product of the educational effort is performance by the child, and this performance is measured by using various evaluative devices. Such tests can describe the child's performance in detail; yet, they do not portray the strengths and weaknesses of the educational context and procedures that influenced the youngster's achievement. Thus it is vital that educators develop procedures for evaluating the educational environment, including the instructional processes that are employed by each teacher. If a child's performance is poor, and if the environment has caused that problem to some degree, it is of inestimable importance to learn as much as possible about that restricting educational environment so that appropriate changes can be made.

There are at least three possible explanations for poor educational achievement by a child.

1. A youngster does poorly in school because the cause(s) for the problem(s) are solely within the child;

2. A child has trouble functioning in school because the causes for the problems are completely external to the youngster; or

3. A youngster performs poorly in school because of a combination of problems within the child and problems within the child's environment.

As an educator, you must decide which one of these three alternative explanations you are willing to accept. You cannot choose more than one, but you must make a choice. You may not consciously decide one way or another, but your actions as a teacher will clearly reveal how you stand on this key issue. If you say that the causes for the child's poor school performance are within the child, your instructional procedures will need to be focused on attempting to deal with those internal conditions, many of which defy description, verification, and direct measurement. Secondly, if you believe that the problems are completely external to the child and are in no way influenced by internal conditions, your instructional procedures will be exclusively directed to changing the external environment. Thirdly, if you subscribe to the proposition that a child's achievement in school is caused by an interaction which occurs between the child and context, your program of evaluation and intervention will focus on the educational context as it is appropriate to a given child.

This text does not minimize the importance of or substitute for the evaluation of the educational characteristics, achievement, and difficulties of children. Changes in student performance must be assessed in order for teachers and other educational specialists to know how the instructional program is going. However, we believe that it is now imperative to stress the extraordinary importance for educators additionally *to evaluate the educational environment and the processes of instruction that are employed*. While we have adopted the view that learning is the result of an interaction between a child's unique characteristics and his/her environment, we acknowledge that primary emphasis is given in this text to suggesting procedures for estimating the attributes of the instructional environment.

A full discussion of the role of the environment in shaping human characteristics would take us far afield from the major focus of the text. Yet it is appropriate to review briefly some philosophical, theoretical, and empirical bases for stressing the importance of our environment and, thus, its evaluation.

Historical Positions on the Role of Environment

For centuries, the functioning of the human was considered a mystery and quite insulated from the rest of the universe. Indeed, inquiry into the basis or causes of human activity was taboo. One did not question that which was divine. Eventually departures from orthodoxy occurred and the human became increasingly the subject of objective study.

Mind-Body Dualism

Descartes (1596–1650) has been identified as the originator of "dualism." He proposed that the human consisted of two parts: the body and the soul, or the physical and spiritual. The purely physical portion included involuntary and automatic functioning, such as blinking, jerking, coughing; that is, reflexive activity. By formulating this dichotomy, Descartes opened the door to objective investigation of a portion of human activity without raising serious religious objections.

As a dualist, Descartes and his colleagues depicted the operation of the body in mechanical and hydraulic terms. The human interacted with the world in ways that resulted in various predictable actions. Interaction with the environment was seen as necessary and influential in establishing automatic activity. Consequently, advocates of this school of thought accepted and encouraged observation and speculation about human behavior.

Contrariwise, it was held that voluntary or conscious activity was not subject to investigation since it was controlled by the operation of free will. The doctrine of free will was formulated by church scholars to resolve a dilemma in logic. How could God be all-knowing, powerful, and good and yet have created humans, who frequently choose to commit acts of evil? By positing free will, it was argued that people were endowed with free choice and responsible for conscious, voluntary decisions. Commission of sin, then, was the full responsibility of the person. No determining influence was given to the environment for triggering conscious activity. Only reflexive, "physical" responses were a result of interacting with the environment. Conscious, voluntary acts were exclusively a function of "will" or personal "volition."

Within contemporary scientific circles, mind-body dualism has not been predominant. The natural sciences, such as biology, chemistry, anthropology—and application of the principles within these disciplines in solving problems related to medicine, pharmacy, and engineering—have abandoned dualistic explanations. The social sciences (such as education) have also moved in the direction of scientific objectivism.

A New Dualism

A new kind of dualism has been promulgated which, in the long run, has proven to be just as futile and nonproductive. Person or environment? Nature or nurture? Child or context? Concern regarding the importance and relative contribution of each of these domains has appeared throughout the professional literature.

The role attributed to the environment has changed over the last several centuries and three different positions have emerged as expressions of person-environment dualism. A fourth view, interactionism, serves to resolve many of the problems characteristic of the dualism issue.

Environment Has No Influence.   *Preformationism* has no contemporary support. It states that most activity is determined by inherent bodily factors, that is, heredity or nature rather than nurture. As such, then, the environment contributes nothing toward one's development.

The child's developmental destiny is sealed at conception. The ancestral traits, carried through the parents, are contributed to the offspring. Simple traits, such as hair and eye color, as well as complex characteristics, are all set by genetic nature. Intelligence, talent, temperament, and other such global attributes are viewed as the result of a genetic master plan created at birth and unfolded through maturation. An extreme statement of the position gives no credit to the environment except as being a mere place to develop. An extremely antagonistic or impoverished environment could prevent the "natural" course of development. Accordingly, in this view, nature is all, and environment can do nothing except perhaps warp or retard the inborn direction, content, and pace of development.

You can imagine that the role of educational evaluation within a preformationist context would certainly be minimal. Exclusive focus would be on evaluating the characteristics, alleged to be innate, of the child. Little or no attention would be directed to the instructional environment, since it is not seen as critical to learning. Learning capacity, motivation, creativity, talent, and achievement motive are either "in a child's bones" or not.

Environment as Catalyst.   A *maturational* model shares much of the biologic emphasis of the previous view, with one distinguishing and critical difference. It holds that while personal characteristics originate in the constitution of the person, features of the environment are necessary for traits to emerge. Essentially this approach characterizes *environment as a releaser*. Not only can the child's world distort and impede "natural" development, but features of the environment constructively function to trigger or release native dispositions and attributes. Here, then, is an important role for the environment, although not a very creative one. The maturational model had strong support during the first half of this century.

Proponents such as Arnold Gesell and his colleagues, Frances Ilg and Louise Ames, strongly advocated support of the importance of quality environments and facilitating child-rearing practices for optimum development to occur. Permissive child-rearing, child-centered curricula, client-centered therapy, and other approaches to education, guidance, and therapy have been based on this maturational model.

Using the environment-as-catalyst model, educational evaluation would assume a more important role than was true under preformationism. Some aspects of environment would of necessity be evaluated along with assessing the child. Indeed, devotees of this philosophy stimulated research that was aimed at identifying and measuring aspects of childrearing environments that were considered to be crucial. Maternal closeness, general sensory stimulation, and opportunities for exploration were viewed as important for releasing native qualities.

Within education, emphasis was placed on the classroom "atmosphere." A number of useful studies have described and assessed characteristics of democratic, autocratic, warm, and cold educational settings. Such research concluded there is a differential influence of various types of settings on the development of certain traits in different individuals.

Environment as Total Influence.   A third view of environment found its strongest expression in the words of John Watson:

> Give me a dozen healthy infants, well formed, and my own specified world to bring them up in and I'll guarantee to take any one at random and train him to become any type of specialist I might select—doctor, lawyer, artist, merchant, chief, and yes, even beggerman and thief, regardless of his talents, peculiarities, tendencies, abilities, vocations, and race of his ancestors. (1925, p. 82)

Clearly, the position emphasizes that the environment is the total cause for development. Constitutional factors are considered irrelevant; environmental variables are paramount. Assuming that a child is biologically intact, any and all variability in development would be caused by differences in the child's context. This *tabula rasa* or environment-only point of view places extreme accountability on one's physical and social environment. As such, defects and delays in the child's development inevitably cast unremitting suspicion on parental behavior, the child's home, and educational practices.

A smaller (but perhaps more vocal) band of advocates has asserted that humanity's destiny lies in environmental analysis, planning, and change, while little concern should be directed toward genetic planning or eugenics and other biological schemes which have been proposed to improve or save mankind.

Clearly, a *tabula rasa* view places all accountability for educational progress— or lack of it—with the teacher and the instructional environment. Tests of the child's characteristics are viewed as irrelevant since they have no direct pertinence in effecting changes. The purpose of assessing a child is to detect the impact which the environment has made on development.

The *environment-is-all* position, then, is the other side of the nature-nurture coin. The preformationism view gives total credit to constitution and none to context;

the *tabula rasa* environmentalist reverses this assertion; and the maturationist proposes that environmental factors are necessary for the release and emergence of constitutionally based and regulated attributes.

A fourth model, *interactionism,* provides a more comprehensive and acceptable view of the determinants of human capabilities. It is especially important for educators to be conversant with the interactionist position, for it provides a strong rationale for educators focusing on instructional intervention and environmental evaluation.

Environment as Codeterminant: A Case for Interactionism

The three prior positions on the role of the environment provide no formulation for an active exchange and interplay of the environment with one's constitutional makeup. The *interactional viewpoint* postulates that development and behavior result from an interchange of one's unique characteristics with the environment. Regulation resides in the type and quality of the interface between a child and the context. According to this transactional position, virtually all human traits result from active reciprocity between biologic and environmental variables. Questions regarding which is *more* important become somewhat irrelevant. Any performance is a product of the interchange of heredity, history, and situational determinants.

The expanding acceptance of interactionism is of significant importance for education for it places emphasis on the need to evaluate the educational context with which each child interacts. As illustrations of the increasing interest among educators in adopting the interactionist approach, the following developments summarize several contemporary scientific trends that have pertinence to teaching and learning.

Operant Psychology

B. F. Skinner, perhaps the most influential psychologist of this century, is the leading proponent of the operant, functional analysis of behavior. One of his latest books on the topic, *About Behaviorism* (Skinner, 1974) is a highly readable presentation of the focus and substance of an operant approach. This point of view stresses that a behavior is not important in its own right, but rather in its *effect* or function on the environment. Likewise, the environment has little importance unless it influences behavior. Accordingly, the *relationship* between behavior and environment is crucial and not the individual components in separate isolation. These critical, controlling relationships are the *contingencies* of reinforcement. To illustrate, no event can properly be called a "reinforcer" unless it has a reinforcing effect on a behavior. That is, the event must have a subsequent influence on the behavior in question.

A similar situation exists when defining prompts or cues for eliciting behavior. No stimulus, for example a sign or a signal, can be considered a "prompt" unless it functions in a fashion which sets the occasion for a behavior. If a "Quiet Please" sign has no control over Billy's boisterous activity, it is not a prompt for quiet behavior by Billy!

The emphasis on the *contingencies* between antecedent stimuli (prior environmental events) and behavior, and between behavior and environmental consequences is perhaps Skinner's greatest contribution. The operant approach makes clear the need for assessing the person's behavior and the environment with which it dynamically interacts; with special attention given to evaluating the environment before and after a behavior.

Counseling and Therapy

For years psychologists have attempted to identify and measure individual traits for purposes of predicting and managing human behavior. The assumption has been that the mainsprings for functioning reside within the individual. Discover the attributes that make the difference, and you will be able to predict and perhaps control the functioning. Thus clinicians and educators have "discovered," measured, and labelled an array of traits presumed to have utility in forecasting individual performance. But there are diminishing returns in piling up measurements on the child alone or in isolation because

> . . . no matter how much information about the individual one adds to the predictive equation, one cannot bring the correlation coefficient between individual characteristics and prediction criteria much above .40. (Arthur, 1971, p. 544)

Familiar trait labels identified and assessed in education include *retarded, overachieving, gifted, learning disabled, talented, hostile, acting-out, motivated, creative,* and *curious.* The trouble with estimating future performance based on measurement of personal traits is that "it all depends." It depends on what setting will be available to interact with the trait. It is necessary, therefore, to evaluate

Evaluating and planning the instructional environment should include student input.

and recommend settings in relation to an educationally relevant trait. Generally, it appears that people can behave quite differently in different settings and that *variables of the setting and its interaction* with the person play a major role in accounting for variability in behavior (Ekehammar, 1974).

Similar urging can be found in the literature outside the field of education. Increased accuracy in predicting recitivism is made possible by considering the environment to which an inmate is returned. The same conclusion was reached by Sinclair (1971) concerning the success of probation home programs for adolescent boys. In this British study it appears, again, that it is not so much the type of program itself that makes the difference, but rather differences in the boy's environment after release from prison. Indeed, a common problem among counselors and therapists is the difficulty in generalizing and maintaining treatment effects in prison to real-life settings in the community. It is evident that teachers cannot assume that transfer of training will automatically occur from one environment to another, even though substantial changes may have been observed in students in the first setting. Failure to generalize or "reversion" is all too frequent. Instead, it appears that educators must intentionally plan and teach for generalization and maintenance of learning from one environment to others (see Kazdin, 1975).

Consider the condition or trait of motivation. There are numerous tests and clinical procedures for assessing a child's motivation. Yet, most teachers have observed over and over again that the unmotivated child in the classroom can often be exuberant and persistent when it comes to personal hobbies and after-school friends. Motivation does not reside exclusively within the child or within the setting. It depends on a match or interplay between the two. It is a quality or set of behaviors that we see arise as a result of the right child characteristics with the right environmental variables.

Child Development

The case for evaluating the environment as well as the child is vivid in recent research with hyperactive children. In discussing their problems, Battle and Lacey (1972) state:

> High levels of motor activity in children may not in themselves, be detrimental; rather the effects of high activity levels on the child's interactions with his environment may sometimes be damaging. The reactions and reinforcements he receives from peers, parents, and other adults may result in the kind of negative behaviors (aggression, defiance, discipline problems) which have been observed in clinical samples. (p. 758)

Other investigations of problems in child development provide convergent evidence. It has been known for sometime that children whose mothers experienced a complicated pregnancy often developed difficulties during childhood. But some children do and some do not have problems later in life. Again, it depends "on the caretaking environment in which they are reared" (Ross, 1976, p. 90). It may be, as Sameroff and Chandler (1974) suggest, that annoying temperamental characteristics in children result when their mothers experienced a difficult reproductive history. These characteristics then interact disadvantageously within the home and elicit poor child-rearing practices.

Dimensions of the Instructional Environment

By now we hope that you concur with our assertion that evaluation of the *conditions or context for learning* is an indispensible and necessary partner to evaluation of a *child's characteristics.*

The Product of Teaching

When the status of a student is evaluated, we find where the youngster is performing in contrast to other children or how much progress he/she has made over a period of time. Checking on changes in child performance is indicative of the *product* of teaching. This evaluation is of highest priority. It doesn't matter how professional, learned, or up-to-date the teacher may be if children aren't learning. Again, good teaching produces good learning!

While this all may seem simple, it is far from the case. What constitutes "learning" is not always agreed upon. And second, learning can take place *without* teaching. *Incidental learning, latent learning,* and *self-learning* are examples of terms describing learning that does not involve deliberate teaching. Further, controversy abounds among theorists who have offered definitions for *learning.* Process and product definitions are found throughout the professional and lay literature. If we can lay aside some of the controversy, perhaps we could settle for the following characterization of teaching and its relationship to learning: *"Teaching" refers to the arrangement of conditions deliberately designed to effect relatively permanent demonstrable changes in behavior.*

The accountability movement has emphasized that change in the pupil must be demonstrated so that one can evaluate the impact of teaching. Product evaluation historically has been the primary focus of evaluation. The demonstrable changes in behavior are the product of teaching.

The Process of Teaching

Despite our support for emphasis on the product, there is much to be said for directing one's attention to the tools and tactics for teaching; that is, to the arrangements of conditions deliberately designed. There is, admittedly, little firm evidence about the exact characteristics which are necessary for good instruction. For example, it is not precisely known what room designs, social circumstances, instructional materials, and teaching strategies are most effective with a given child, under certain circumstances, at a particular level of sophistication. Less than complete knowledge, however, is not excuse for neglect. There is sufficient research available to enable educators to develop reasonable guidelines for conducting a general evaluation of the conditions for learning. *Some* important information is known about good and bad teachers, instructional methods and materials, and the qualities of the educational context.

> Having partial answers does not mean that we are helpless, nor does it keep
> us from attempting to put what we do know into practical application; it
> does mean that we must be aware of the limitations of our knowledge of
> where facts leave off and belief begins. (Stevenson, 1972, p. 1)

Imagine that an educational consultant has been asked to help examine a teaching situation. Assuming the purpose is to optimize student learning, the consultant might suggest very early in the consultation that tests or other assessment devices be used to detect changes in student performance. Achievement tests, of course, have been widely used for this purpose. Such summative measures are indeed useful, but they must be accompanied with frequent feedback assessment throughout the period during which learning is presumed to be occurring. This process is called *formative evaluation.* Assume, then, that our consultant has specified summative and formative tests of learning. These may include checklists, rating scales, and objective tests of student knowledge.

After we all agree that measuring student learning is necessary at the end and throughout the process of instruction, the next questions for our consultant quickly emerge, such as: What about the classroom? Could it be better arranged to improve teaching and learning? What new materials might be purchased? What guidelines are available for screening the quality of educational materials? Despite the fact that good teaching shows up in good learning, aren't there some things we know about good teaching methods?

In brief, how can the circumstances of teaching/learning be evaluated? These issues are the focus of this book.

In the pages that follow, you will study five major dimensions of the conditions for learning that you need to evaluate as much as you need to evaluate the performance of children. These are

1. *Physical environment,* that is, architectural, design, and arrangement considerations for the school and particularly the instructional space.

2. *Instructional arrangements,* that is, curriculum content and characteristics, teaching methods, and materials and media for instruction.

3. *Social situation,* that is, teacher-child, child-child, interactions, group dynamics, classroom, school, and community social aspects.

4. *Evaluative instruments and evaluative practices,* that is, placement, summative, and formative devices and procedures used by school psychologists and others.

5. *Supportive services,* that is, in-school (health, speech, counseling) and out-of-school (employment counseling, follow-up) facilities.

For each dimension, there is a chapter-length discussion of its importance to effective teaching. Variables to consider in designing and evaluating that dimension are detailed. Finally, suggested assessment checklists for beginning the process of evaluating the environment and profiles for charting your evaluations are given.

You should consider the evaluative devices offered in this book as *screening* instruments for roughly detecting strengths and weaknesses of components within the educational context. Hopefully, they will be useful to you as you initiate adjustments in various aspects of the educational setting.

Remember:

> No enterprise can improve itself to the fullest extent without examining its basic processes. A really effective educational system cannot be set up until we understand the processes of learning and teaching. (Skinner, 1968, p. 95)

How to Use the Assessment Checklists and Profiles

As an aid to you and others in conducting evaluations of educational environments, two assessment instruments have been included at the close of chapters 2–6: a self-assessment checklist and an environmental profile. While these tools are not designed to provide a comprehensive or complete evaluation of all aspects of the educational environment, they will help you to gather, summarize, and interpret information on the use, misuse, or neglect of important environmental influences on education.

Assessment Checklists

Each checklist has a series of questions designed to focus your attention upon important specific attributes of the overall environment. There has been no attempt to favor or place more importance on any one or several attributes over any of the others. These patterns of priorities should be established by the persons who are designing and implementing the arrangement of the educational environment and will be as unique and diverse as are the people within them. You may find that the Assessment Checklists are not comprehensive in their coverage of all the environmental variables which you may believe are important to good educational planning and delivery. Once you are familiar with the process of evaluating the influence of the environment, you may wish to extend and expand the coverage of the checklists by adding additional items. You should regard the Assessment Checklists as screening instruments that roughly size-up the quality of aspects of the instructional environment.

Environmental Profiles

The Environmental Profiles are included to aid you in summarizing and interpreting observations recorded on the Assessment Checklists. The profiles add no new information; they simply graphically display the results of the Assessment Checklists. If you find that the profiles are not helpful, you may decide not to complete them. Many evaluators, however, find the profiles provide quick, visual summaries of data.

Again, it should be pointed out that, like people, environments are continuously growing and changing. Systematic periodic *reassessments* will be the key to improving the impact the environment is having on the educational context. Any plan for environmental change in one or several areas should include a reevaluation of the environment. This will not only document that the change has met its desired goal but will also help monitor continued successful functioning in the areas which were not changed.

How to Complete the Assessment Checklists

You may wish to conduct a total assessment of an educational environment or perhaps just focus upon a specific aspect of assessment. The checklists may be used for either purpose. In answering the questions on the assessment checklists, you will draw from many sources of information: personal observations, memory critiques, class record anecdotal records, and interviews with personnel responsible for the management of the environment. Each question should be answered objectively and honestly, for whether the answer is *yes, no,* or *undecided,* you will gain useful information. *Yes* answers indicate that the impact of that environmental attribute is probably desirable. *No* answers suggest that certain aspects of the environment are not being used or are being misused. Just as an environmental arrangement can aid and promote learning, a bad or misused circumstance can hamper or deter learning. It is, perhaps, more important to identify these *no* areas so they can be changed and improved.

Finally, questions which are answered with *undecided* may reflect aspects or attributes of the environment which were previously overlooked. These *undecided* answers reveal where more systematic observation may be needed to make you more fully aware of the environment's influence on children's learning.

Once all the questions have been answered, tally the number of *yes* answers and enter these figures in the designated boxes. (See Figure 1.) These boxed figures represent subtotals, which are calculated in addition to a single total instructional environmental score. A subtotal score is given for each major variable (component); this permits you to assess each variable independently. For example, in assessing curriculum and methods, you may find your classroom program has a strong "learning environment" but is weak in the areas of "consequating behaviors" or "selecting appropriate objectives." Subtotal scores from the boxes should be transferred to the summary section of the checklist. These will be used to complete the Environmental Profile.

FIGURE 1   Example of completed assessment checklist

ASSESSMENT CHECKLIST: CHILD ASSESSMENT

Components	Question	Yes	No	Undecided

A. The Instrument

1. Reliability	1. Is there evidence that provides a stable score over time?	✓		
	2. Are alternate forms available that are shown to be equivalent?	✓		
	3. Are data available on acceptable internal consistency (slithalf)?			✓
	ENTER NUMBER OF QUESTIONS ANSWERED YES	2		
2. Validity	4. Does the test cover the content that it is supposed to?	✓		
	5. Are results on this test comparable to results on other tests that purpose to assess the same thing?	✓		
	6. Does the test have demonstrated high-predictive capaability?		✓	
	ENTER NUMBER OF QUESTIONS ANSWERED YES	2		

14

Summary Section

A. The Instrument

1. Reliability (questions 1–3)   *2*

2. Validity (questions 4–6)   *2*

3. Objectivity (question 7)   *1*

4. Norms and Standardization (question 8)   *1*

5. Utility (question 9)   *1*

Subtotal: The Instrument   *7*

How to Complete the Environmental Profiles

Profiles have been included to help you translate the results of the Assessment Checklist into graphic summations of data. There is a profile for each checklist. The components (subareas) from the checklist are designated along the left margin of the profile. Across the top of the profile are numbers that show the number of *yes* answers (based on the questions in the checklist). Maximum bar lengths are already drawn on each profile. Remember that these bar lengths vary because of differing numbers of maximum *yes* answers associated with the components.

Using the summary section of the Assessment Checklist, you should plot each component on the profile. Place an X under the number which corresponds to the appropriate subtotal score. When all the subtotal scores are marked on the profile, you should consider the discrepancy between your X and the maximum possible bar length. (see Figure 2.)

As mentioned earlier, the profile is a graph with a series of bars that display *yes* answers for the components of major environmental dimensions. When interpreting your results with the bars already drawn, remember that the subareas involve differing numbers of questions and differing total possible *yes* answers. Therefore, the bars corresponding to the components have differing maximum lengths. Some components involve up to 20 possible *yes* answers. A perfect score would be 20. Scoring only 5 out of 20 would suggest a substantial deficiency (75 percent) and should alert you to a problem area. On the other hand, there are components that involve only 5 possible *yes* answers. A score here of 5 would be a *perfect* score,

FIGURE 2   Example of completed environmental profile

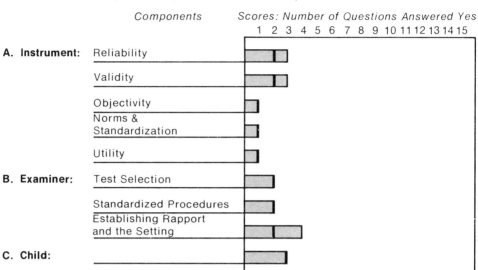

while a score of 2 would indicate a 2 out of 5 rating or 60 percent deficiency. When considering the discrepancy between your *yes* answers and the maximum possible *yes* answers, you must judge if the gap is great enough to cause concern.

To briefly review these procedures:

Step 1.   Answer each Assessment Checklist question as objectively and honestly as possible.

Step 2.   Tally the *yes* answers and enter that number in the designated box.

Step 3.   Transfer the box totals to the summary section of the checklist and then calculate the subtotal and total score.

Step 4.   Plot the results of the Assessment Checklist on the Environmental Profile.

Step 5.   Compare the bar lengths you have plotted with the maximum possible lengths.

Step 6.   If, in your judgment, some areas are substandard, refer back to the appropriate section in the Assessment Checklist and begin planning how you will change circumstances. Or if your X's are at or close to the maximum, GREAT! You are making successful use of your arrangement of the environment.

How to Complete the Comprehensive Environmental Profile

At the end of this book, a Comprehensive Environmental Profile is provided to give you a total view of your evaluation of all environmental areas. Since it does not include the various subareas, it will not offer the close-up that the separate chapter profiles provide. The Comprehensive Profile will, however, display in summarized form the evaluation of all areas. You can complete it by entering the appropriate total scores from the end-of-chapter profiles.

Summary

Evaluation of child progress is an essential and inextricable part of good teaching. Effective, efficient teaching also requires evaluation of the qualities of the instructional context, materials, and methods. Views of the importance of environment in bringing about child characteristics have evolved over time from a presumption of no influence to one of paramount importance. An interactionist position asserts that the variables controlling learning and development are not to be found in the child or environment, but they are embedded in the relationship that exists between the two.

Factors of the educational environment that influence the effectiveness and efficiency of teaching include: physical arrangements, instructional methods and materials, the social setting, evaluative practices, and supportive services. Guidelines and criteria are available for identifying and estimating the qualities and utility of each of these primary dimensions of the educational environment. The Assessment Checklists and Environmental Profiles are examples of such evaluative instruments.

2

Evaluating Child Assessment

Evaluation of a child's performance is a prerequisite of effective education. Information obtained from tests, observation, and other measures of behavior form the basis for all of the major decisions that direct the child's progress in school, including classroom placement, curriculum selection and every phase of diagnostic/prescriptive teaching. Many of the decisions made have long-lasting effects and frequently are irreversible. Considering the impact which this essential element of instruction has on children, it is critical that teachers frequently and carefully examine the evaluative practices on which they so heavily rely. The purpose of this chapter is to assist the teacher in this process.

The evaluation of children within the context of the school environment is extraordinarily difficult, ambiguous, and obtuse for many teachers and school administrators. There are numerous reasons for this. First, educational evaluation has roots in psychological measurement and has developed from complex theories and statistical concepts. Scientists within these fundamental disciplines have disagreed on many of the basic propositions that have served for so long as foundation blocks on which educational evaluation procedures and practices are based. Teachers are often confused over the meaning of such scientific debates. Second, practitioners believe that some form of educational evaluation of children is necessary (even required); however, it is often not very clear what type of evaluation is most appropriate for a given situation. Third, teachers and administrators are becoming increasingly more aware of the potential negative consequences arising from the inappropriate collection (and misinterpretation) of psycho-educational information on children within a restricted and contrived testing environment. Fourth, professors who train teachers are frequently inclined to push or advocate a certain theory, perspective, and/or test battery. Their students are urged to adopt that same viewpoint. However, confusion inevitably arises when a school system chooses to use another approach for evaluating students—one that either conflicts with the new teacher's previous training or one that is unfamiliar to him/her.

There are numerous other reasons for the confusion that exists among educators in the general subject of evaluating children. This chapter is not intended to debate the advantages or disadvantages of subscribing to any one position or philosophy as contrasted to others. Instead, it will attempt to present in a straightforward and simple manner certain basic considerations and procedures related to evaluation that have direct implications and utility for teachers in the classroom.

The first section of the chapter is designed to help readers assess their own comprehension of the evaluation process and awareness of the changes that have taken and are now taking place in this area. In recent years there has been a steady growth of uncertainty and discontent among educators concerning the tests and evaluation practices traditionally employed in instruction. Public demands for accountability and key legal decisions are precluding the unmodified use of these approaches and forcing resolutions of a wide range of related issues. Classroom teachers must familiarize themselves with these developments. They must make every effort to identify and delete any misconceptions or outdated ideas which may have characterized their thinking and approach to evaluation in the past.

The second section of the chapter focuses on the more technical aspects of evaluation. Administrative factors, common to most widely used approaches, that deserve close attention are identified and procedures for their examination are suggested. Once sensitized to the numerous errors that can affect the evaluation process, the teacher should be able to establish procedures which avoid many sources of error. At the same time, the test results of students, which have been obtained and reported by other teachers or psychologists, can be interpreted with a degree of caution more fitting to the level of accuracy and validity which typifies the instruments and procedures employed.

Testing Is Integral to Instruction

Every course of action which a teacher determines to follow in connection with a child's educational needs is predicted on some basis. Essentially the teacher predicts that the child's performance will be enhanced by arranging the instructional setting (for example, the curriculum, methods, and/or materials) in a certain way. And the presumption is that the approach the teacher has chosen will result in a better performance by the child than other approaches. In addition, it is presumed that, if requested, the teacher could articulate the reasons for, rationale behind, and basis on which the decision was made to approach a child's educational problem in a certain way. The process involved in responding to instructional problems includes the following steps.

1.   A problem appears. For example, a child is inconsistent in discriminating *b*'s from *d*'s, has trouble with multiplication tables, or speaks in a voice that is so soft that others have difficulty hearing.

2.   Information is obtained about the problem. Evidence that describes the child's educational difficulties is gathered from a variety of sources. The first and most important step is to have actual samples of classroom performance relative to the problem area over an extended period of time. The teacher may also want to include achievement-test data and other appropriate information from formal psycho-educational evaluations.

3.   The problem is described and judgments are made about how best to manage it. All of the data are reviewed, similarities in responses among the various information sources are clarified, and possible correlates of the performance weaknesses are identified. Judgments are made as to possible causes of the performance inadequacies, predictions are advanced about the consequences of such weaknesses, and decisions are reached on a remedial program that is presumed to be most appropriate.

4.   The program of educational management is implemented. Based on decisions reached at the previous stages in the process, a specific program of intervention is established and made operational. This program should involve clear and specific indications of the curriculum, methods, and materials to be used. The precision of the educational prescription should be of such a magnitude that any competent teacher could understand, interpret, and implement the program. This assures maximum reliability among teachers in the delivery of the instructional program to the student.

5.   Continuous assessment process is instituted. Reliable and valid procedures for assessing how effective the management techniques have been in remediating the child's educational weaknesses must be an integral part of the instructional program. No time should be lost in altering or properly tuning the curriculum, methods, and materials when progress by the child has not occurred. This continuous process of assessment will provide a mechanism for obtaining the necessary documentation to make whatever adjustments are appropriate.

Quite obviously, the ultimate test of a special educational program is the rate and extent of progress that the youngster makes after the intervention has been implemented. If the child progresses at a rate that exceeds the pretreatment level, one could justifiably assume that the special instructional program is effective. Of course, how well the child's teacher delivers the instruction has profound implications for how well the child does. But there is a more basic consideration. If an error has been made at the point of gathering information about the child—if the characterization of the problem has been off-target or clouded by irrelevancies, or if the judgments about the nature of the problem and how best to manage the difficulty are in error—any educational program, no matter how well delivered, will falter.

Of key concern, then, is that utmost care be given to describing accurately the child's problem, condition, and characteristics. This most frequently involves rendering a judgment based on something—hunch, intuition, speculation, hard data, or combinations of these and others.

Clinical and Objective Approaches

In education, the most frequently used bases for making decisions about the nature of an instructional program for a child are clinical and/or objective. In the latter instance, objective predictions and decisions are made by way of using quantitatively oriented techniques. There are standardized tests, computer diagnostic programs, actuarial-type tables, statistical probabilities, or decision rules that had been documented through empirical research, flow charts, decision trees, and functional analysis techniques. All these represent the armamentarium of those professionals who approach judgments and decision making about educational difficulties in children from an objective perspective.

Clinical approaches in decision making, in contrast to objective approaches, are more of an art form and not primarily focused on quantitative techniques. Judgments are made by more informal and qualitatively focused procedures. A major argument advanced to justify the use of a clinical approach in decision making is that the subtle characteristics and patterns expressed by people can best be identified and the conflicting evidences weighed with more sensitivity than is possible with a strictly statistical or actuarial approach. The clinical approach strives to provide what is best for an individual child. And, in that no two children are identical, those who are subscribers to the clinical approach feel that describing characteristics of populations has relatively less appropriateness for dealing with the day-to-day educational problems of children. Clinicians feel that their judgments concerning a child or a situation are difficult to quantify since they involve identifying subtle patterns, weighing conflicting evidence, analyzing complex interrelationships among multiple factors, and dealing with atypical situations.

In reality, most skillful teachers use a combination of the objective and clinical approaches in identifying, describing, and remediating educational problems. Usually data on student performance are gathered from tests, hypotheses generated from this information, and a final judgment eventually made on the most appropriate instructional procedure. Too little or too much test data can have an adverse affect on the diagnostic interpretations and judgments made in a clinical context. In addition, of course, the wrong kinds of information or data that are in error can be equally debilitating. Computer devotees have coined the expression, "Garbage in—garbage out," to emphasize that the output from a computer run is only as good as the quality of the information that was inputted prior to the computer analysis. This is similarly true with evaluative and diagnostic procedures.

Identifying Misconceptions About Evaluation

Due to the rapid growth in the number and variety of standardized and informal educational and psychological tests that are being used in public schools, it is understandably difficult for teachers to keep abreast of all the current developments. In fact, considering the demands of the average school day, this is all but an impossible task. Nevertheless, teachers cannot afford to be naive about those aspects of evaluation that directly affect the educational well-being of their students. Misconceptions about the use of interpretation of commonly used evaluation practices can be and are extremely harmful to a vast number of youngsters.

Testing and Evaluation Are Synonymous

Testing, according to Newland (1971) denotes:

> . . . the exposure of a client to any given device, whether group or individual, essentially for the purpose of obtaining a quantitative characterization of one or more traits of that client. (p. 116)

While tests of every description, ranging from general intelligence and achievement tests to specific diagnostic instruments, are employed in the evaluation process, they represent only one aspect of it. Evaluation also necessarily involves a variety of other diagnostic approaches. As described by Smith (1974), the profiling and analyzing of scores on general and/or specific achievement tests, as well as those obtained on specific diagnostic devices, are combined with the systematic and direct observation of the child. In addition, the learning environment must be evaluated carefully to identify those factors which may be causing the functional deviations manifested in the test and observation data. While there are educators who believe that the administration of a battery of tests completes the evaluation process, they are mistaken. This entire text focuses on many equally critical but often neglected facets of educational evaluation.

Misconception: Ability Must Be Stated in Subjective Terms

For those accustomed to reading the cumulative folders of their students, or the psychological reports obtained through the referral process, it may be difficult to believe that "psycho-speculation" is unnecessary. For years there has been, and continues to be, a dependence on impressionistic, hypothetical explanations for problematic student behavior. Despite their omnipresence, such inferences as *minimal brain damage, cultural disadvantage,* or *weak cognitive structure* are not only unnecessary but, in fact, can seriously damage a child's program in school. They provide no meaningful information on the child and no practical, concrete suggestions to the teacher. Worse than that, such speculations invariably focus on the inadequacies of the child rather than on environmental conditions which contribute to the child's learning difficulty.

Subjective speculations about a child's ability should be replaced by evaluation procedures that focus on the observable, functional qualities of each learner. Information on current level of performance and the rate and style of learning obtained accurately and reliably through direct observation would provide a much more logical and efficient basis on which to make major, as well as minor decisions.

Misconception: IQ Scores Accurately Estimate Innate Ability

An IQ score is neither a synonym for intelligence nor an accurate estimate of ability. Rather, it is a numerical score earned on a test which, for all practical purposes, measures little more than achievement. In fact, many of the tasks found on an intelligence test are similar if not identical to tasks which a child must perform on a general achievement test. Understanding this, it is not surprising that the IQ scores of children vary systematically with a variety of background conditions which generally promote or restrict opportunities for learning—such as socioeconomic status, educational circumstances, or home life. While there have been studies, such as those by Jensen (1969), which have employed the IQ to assess differences in innate intelligence, it is critical that educators recognize how misleading and dangerous this can be. The IQ is an estimate of a child's *current* performance only, and any inference about innate ability, on this basis, is unjustifiable.

Misconception: Cultural Bias Is Not Inherent in Most IQ Tests

Educational literature is permeated with studies that report that children from disadvantaged areas or culturally different backgrounds attain lower intelligence and achievement test scores than do their contemporaries from middle- and upper-socioeconomic levels. Most agree these results occur because most of the tests do not sample the experiences common to the black youngsters, Spanish-speaking children, poor, rural white students, or any other children whose backgrounds differ from the mainstream American culture. Low scores, in and of themselves, are not necessarily bad if they are used for diagnostic purposes and as an aid in establishing meaningful educational programs for such children. If, on the other hand, they are used to place minority children into special education classes with little or no chance for a return to the regular program, such practices are legally and ethnically indefensible. Nevertheless, there are reports which indicate that a disproportionate number of children in the special education system of at least two states came from minority and/or low income populations (Chenault, 1970; Mercer, 1970).

Evaluation of testing procedures will increase the quality of child assessment practices in the schools.

Misconception: IQ Scores Are Fixed and Remain Constant

While many teachers think the IQ score is a fixed and unchanging quantity and categorize their students accordingly, this belief is unsupported by the facts. To the contrary, there is a substantial body of evidence which indicates that changes in a child's environment can produce significant changes in intelligence test performance. Bloom (1964), for example, in an examination of various studies of identical twins, found that while they typically attain similar IQ scores, twins' performances are often quite different if they are raised in very different environments. Similar differences have been produced, in far less time, through infant intervention programs (Heber, Garber, Harrington, Hoffman, & Falender, 1972) or by providing more adequate educational programming. Some children increase their IQ scores by as much as 20 points.

Considering the fact that most IQ scores are obtained in about an hour and a half, and not frequently repeated, it is highly conceivable that significant changes could be found from day to day. As Green (1975) points out, any number of factors, from having a cold to being oppressed by daily stresses in a poor urban environment, can produce unrepresentatively low scores on any given day.

Misconception: IQ Scores Accurately Predict Performance

If we are concerned with predicting a child's success in a static learning environment, test scores may be fair predictors. If, for example, the factors that contributed to a minority child's low IQ score, such as lack of motivation or difficulty with English, continue to dominate school experience, it is very likely that test performance will accurately predict subsequent achievement. The constancy of the IQ score is dependent, in large part, on the fact that children remain in the same general environment in which they have always lived and learned. If, on the other hand, deliberate attempts are made to provide educational programs and settings which are more conducive to learning, tests may lose their predictive accuracy. In all probability, more relevant subject content, more meaningful and effective incentives to learn, and better remedial help in problem areas would result in far greater progress than expected for children with low IQs. When children do better than predicted, it is a case of a test's *under prediction,* rather than one of a child's over achievement!

Misconception: IQ Scores Are Not Affected by Testing Situations

The score that a child obtains on an intelligence test or an achievement test is always affected to some degree by the circumstances which surround the test administration. Sometimes this effect can be dramatic. The second half of this chapter focuses on several sources of error which include the test itself, the person giving the test, the physical setting, and the youngster himself/herself. Among other things, the test may be an inadequate measure of the behaviors in question. It may be inappropriate for the age and interest level of the student. If untrained to use a particular instrument, or if biased against the child, the testor likewise would deflate a youngster's score. The physical settings—including the lighting, the seating arrangement, or the presence of distractions—can also hinder performance. Finally, the child's attitude toward testing, as well as his/her mood and health on the examination day, are factors which cannot be overlooked when interpreting scores. Once aware of these various conditions and the very significant impact which they can have on the accuracy of the scores, teachers should be much more cautious in their interpretation of the scores and the way they use them.

Misconception: Misdiagnosis and Mislabeling Do Not Lead to Lowered Teacher Expectations and Student Performance

As long as there are teachers who think of the IQ score as an accurate and permanent measure of a child's cognitive ability, there will be teachers who consistently expect and demand less from children who have, for any number of reasons, attained low scores on intelligence tests. Such lowered expectations are very probably accompanied by a degree of fatalism by the teacher, less effort being expanded in the student's behalf, and materials and subject content which are not challenging being presented to the child. Ultimately there will be a downward shift in the child's own expectations, confidence and performance. The damage to the child resulting from this insidious process may be irrevocable. Thus labelled and tracked in a watered-down program, the child has little chance of returning to the regular program in which he/she previously participated. Largely in recognition of this danger, New York City banned the use of group intelligence tests in public schools in 1964 (Gilbert, 1966). Other cities and school systems are joining in this movement.

Misconception: IQ Scores Are Indispensable to Prescribe Educational Treatments

While intelligence tests can assist educators in a variety of undertakings, including research, the evaluation of group performance, and general selection and placement decisions, they are of no value to the classroom teacher faced with the everyday decisions of individual instruction. This is true for at least two reasons. First, since numerous sources of error can affect the score of a child, the accuracy and validity of the results provide a dubious foundation for specific educational decisions. Second, the general, abstract nature of the scores obtained prevents their translation into relevant, meaningful steps which might be taken to facilitate the educational progress of the child. In light of these facts, it makes little sense automatically to provide teachers with IQ scores for each child. While not providing any practical assistance in devising instructional programming, the widespread dissemination of scores simply increases the risk of misinterpretation and misuse.

Misconception: Continuous Evaluation Is Not Essential

The particular combination of content, structure, and motivation needed to encourage high levels of educational performance and progress depends on each child. Through a variety of diagnostic instruments and systematic observation, the teacher tentatively can decide on those strategies which seem best suited to the needs and characteristics of the student. The evaluation process, however, must not end at that point. The suitability of these early instructional decisions can only be determined by an ongoing system of feedback for the teacher. Maintaining a daily record of the degree and rate of progress made by each child provides a sound basis for subsequent modifications in his/her program. Changes in student interest or performance quickly become evident, and continued use of inappropriate or ineffective teaching approaches can be avoided.

The purpose of this chapter, as indicated earlier, is to help teachers examine the evaluative practices which they employ in the classroom. The importance of effective procedures cannot be overestimated and the remainder of this chapter focuses on the various sources of error which can distort the data used in determining a youngster's program. The most important source of error, however, is the teacher. If the teacher does not understand the evaluation process or is mislead by any of the common misconceptions in this area, his/her students can be seriously harmed. Hopefully, the statements of these misconception just presented will help the teacher identify these problems. Any reader having difficulty with them should try to read as much as possible about current evaluation procedures. Special emphasis should be given to those issues covered, since they all so directly affect the well-being of each student. To assist those needing this extra study, the following list includes several recent and easily understood sources which deal with the subject.

Ebel, R. L. Educational tests: Valid? biased? useful? *Phi Delta Kappan,* 1975, *15,* pp. 83–88.

Green, R. L. Tips on educational testing: What teachers and parents should know. *Phi Delta Kappan,* 1975, *12,* pp. 89–93.

Kirkland, M. C. The effects of tests on students and schools. *Review of Educational Research,* 1971, *41*(4), 303–350.

Neisworth, J. T. The educational irrelevance of intelligence. In R. M. Smith (Ed.), *Teacher diagnosis of educational difficulties.* Columbus, Ohio: Charles E. Merrill Publishing Co., 1969, 30–46.

Sax, G. *Principles of educational measurement and evaluation.* Belmont, Calif.: Wadsworth Publishing Co., 1974, 25–41.

Sources of Error in Evaluation

The essence of evaluation is information. Every evaluation model employed by educators is designed to somehow generate information about the students which will assist the teacher in the development and continuing adjustment of what is hoped will be an optimum learning environment. Countless strategies can be identified. They range tremendously in complexity and focus, but all produce large amounts of data on the students. How accurate is this information? Which test scores offer the most relevant and dependable estimate of a child's performance? What information should be disregarded by the teacher? These and numerous similar questions must be faced by all classroom teachers. To answer them effectively, they must be aware of the common sources of error which plague educational evaluation. This will not only insure a more accurate interpretation of the test data already accumulated but will also help to avoid circumstances which will distort the students' performance on tests and other evaluative devices administered informally in the classroom. The remainder of this chapter, therefore, focuses on those sources of error and distortion which most frequently affect educational testing and evaluation.

Most errors in evaluation can be grouped into five main categories. First of all, there are problems which are inherent in the design of many evaluative instruments. They vary greatly in terms of reliability, validity, ethnic bias, ambiguity of items, and many other important variables. The second category consists of examiner error. Examination results can be greatly distorted and meaningless if the testor lacks training, is affected by inappropriate expectations for performance, or is simply careless when administering the device. Third, the setting in which evaluation takes place is yet another common source of error. If unpleasant, uncomfortable, distracting or unnatural, the scores achieved may be unrepresentative of the youngster's normal performance. A fourth category considers the ways in which the child, himself/herself, can contribute to misleading results. Attitude and health on the day of a test are but two of the many factors which can drastically deflate test scores or produce incorrect profiles of strengths and weaknesses. Finally, numerous problems can be found in the interpretations, impressions, and explanations which are preferred by persons involved in the evaluation process. Frequently faced with cumulative folders or referral reports which are replete with hypothetical explanations or unsupportable conclusions, the teacher must be prepared to glean out only the relevant information.

As depicted in Figure 3, each of these five sources of error must be considered before the information generated from testing and other evaluation practices can be accepted as a sound basis for educational decision making. Of course, some error will be present in any attempt to measure human behavior. It is the degree to which it is present that is critical. The remainder of this chapter will examine each of these five categories, and then suggest practical ways to help the teacher recognize them and avoid their negative impact.

Possible Error: The Instrument

Any search for error or distortion in the evaluation process should begin with an examination of the tests used. Even if there is little or no contamination from the other common sources of error, serious problems with the assessment devices themselves will totally invalidate the results. While tests vary tremendously in design and purpose, they share several characteristics. Listed and briefly described here, they offer the basis for comparison or judgment of test appropriateness and accuracy.

Reliability

Reliability refers to the extent to which tests can be depended upon to provide consistent information. The more consistent and unambiguous the results are, the more reliable is the test. This critical feature is achieved to the degree that change or random conditions are minimized in the testing situation, thus allowing the true differences in performance to be reflected in the scores.

No test is totally reliable. Even when administered under standardized procedures, irrelevant factors such as the carelessness of the examinee, the ambiguity of
test items, or mistakes by the tester can all influence the score. Nevertheless, some
instruments are more reliable than others. Testers must be aware of this and take into
account the degree of reliability when interpreting scores.

Test-Retest Reliability.   Most test manuals provide an estimate of reliability, called the *standard error of measurement*. The test is administered to the same
children at two different times, and the results of the two administrations are analyzed
for consistency or stability. Those children who obtain high scores on the first examination would be expected to score similarly on the second. Those obtaining low
scores would be expected to obtain low scores again on the second examination. The
standard error of measurement indicates the range of variance in this test retest
procedure, thereby suggesting the confidence with which the scores could be interpreted.

Alternate Forms Reliability.   Many tests are available in more than one
form. This is useful when repeated testing is necessary and it would not be wise to
use exactly the same items. Instead, a *parallel* or *equivalent form* is employed. One
kind of reliability, then, relates to the degree of consistency across forms. When the

FIGURE 3   Identifying errors in evaluation data

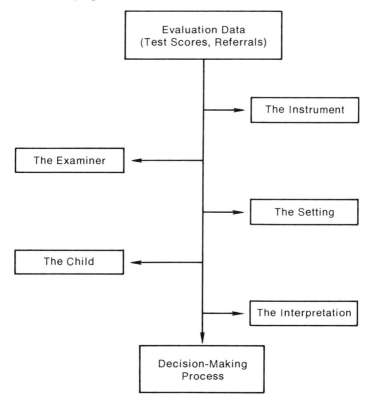

reliability is high, children who have taken different forms of a test can be considered to have taken the same test, and there should be no concern when a child who has taken Form A has been retested with Form B.

Internal Consistency.   The reliability of internal consistency is quite similar to alternate forms reliability, except that it is concerned with equivalence of test parts *within* a test form. A frequently used analysis is the *split-half technique,* where odd versus even items are compared just as one might compare two separate forms. Again, this reliability determination gives an idea of the test's consistency across itself, from beginning to end.

Validity

While a test may be highly reliable, it still may not produce valid information about the child. Consistency and freedom from measurement error are necessary prerequisites, but there are more. The test must measure what it is supposed to measure. It must serve the purposes for which it was intended. Typically, in education, this involves two basic objectives: estimating a child's current level of performance in some area and predicting future performance.

To judge an instrument's ability to achieve these objectives, that is, to judge its validity, a number of procedures are commonly used. For example, the content of the test is compared in range and depth to the subject matter that it purports to measure *(content validity).* In addition, the scores on the test are compared with those obtained on other instruments which claim to measure the same characteristics *(concurrent validity).* Similarly, the ability of the test to predict future performance *(predictive validity)* is ascertained by comparing the measures it produces with the youngster's subsequent achievement in the area. The quality and ultimate value of a test to educators is largely dependent on how close these comparisons are.

Objectivity

Closely related to the reliability and validity of the instrument is the objectivity which is inherent in its design and the administrative procedures employed with it. Generally speaking, even if differently trained people administer a test, they should obtain approximately the same results. If they do not, then it is likely that the subjective biases and judgments of the testor have not been sufficiently eliminated in the examination. This, in fact, is the case with many individual intelligence tests. In contrast to the relative objectivity and precision which typify the instructions, questions, and acceptable answers in group intelligence tests, much more latitude is given in the individually administered exams. Among other things, the rapport established between the testor and the child can differ dramatically and the questions asked can be answered in a variety of ways.

To avoid serious problems of this kind, most tests are accompanied by manuals which spell out, in great detail, every aspect of examiner behavior. The exact statements to be used to elicit responses are specified and often emphasized **in boldface type.** Scoring directions are hopefully clear and specific and include procedures for dealing with such problems as omitted items and ambiguous answers. Such steps can significantly reduce subjectivity in testing and should accompany any device used in the evaluation of children.

Norms and Standardization

Tests and other evaluation techniques are valuable only to the degree to which they assist teachers in making effective decisions about each student's program. Great emphasis, therefore, must be placed on the probability that a meaningful interpretation can be made using a particular device. The raw scores, in and of themselves, have relatively little meaning. It is only when they are compared to the scores of other children of the same age that an estimate of relative standing and performance level can be made.

To assist in this process and facilitate meaningful interpretation, most standardized tests provide age norms. Based on the performance of a sample of children from various age levels, the resultant norms provide a yardstick by which to evaluate each youngster's performance. In using these norms, however, the teacher must carefully study the representative sample on which they were standardized. If they differ significantly from the child tested, in such areas as ethnic background, socioeconomic level or geographic location, a direct comparison will probably not be appropriate. For this very reason, it is important that an IQ or any other score always should be consciously associated with the test on which it was obtained. While such scores are commonly used interchangeably, they are not necessarily equivalent. You should state, for example, that a child ". . . has a Stanford-Binet IQ of 110," rather than ". . . an IQ of 110."

Utility

Currently so many different types of tests are used in evaluation that it is exceedingly difficult for most teachers to assess accurately the value and dependability of each one which they encounter. This is reflected in the many criteria for test evaluation listed in *Standards for Educational and Psychological Tests and Manuals* that is published by the American Psychological Association (1974). While the preceding discussion should help teachers to focus their efforts on the most important factors, it is still a very time-consuming and complex task. Therefore, teachers use the information already gathered and disseminated about commonly used tests. One of the best sources for such information is the Center for the Study of Evaluation at the University of California at Los Angeles. It has developed a procedure for evaluating standardized tests. In that it looks closely at the *m*easurement validities, *e*xamines appropriateness, *a*dministrative visability, and *n*ormed technical excellence of each instrument, it is called the *MEAN Rating System.* In Table 1, the MEAN criteria used to judge a number of critical dimensions is presented.

As pointed out by Smith and Neisworth (1975), the efforts of the Center for the Study of Evaluation can be of great assistance to teachers in two primary ways. First of all, the Center staff has characterized the commonly used standardized tests according to their educational objectives. Accompanied by the analysis and evaluation of each instrument, this compendium of tests will assist the teacher in selecting those measurement devices which purport to evaluate a particular cluster of characteristics or problem. The teacher, from the type of information illustrated in Table 1, can move quickly and efficiently ascertain the strengths and weaknesses of the various tests. The second advantage relates to the guidance this rating procedure can provide for the teacher desiring to develop one or more informal evaluative devices. The factors included in the scale are critical to the accuracy and ultimate value of any such instrument.

TABLE 1   Criteria used in the mean rating system.

Dimensions	Total Possible Points	Criteria or Relevant Questions
1. Measurement validity	0 to 15 (total)	
A. Content and con-struct	0 to 10	Does the test appear to measure the specific educational objective? Examination of instructions and items with psychological (content) insight, and consideration of re-ported construct-validation re-search resulted in assignment of a rating between 0 and 10.
B. Concurrent and pre-dictive	0 to 5	Is there direct or indirect evidence for predictive or concurrent valid-ity? Examination of technical and administration manuals for suppor-tive research on the test led to a subjective judgment on a scale from 0 to 5 points. No attempt was made to comb the research litera-ture for additional or more recent supportive findings.
2. Examinee appropriate-ness	0 to 15 (total)	
A. Compre-hension	0 to 4 (in each of 2 subareas)	Is the comprehension level correct for the age and educational level to which the test is directed? Exami-nation of the instrument that the ex-aminee sees or hears in terms of comprehension, both of items and instructions, led to two subjective judgments of 0 to 4 points each.
B. Format	0 to 2 (in each of 2 subareas)	Is the test printed and organized for ease of the examinees or is taking

Source: The material appearing in this table was extracted from *CSE Elementary School Test Evaluators,* Center for the Study of Evaluation, UCLA Graduate School of Education, 1970, pp. xvii and xviii. It is reproduced here with the permission of the Center.

Dimensions	Total Possible Points	Criteria or Relevant Questions
	0 to 1 (in a 3rd category)	the test a test in itself? Examination of test-page format in terms of effective usage of gestalt visual principles resulted in a subjective rating from 0 to 2 points, and appropriateness of pacing in a rating from 0 to 1 point.
C. Recording answers	0 to 2	Is the response recording procedure simple and direct for the examinee?
3. Administrative usability	0 to 15 (total)	
A. Administration	0 to 2 (in 1 subarea) 0 to 1 (in 2 subareas)	Is the test easily and conveniently administered? Administration of the test from individual situations to small groups to large groups resulted in credit of 0 to 2 points. The need for training of the test administrators was credited 1 point if school staff were sufficient and 0 points if a psychometrist were needed. Tests needing more than 43 minutes were credited 0 points; tests needing less time, 1 point.
B. Scoring	0 to 2	Can the test be easily and reliably scored? Simple, objective scoring that can be done by the administrator or a scoring service received 2 points, while more difficult but objective scoring earned 1 point and subjective scoring received 0 points.
C. Interpretation	0 to 1 (in 3 categories) 0 to 2 (in 1 subarea)	Is the score interpretation simple, through use of clear and adequate norms and descriptions? If the norm range is broad, 1 point is credited: if restricted, 0 points. Common and simply interpreted scoring systems receive 1 point, while uncommon or abstruse systems receive 0 points. If conversion from raw to normed scores is clear and simple with graphs or tables, 2 points are credited. Simple, but not well-presented conversions receive 1 point and complicated conversions

Dimensions	Total Possible Points	Criteria or Relevant Questions
		receive 0 points. One point is credited for national and well-sampled normative groups and 0 points are credited for normative samples that are local, outdated, or poorly sampled.
D. Score interpreter	0 to 1	What qualifications must the score interpreter have? If school staff can interpret the scores accurately, 1 point is earned; if a psychometrist is necessary for accurate interpretation, 0 points are credited.
E. Can decisions be made?	0 to 3	Can decisions be made or aided on the basis of the scores? Tests with manuals providing tables or charts for educational decision making were credited 3 points. If the claim is made and appears to be reasonable that decisions can be made, 2 points are earned. The possibility or implication of decision aiding earned a test 1 point, while the doubtful nature of a test in decision-making potential earned it 0 points.
4. Normed technical excellence	0 to 15 (total)	
A. Stability	0 to 3	Is the test reliable? Three reliability ratings were made; one each for stability (test-retest), internal-consistency (Kuder-Richardson, alpha, split-half, or odd-even), and alternate-form reliabilities. Points were assigned according to the size of the reported reliability coefficients, computed from a specific, limited age group. An appropriate coefficient of .90 or more earned 3 points; .80 to .90 earned 2 points; .70 to .80 earned 1 point; and less than .70 earned 0 points.
B. Internal consistency	0 to 3	Same as *A* above.

Dimensions	Total Possible Points	Criteria or Relevant Questions
C. Alternative forms	0 to 3	Same as *A* above.
D. Replica-bility	0 to 1	Are normed scores obtained under replicable conditions? If so, 1 point is earned; if not, 0 points are earned.
E. Range of coverage	0 to 3	Does the test have an adequate range of coverage? Test score distributions with more than adequate ranges received 3 points, and distributions with adequate floor and ceiling for the specific group received 2 points. Whenever examinees appeared to have reached the floor or ceiling, or there was evidence of score truncation, 1 point was assigned. If no information was given to make an evaluation, or even to extrapolate one from centile conversion tables, 0 points were assigned.
F. Scores	0 to 2	Are the scores well-graduated, interindividual comparison scores? Scores that are well graduated but perhaps not easily understood, or poorly graduated but commonly utilized, were credited with 1 point. Scores that are poorly graduated and poorly obtained, or are poorly graduated and difficult to understand were given 0 points.

When using the MEAN Rating System it is important first to clearly identify the educational goals or problem areas which the teacher wishes to assess. Overused generalities and a shotgun approach to testing are incompatible with this selection procedure as well as with sound evaluation of behavior in general.

In addition to the approach used by the Center for the Study of Evaluation and the data it has disseminated, there are numerous other sources of information available to teachers interested in assessing evaluative devices and procedures.

1. Psychological Corporation, 304 East 45th Street, New York, New York, 10017.

This group publishes an extensive series of effectively written bulletins on various subjects relevant to the evaluation of testing and assessment practices. As the sample selection of titles listed here indicates, these *Test Service Bulletins* focus directly on many of the key issues.

How Effective Are Your Tests? (37)
Norms Must Be Relevant (39)
Reliability and Confidence (44)
How Accurate Is a Test Score? (50)
Comparability Versus Equivalence of Test Scores (53)
On Telling Parents About Test Results (54)

2.   Educational Testing Service, Princeton, New Jersey, 08540.

This service publishes a bulletin entitled *The Test Collection Bulletin* that contains up-to-date information on new tests which have been published in the United States. ETS also publishes a test and measurements kit which includes the following sections:

"Multiple Choice Questions: A Close Look"
"Selecting an Achievement Test: Principles and Procedures"
"Making the Classroom Test: A Guide for Teachers"
"Shortcut Statistics for Teacher-Made Tests"

3.   Buros, O. K., *The mental measurements yearbook* (7th ed.). Highland Park, N.J.: Gryphon Press, 1972.

This book is a widely used source of current information and critical evaluations on an extensive listing of tests. It includes technical information, such as cost, time required for administration and availability of alternate forms, as well as reviews of the instruments by leading authorities in the field.

Possible Error: The Examiner

Another critical source of error and distortion is the person who administers the test. While the human factor can never be completely eliminated from testing and evaluation, gross fluctuations in the examiner's behavior can very dramatically affect the results of a test. Such behavior should be controlled in order to increase the accuracy of any evaluative effort. Those who employ test data to make judgments about a child or to plan the child's program must be sensitized to this profound potential problem. The most common examiner mistakes will now be described; we urge you to study each carefully before accepting any test results on a youngster.

Test Selection

Given the tremendous number and variety of tests which are available today, it is imperative that the examiner select the most appropriate and effective device. The examiner must be aware of strengths and weaknesses of each instrument, and it is important for the examiner consistently to avoid using tests which are unreliable and lack validity. As suggested by Smith and Neisworth (1975), the selection of tests should be guided by two critical rules of thumb. First of all, the examiner should select procedures which permit a direct and easily observable measure of the child's performance of the dimensions of behavior which the examiner wishes to assess. Second, the examiner should employ instruments that provide direct information, rather than unobservable and unverifiable inferences concerning the child's performance, the causes for any problem areas, and the specification of instructional strategies that might most effectively deal with problems. Both those who give tests and those who use the information should consider these points carefully.

Use of Standardized Procedures

The reliability and validity of an assessment instrument depends on strict adherence to the standardized procedures typically identified in the manual which accompanies the instrument. For example, examiners should employ the exact instructions specified by the author of the test. They must refrain from adding, deleting, or otherwise altering the words used in the test procedure. Similarly, they must take care to abide by special rules concerning the repetition of test questions. Usually, questions can be repeated if the child was distracted or failed to hear the direction correctly, but there are some test situations (such as memory questions) which can never be repeated. Recording the child's answers accurately and completely, keeping an exact record of the time required on timed items, and noting any unusual circumstances which may affect the results are also essential to assure the adequate standardization of the test administration. If an examiner, due to a lack of preparation or training, does not follow these designated directions and procedures, the results obtained will probably have little validity.

Many of the evaluative devices that are used today involve a complex scoring system in which there are numerous opportunities for error or careless mistakes. On most of the individual scales, for example, the examiner must score the responses, determine the total number of correct responses, and with the appropriate tables obtain a score. This procedure usually requires familiarity with the scale and the procedures stipulated in the manual, as well as the careful computation of each score. With training this is not especially difficult, but the complexity inherent in the task is clearly illustrated in the calculations required to determine a child's chronological age. And numerable mistakes have been made in simply subtracting the child's birthday from the testing data. Therefore, those who use the test data must be aware of this possibility and even check the scoring of critical examinations whenever possible.

Establishing Rapport

For many children tests and examinations are a frightening experience. When they are administered by a stranger, as is usually the case, this is even more likely. It is especially critical, therefore, that examiners take time to establish good rapport with the children they are testing. A warm, friendly examiner will obtain a much better response and more accurate results than one who is cold or aloof.

There are several ways in which an examiner can establish rapport and help a child to relax. The youngster should be greeted with a smile and a little friendly conversation at the outset. It is also helpful, in the beginning, to provide some simple explanation of what the test is for and how it will be administered. Throughout the examination, the testor should be patient and occasionally give encouragement. Calling the child by his/her first name further enhances the feeling of familiarity. With these and other techniques a skilled examiner can usually help the child relax and elicit good work from the youngster. When it is apparent, however, that the child is too shy, upset, or uncooperative, the examination should be postponed and perhaps even administered by someone else.

Objectivity

It is always assumed that a trained and competent examiner will maintain an objective attitude toward the child being evaluated. This, however, is not always the case. For example, when a child's teacher is the examiner, he/she will often be so interested in the student that he/she will inadvertently assist the child by giving the youngster the benefit of the doubt in ambiguous response situations. On the other hand, an examiner may be biased against a particular child and expect and receive a poor performance. This could happen if the child is poorly dressed, unclean, exhibits annoying mannerisms, or is simply the sibling of another child with whom the testor has had previous difficulty. There is also evidence that socioeconomic and/or racial differences between the examiner and the child can result in unrepresentative results (Deutsch et al., 1967 pp. 303–314). Whatever the reason, any lack of objectivity may seriously distort the test results and ultimately harm the child.

Checking for Examiner Error

While few would deny that examiner mistakes represent a very serious source of error in the evaluation process, many question what can be done to prevent such mistakes. If a teacher does not actually observe the administration of a test and the interaction between the examiner and the child, it is difficult if not impossible to determine whether serious mistakes have been made. Probably the best insurance against such mistakes is to obtain more than one test score on a child. If different examiners, on different occasions, report similar results using the same test, usually the teacher can use the information with confidence. Whether or not more than one score is possible, every teacher should be alert for any indications of examiner error. While reviewing the test data reported on a child, it would be beneficial automatically to ask questions such as those listed in the following checklist for examiner error.

√ CHECKLIST FOR EXAMINER ERROR

1.   Do you know whether the examiner was trained to use the instruments on which the child was evaluated?

2.   Does the examiner have a reputation for thoroughness, accuracy, and a pleasant manner with children?

3.   Does the examiner differ in ethnic or socioeconomic background from the child being evaluated?

4.   What is the reliability and validity of the test the examiner employed?

5.   Were the child's responses recorded carefully and completely?

6.   Was the child's chronological age correctly calculated?

7.   Was there a long period of time (such as more than a week) between the date of administration and the day on which the evaluation was scored and written-up?

8.   Are there any prejudicial comments in the examiner's report which might indicate a bias against the child?

9.   Was the child in any way upset or anxious after the testing session?

Possible Error: The Setting

A third important source of error which must be taken into account is the physical setting in which the testing or evaluation takes place. Whether due to a lack of space or poor planning, children are frequently tested under circumstances which preclude their best performance. It is helpful, therefore, for a teacher to be aware of this possibility and to determine whether the testing situation for the youngster is appropriate.

The teacher might first inquire about the room in which the testing was conducted. It should be relatively small, with adequate lighting, ventilation, and a comfortable temperature level. While this seems obvious, the only space available in some overcrowded schools may indeed not meet these very minimum standards. And numerable tests have been given in cramped storage closets, stuffy rooms located near a furnace, and other similarly inappropriate locations.

It is equally important that the test be administered in a setting which is free of distraction. The room should be devoid of any toys, interesting posters, or any other materials which might detract from the testing stimulus. It should also be protected from outside noises, such as traffic in the hallways, office noise, telephone conversations, and noises generated in typical classroom activity. Obviously, a room adjoining the gymnasium or facing the playground would be vulnerable to frequent shouts and laughter and would certainly not be conducive to concentration. Finally, the various testing materials should be organized ahead of the testing time and should be easily accessible to the examiner. This helps to minimize the distraction of fumbling and searching for materials. Steps should also be taken to prevent interruptions. A sign should be posted on the door of the testing room and people working in the immediate vicinity should be informed of the examination schedule.

Even if the above conditions are met, the teacher and the examiner must both remember that the setting is still probably somewhat unnatural for the child. The degree to which this is true has a direct bearing on the accuracy of the measures of change therein. As stressed by Smith and Neisworth (1975), an evaluation in a foreign environment can produce an atypical performance by the child and result in erroneous conclusions and recommendations. Whenever possible, therefore, the testing environment should be designed to resemble closely those conditions of the child's normal educational program. Any unusual conditions should be carefully reported.

Possible Error: The Child

The individual youngster being tested is another important source of error. The child's performance may be affected dramatically by circumstances unique to the testing situations or by personal difficulties the youngster experiences on the day of the examination. In either case, the resulting scores will not accurately reflect what the child can or does accomplish in nontesting situations. The most common of these problems now will be described.

Test-Taking Ability

It is not uncommon for two children, known to be working at equal levels in the subject area, to obtain significantly different scores on the test covering that content. One explanation for this is that some children are better in taking tests than others. Usually benefitting from prior experience with similar tests, such children are more familiar with test-taking procedures, question-and-answer format, and know a great deal about how to behave in the examination situation.

Text-Taking Anxiety

While some degree of anxiety is probably a necessary and desirable stimulant for learning and for achievement, children who manifest chronically high anxiety levels will often have difficulty in school. In test-taking situations, they frequently perform more poorly than they might in a more relaxed setting. This is especially true for children who have already experienced failure and frustration in previous test situations.

Test-Taking Motivation

A student's attitude toward the examination is always an important factor. Whereas some children are too concerned about their performance as noted above, others care little about the test outcome. Their lack of attention, minimal cooperation and occasional open hostility can very dramatically affect the scores they receive. While not the case for many middle-class American school children, such motivational problems are frequently encountered with children of different ethnic and socioeconomic backgrounds.

Because some individually administered tests require rather long testing sessions, already existing attitudinal problems are usually exacerbated. Even with motivated students, fatigue or boredom can and does adversely affect their scores.

Immediate Personal Circumstances

Since most mental and achievement tests are given at infrequent intervals, sometimes not even once a year, it is always possible that their results are not at all typical of the child's performance. On the day of an examination, the child may have had a cold or not slept well the night before. The youngster may have had a confrontation with the teacher that morning, overheard marital squabbles between parents which preoccupied him/her during that day, or the youngster may simply be in a bad mood. Whatever the reason, children, as adults, have good days and bad days and cannot be fairly examined with "one-shot" examinations.

Minimizing Errors by the Child

There are a number of simple, common-sense steps which can be taken by the teacher and/or the testor to eliminate or at least reduce these errors. While, obviously, the ability of the examiner to establish rapport and to maintain a relaxed atmosphere during the test is critical, the following suggested measures should further insure a more natural and typical performance by the child.

Test-Taking Practice.   The teacher can provide numerous, nonthreatening test-like situations which introduce students to the format and procedures typical of most formal examinations. These will give the child an opportunity to practice responding under test restrictions, listening carefully to instructions, and using data processing sheets before their performance really counts. Such test-taking practice, however, is not to be confused with coaching children on specific test items or on material closely related to that covered on the test. This latter approach may result in better test scores, but those scores will not be representative of the student's performance and will be of little use for educational evaluation or planning.

Observation of the Child's Behavior.   Throughout the day of the test, before, during, and after the actual examination, the teacher and the testor should watch for any unusual or atypical behavior on the part of the child. If it is apparent before the test that the youngster is extremely anxious about being tested or, perhaps, upset about something else totally unrelated to the examination, it would be advisable to postpone the examination until a later date. If any such behaviors appear during the test, or even afterwards, careful note should be made and included along with the child's score. Interpretation from those scores should be guarded in cautious situations.

The following checklist of questions should be used by the examiner. It focuses on the types of issues which should be of particular concern. Affirmative answers on any of these questions should alert both the teacher and examiner to the possibility of unreliable and invalid results on the examinations.

√ CHECKLIST FOR STUDENT'S BEHAVIOR

Before the Test

1. Was the child noticeably upset for any reason during the day of the examination?

2. Was the youngster irritable or did he/she show any signs of not feeling well?

3. Was it necessary at any time before the examination to reprimand or discipline the student for misbehavior?

4.   A pretest questionnaire for examinees:

   a. Did you eat a good breakfast this morning?
   b. Do you feel well today?
   c. Has this been a good day for you so far?
   d. Do you worry a lot about how you do on tests?
   e. Have you worried much about taking this test?

(With young children, these questions can be administered orally before the test. For older students, they can be stapled to the test booklet and filled out along with the child's name and date.)

During the Test

1.   Did the child have to be prodded frequently or encouraged to stay on task?

2.   Did the child look confused or frequently ask for help or clarification?

3.   Did the student complain about anything related to the test itself or something else within or outside of the room such as noise, an earlier event with which this child may have been associated, or physical comfort of the room?

4.   Did the youngster do or say anything which reflected negativism or hostility toward the test or the examiner?

5.   Did the student complete the examination so quickly that guesswork and carelessness was probable?

After the Test

1.   Did the child say anything about the test or the examiner which would suggest that it was a bad or disturbing experience for him?

2.   Did the youngster act differently after the test, i.e. that is, was the child unusually quiet, disruptive, or sad?

Possible Error: The Interpretation

Until now, this chapter has focused on the process of evaluation rather than on the product. By examining the instruments used, the skills and practices of the examiner, the adequacy of the setting, and the readiness of the child, it is assumed that more accurate and effective data can be obtained. And this is true. If, as earlier described, the examiner selects and properly administers valid, reliable, and practically oriented tests, most problems associated with the product or results of the testing can be avoided. Nevertheless, it is necessary to look briefly at one last source of error—the interpretations provided by both examiners and teachers which are purportedly based on the test data.

Cumulative folders and psychological referrals are replete with interpretations of test data which are subjective, imprecise, and of no educational value. Very often, this is due to the abstract or vague nature of the evaluative instruments employed. But even when such tests are avoided, professionals still often engage in fruitless conjecture. How often have you seen scores falling below the norm explained in terms of cultural deprivation? How often have particular patterns of test scores convinced professionals that the child is minimally brain damaged? Once such conclusions are made, what differences do they make to the teacher charged with designing that child's instructional program? The answer is little, if any. On the other hand, the labeling and stereotyping which result can be a serious source of error. Once a child's performance is "explained" in this way, a more careful and discerning analysis of the test scores is precluded.

Teachers must recognize and discourage this practice by others and refrain from the same preoccupation themselves. Instead, they must use the accumulated test data to develop specific hypotheses about the child's performance and the instructional conditions which might facilitate improvement. Is it possible that the specific curricular objectives are too difficult? Would a more detailed task analysis be beneficial, allowing the child to progress through smaller, more gradual steps? Are there any materials or devices which could be employed to increase performance in particularly low areas? Is the child's current placement best suited to his/her particular patterns of strengths or weaknesses, or would some other arrangement be better? By asking such questions, a new and hopefully more effective educational program can be formulated for the child. Subsequent evaluation, using the same or similar measures, can be carried out to determine whether the new measures are increasing the youngster's rate of progress.

ASSESSMENT CHECKLIST: CHILD ASSESSMENT

Components	Question	Yes	No	Undecided

A. The Instrument

1. Reliability

    1. Is there evidence that provides a stable score over time? _____ _____ _____

    2. Are alternate forms available that are shown to be equivalent? _____ _____ _____

    3. Are data available on acceptable internal consistency (split-half)? _____ _____ _____

ENTER NUMBER OF QUESTIONS ANSWERED YES ☐

2. Validity

    4. Does the test cover the content that it is supposed to? _____ _____ _____

    5. Are results on this test comparable to results on other tests that purport to assess the same thing? _____ _____ _____

    6. Does the test have demonstrated high-predictive capability? _____ _____ _____

ENTER NUMBER OF QUESTIONS ANSWERED YES ☐

3. Objectivity

    7. Are test instructions and scoring criteria so clear that different administrators will

44

Components	Question	Yes	No	Undecided
	obtain about the same re-sults with the same child?	____	____	____
	ENTER NUMBER OF QUES-TIONS ANSWERED YES			
4. Norms and Standardization	8. Does the test include infor-mation on results across a large number of children similar to the child being tested? Are the norms ap-propriate for comparison purposes?	____	____	____
	ENTER NUMBER OF QUES-TIONS ANSWERED YES			
5. Utility	9. Are the effort and time re-quired to administer the test justified relative to the use-fulness of the results in helping the child?	____	____	____
	ENTER NUMBER OF QUES-TIONS ANSWERED YES			

B. The Examiner

1. Test Selection	10. Has the examiner chosen the test with care, considered the child, circumstances, and other available test options?	____	____	____
	11. Is the selection of the test good when the context of			

Components	Question	Yes	No	Undecided
	other tests in a battery is considered? Could an oral rather than written test be used if other tests are written?	——	——	——
	ENTER NUMBER OF QUES- TIONS ANSWERED YES	☐		
2. Use of Standard- ized Procedures	12. Does the examiner follow standard procedure in ad- ministering the test?	——	——	——
	13. Is the scoring computed in the appropriate way? Do you have confidence in the ac- curacy of the computations?	——	——	——
	ENTER NUMBER OF QUES- TIONS ANSWERED YES	☐		
3. Establishing Rapport and the Setting	14. Does the tester smile at the child, use a first name, and use other ways to reduce the unfamiliarity of the situation?	——	——	——
	15. Is the testing location com- fortable and adequately lighted?	——	——	——
	16. Is the location free of dis- traction?	——	——	——
	17. Is the testing situation part of or does it at least resem-			

Components	Question	Yes	No	Undecided
	ble the child's usual environment?	___	___	___
	ENTER NUMBER OF QUESTIONS ANSWERED YES			
C. The Child	18. Does the examiner consider the test-taking skill of the child?	___	___	___
	19. Does the examiner note whether the child evidences any unusual level of anxiety during the testing?	___	___	___
	20. At the time of testing, is the child free of unusual, aversive circumstances in school or at home?	___	___	___
	ENTER NUMBER OF QUESTIONS ANSWERED YES			
D. The Interpretation	21. Does the examiner report test results in a fashion that avoids unwarranted interpretation and conjecture?	___	___	___
	ENTER NUMBER OF QUESTIONS ANSWERED YES			

Summary Section

A. The Instrument (questions 1–9)

   1. Reliability (questions 1–3)   _____

   2. Validity (questions 4–6)   _____

   3. Objectivity (question 7)   _____

   4. Norms and Standardization (question 8)   _____

   5. Utility (question 9)   _____

   Subtotal: The Instrument   _____

B. The Examiner (questions 10–17)

   1. Test Selection (questions 10 & 11)   _____

   2. Use of Standardized Procedures (questions 12 & 13)   _____

   3. Establishing Rapport and the Setting (questions 14–17)   _____

   Subtotal: The Examiner   _____

C. The Child (questions 18–20)   _____

D. The Interpretation (question 21)   _____

TOTAL INSTRUCTIONAL ENVIRONMENT SCORE   _____

ENVIRONMENTAL PROFILE: CHILD ASSESSMENT

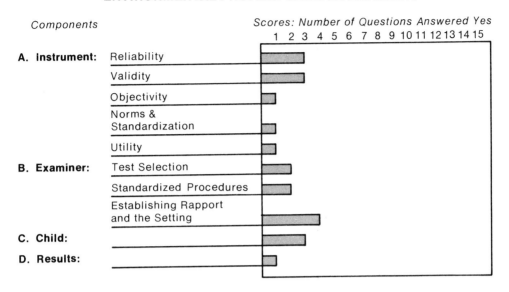

Components   Scores: Number of Questions Answered Yes
                                        1 2 3 4 5 6 7 8 9 10 11 12 13 14 15

A. **Instrument:** Reliability
                    Validity
                    Objectivity
                    Norms &
                    Standardization
                    Utility

B. **Examiner:**   Test Selection
                    Standardized Procedures
                    Establishing Rapport
                    and the Setting

C. **Child:**

D. **Results:**

3

Evaluating the Curriculum, Methods, and Materials

Teachers are obliged daily to make a great number of decisions on a wide range of areas. For example, there are problems related to how best to react to certain negative responses made by a youngster; there are decisions as to what level of instruction in arithmetic computation should be chosen for another child. Choices must be made concerning how to effectively introduce a topic on which children previously have failed or expressed particular disinterest. Pluses and minuses about a reading series for a given class at the beginning of the school year must be weighed. A choice must be made about whether to place a certain child who is especially competent in an academic subject in a leadership role in spite of the child's not being readily accepted by others. Teachers constantly are faced with these kinds of decisions throughout the school day, week-in and week-out. A teacher has the primary responsibility and authority for appropriately orchestrating the instructional environment. This is not the job of administrators, parents, or ancillary personnel. It is a teacher's duty to determine how best to provide an environment in which the children can develop new knowledge and competencies that subsequently can be applied for personal and societal betterment. This is an awesome task, and requires of every teacher a certain attitudinal set toward youngsters. It also requires a tremendous array of technical skills, clinical insight, knowledge, and common horse sense.

Throughout this book the proposition is advanced that a high correlation exists between the level of performance children exhibit and the character and type of environment in which they function. This conclusion has been documented in highly experimental settings using highly scientific methodology. This has also been demonstrated by specialists in child development who have placed orphaned twins or siblings in different environmental settings and subsequently have compared their performance on a variety of tasks. But, at a much more informal and personal level, most of us are aware each day of the highly influential role our past environment at home and at school plays in our present. We all recognize that parents are highly influential in molding a child's behavior as a direct result of the child-rearing patterns and the general family milieu that surrounds each child. These very persuasive influences notwithstanding, there is no question but that the school environment has an inestimatable influence on current and subsequent performance of children. And so, the types of decisions a teacher makes concerning how to react to a child, how to structure the curriculum, what types of methodology and materials to use, and where all of these factors fit into the total sequence of school activities are of profound importance. All of these factors are part of the total, complex environment.

The characteristics that each child presents upon arrival in a given classroom are indeed important contributors to performance and general behavior; however, the extent to which any member of the school team, including the teacher, can significantly alter these unique attributes is minimal. Instead, the major focus needs to be on how best to manipulate the instructional environment to foster in each child increasing levels of understanding, skill development, and overall happiness and satisfaction.

The curriculum, the methods used, and the types of materials that are employed in assisting children to acquire acceptable levels of competence have been and continue to be of major concern. If the curriculum is poorly sequenced, if the methodology that the teacher uses changes from one day to the next, and if the materials used have no relevance to the methodology, it would be reasonable to

Allowing a child to practice errors indicates a faulty instructional environment.

predict that confusion will exist among the children and that they will make little progress. As pointed out earlier, the teacher is the person responsible for making both short- and long-range decisions in each of these key environmental areas.

This chapter is designed to assist teachers in evaluating the curriculum, the methodology, and the materials, all of which constitute the primary factors of an instructional environment. Each of these usually is subject to the direct control of the classroom teacher; and, therefore, each can be manipulated in a fashion that will be directly relevant to the student's performance and behavior. It is, then, incumbent that teachers be able to evaluate the major factors contained within each of these three important dimensions so that they can make judgments concerning areas that require modification.

The Curriculum

The curriculum is the content or the message. It is the information, knowledge, or skills that the schools desire and expect children to acquire. It is predominantly of an academic nature, related primarily to subjects or disciplines; however, it is also social, vocational, communicative, motor, and personal. Each of the subject disciplines, or other major curricular areas, contains an abundance of content. The total content in each area is not always fully known or understood by even the most erudite minds. Certainly the exact-skills sequence by which we learn or are taught is not completely clear. The broad sequence of most subject areas is reasonably obvious. For example, being able to articulate sounds and blend consonants and vowels is clearly prerequisite to uttering skillfully words or expressing a thought. Certain arithmetic concepts are necessary to develop competence in algebraic operations.

The curriculum, then, is broadly organized by levels according to logical rationale, perhaps some theory, but not much data. Certain levels traditionally have been assigned as being within the jurisdiction of specific grades with some local flexibility. Teachers at the different grade levels usually are responsible for working with other grades and classes to assure that the full scope of the curriculum is covered and that an excessive amount of overlap does not exist. Research which has focused primarily on the psychology of learning has provided some general guidelines for assessing curricular sequencing.

Another important factor in the sequencing of the curriculum is a gradual shaping toward difficult or complex tasks. This, of course, involves completing a *task analysis*. Essentially this term means fractioning down a major-skill area into its component parts and then developing a hierarchy of tasks in which the skills build upon each other. Such sequencing is especially critical for children who have learning problems and who are unable to "fill in the gaps" between major segments of a curriculum sequence. In teaching children to tell time, for example, the tasks expected of children should not require that they jump from telling time by the hour to telling time by five-minute intervals. Intermediate steps, such as telling time by half hours and then by fifteen-minute blocks, will make each task only slightly more difficult than the preceding one. This increases the possibility of the young-ster's achieving success.

Another major consideration in sequencing the curriculum is that there be some *spiraling* in the content. This term refers to a sequencing structure in which a certain content matter appears periodically within the curriculum but at a slightly higher level of complexity (Bruner, 1971). The spiraling effect exposes students to basic ideas and processes early in the program and allows for subsequent application of those basic ideas in progressively more complex and broadening contexts. In addition to this more theoretical justification for including the concept of spiraling in the curriculum, some research has examined the maintenace of behaviors after interven-tion programs have been discontinued. Many studies report that behaviors are not automatically maintained when intervention is discontinued (Kazdin, 1975, pp. 216–217). The lack of automatic maintenance suggests that the pattern of reviewing and building skills and information which is characteristic of the spiraled curriculum is fundamental to the success of that curriculum. This is especially important for those behaviors that are not concurrently practiced outside of the school but that will subsequently be useful in an applied context, for example, the computation of percentages.

Sources of the Curriculum

Evaluation of the curriculum should occur within the context of the total school district as well as in terms of the various specific teaching objectives that arise from the task analyses performed in the various curricular areas. There are broad, generic concerns related to the curriculum that should be considered in any evaluative effort. For example, we would want to discern the extent to which the primary source(s) of the curriculum is (are) the individual learner, knowledge, and/or society. Most authorities agree that a well-balanced curriculum should have as its source these three entities.

We can use the *individual learner* as a focus in the curriculum by including problems and major landmarks of normal child development in structuring both the scope and the task sequences of a curricular area. For example, it is important that children not be placed in situations that require the use of certain physical skills that are well beyond their levels of maturational development. *Knowledge* is also an important source in curriculum development. For example, teaching children to follow a scientific method in solving problems or presenting children with activities that require the application of theorems, proofs, or principles are illustrative of knowledge as an important curricular source. Finally, the curriculum should contain major segments that are directed toward making students productive and contributing members of our *society*. Helping students develop skills in making decisions democratically and assisting them to understand appropriate social behavior are illustrative of curricular areas in which society serves as a primary source.

Although it is important that the curriculum be derived from these three sources, it may not be possible objectively to categorize a portion of the school curriculum as to its primary source. For example, the learning of self-management skills may be seen as having its source both the learner and society's needs. There should be some evidence that the state of the knowledge, the needs of society, and the needs and characteristics of the learner have an influence in the makeup of the school's curriculum.

Behavioral Objectives

We now turn from the broad curriculum to consider the specific objectives that teachers derive from the major subject areas that collectively constitute the school curriculum. These are the objectives that teachers write when planning their lessons for both groups of students and individual children. The specific expectations for student learnings are commonly called *behavioral objectives*. However, the nomenclature that is used in the literature to describe the specific student behaviors which teachers desire insofar as the curriculum is concerned is slightly ambiguous. For example, in addition to the term *behavioral objectives,* others have used *curriculum objectives, targets, goals,* and *performance criteria* to describe such expectations. In all cases, however, the message is essentially the same.

In spite of the common use of and emphasis on behavioral objectives in education, there has been some criticism in the professional literature concerning the possible negative effects on children in situations involving programs that place too much stress on behavioral objectives. A common criticism, for example, is that the exclusive teaching of specific behavioral objectives will produce students who are narrowly educated and lack individual initiative. Such critics are concerned that emphasis on specific behaviors, as described in the objectives, will prevent what Dewey (1938) described as *collateral learning.* For example, behaviors that are more difficult to observe and measure than, say arithmetic computation, often are given relatively less attention in curricula which emphasize the specification of behavioral objectives. Attitudinal development, moral teachings, and personality enhancement are illustrative of important curricular areas that may be neglected because of the difficulties encountered in developing specific behavioral objectives in these areas. An additional criticism of the use of behavioral objectives is that the emphasis on performing behaviors properly may dissuade teachers from allowing students to have opportunities to actually make mistakes and thereby learn lessons in a much more dramatic way (Tanner & Tanner, 1975).

Tyler (1973) has reflected on these criticisms and emphasizes that too often behavioral objectives are written with particular emphasis given to limited, specific, and low-level skills. He urges that teachers give equal attention in their specification of behavioral objectives to more generalized, problem-solving skills and to a wider range of patterns of desired behaviors. It is obviously easier to develop behavioral objectives in the tool-subject areas such as arithmetic, reading, and writing than it is in the more complex attitudinal areas. The problem, according to Tyler, is not with the use of behavioral objectives but rather with the emphasis and the types of behavioral objectives that teachers and curriculum developers have selected.

Teachers should assess the objectives that are used in lesson planning. They should consider the extent to which the behavior expected on the part of the child is directly observable by someone else, the conditions within the environment that are expected to foster such behavioral manifestation, and how well the behavior satisfies the preestablished criteria for accomplishment. In addition, it is important for teachers to examine the level of behaviors that are reflected in the behavioral objectives. To as great an extent as possible, the objectives should sample from various levels of complexity. They should range from simple rote learning to highly complex and independent problem solving. They should not assume that very young children should be insulated from activities that require problem-solving skills. For example, a teacher could engage a group of preschoolers in a problem-solving activity such as having them guess what is in a surprise box after the teacher has presented a number of increasingly more obvious verbal clues; they could choose and test wearing apparel that is appropriate for a rainy or snowy day.

It is irrational for teachers to spend a great deal of time doing task analyses of the various subject areas and converting these skills into behavioral objectives. To do so would be like "inventing the wheel again," since subject specialists have analyzed disciplines and converted each task into appropriate behavioral objectives and activities. For example, the Instructional Objectives Exchange (a group of subject-matter specialists) has undertaken the complex task of fractioning down complex subject areas into tasks which become progressively more specific as previous levels are analyzed.

FIGURE 4   Example of a task analysis of language arts by the instructional objectives exchange

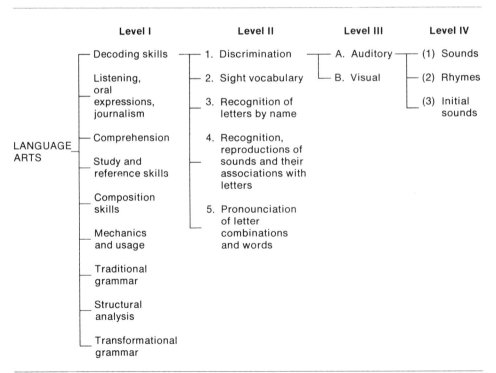

Source: *Language Arts Series,* The Instructional Objectives Exchange, Box 24095, Los Angeles, California 90024.

Figure 4 describes an abbreviated version of a task analysis of language arts as given by the Instructional Objectives Exchange. It is important to recognize that only one trunk of each level of the task analysis has been described in this figure. At *Level I,* decoding skills are viewed as having five subsets. At *Level II,* discrimination is considered to have two major components. At *Level III* auditory is broken down into three factors. To complete the task analysis of language arts, of course, it would be necessary to analyze each of the blocks that emerge from the nine basic skill areas *(Level I)* that are subsumed under the Rubrick language arts. It would be foolish for teachers in a school system, individually or collectively, to devote their energies to task analyzing such major subject areas. They usually have neither the time nor the inclination to tackle a job of such complexity; however, it is well within reason to expect some individual elaboration on or reordering of the skill sequences which are suggested by a task analysis of the sort illustrated in Figure 4.

As soon as the major subject areas have been identified, the teacher can begin to specify the various behavioral objectives contained within each of the tasks. Figure 5 presents an example of a behavioral objective in the area *"Discrimination— Auditory—Initial Sounds."* You will note that the behavioral objective has certain key characteristics, namely:

1.   The stimulus presented to the child (REN) is specified (" . . . a group of commonly used words, a majority of which begin with the same consonant sound . . . ").

2.   The manner in which the stimulus is presented is known ("given orally").

3.   The manner in which the child is to respond is given ("the student will state orally . . . ").

4.   The expected behavior by the child is specified (" . . . will state orally the word(s) having an initial sound different from the majority in the group.").

FIGURE 5   Example of a behavioral objective in the content area "discrimination—auditory—initial sounds"

OBJECTIVE	Given orally a group of commonly used words, a majority of which begin with the same consonant sound, the student will state orally the word(s) having an initial sound different from the majority in the group.
DIRECTIONS	"I will speak four words. One will begin with a different sound from the others. You say which word it is."
SAMPLE ITEMS	1 "house . . . hair . . . mother . . . happy" 2 "light . . . look . . . met . . . luck" 3 "very . . . terry . . . view . . . vex" 4 "doll . . . ball . . . bell . . . bill" 5 "mix . . . map . . . met . . . nap"
ANSWERS	1 mother, 2 met, 3 terry, 4 doll, 5 nap

Source: *Language Arts Series: Decoding Skills K-12,* Revised Edition, The Instructional Objectives Exchange, Box 24095, Los Angeles, California, 1972, pp. 15–16.

In addition, the Instructional Objectives Exchange provides teacher directions, sample items, and answers for each behavioral objective that it has delineated. The materials developed by this organization are very practical and easily implemented in most classrooms. They are extremely time saving and quite current. Of particular significance is the fact that objectives have been developed in attitudinal and affective domains, areas which are difficult to identify and quantify into behavioral objectives. It is important for teachers to select behavioral objectives from the three major educational domains, namely, affective, cognitive, and psychomotor. Bloom (1956), Krathwohl, Bloom, and Masia (1964), and Harrow (1972) have attempted to develop models that specify areas within each of these three domains which should be included in the curriculum in the form of behavioral objectives. A balance among these three overall areas should be established in order that children do not receive an education which is too narrow.

Agreeing with this concern for breadth and depth in the selection of behavioral objectives, Skinner (1968) indicated that it was very important for students to learn without being taught, to have opportunities to effectively solve problems alone, to be given chances to explore the unknown, and to learn to behave in original ways without being directly under the thumb of a teacher or mentor. In addition, Skinner recommended that the behavioral objectives be sensitive to the *rate, intensity,* and *duration of response.* For example, teachers are interested in how long a child can attend in class (duration); how quickly a youngster can write (rate); and how high a child can jump (intensity). These variables are important to consider when writing the criteria part of behavioral objectives.

There are two additional considerations in the evaluation of behavioral objectives to which the teacher should be alert. First, the objectives should be written in a fashion that will lend itself to a practical assessment of the child's learning. This refers to the minimum criterion that is acceptable by the teacher as the child responds to activities that relate directly to a behavioral objective. Criterion measures that suggest simple, quickly accomplished assessments are best. It is simply not feasible, for example, to use a criterion measure of nine-of-ten trials correct when teaching a verbal response to a class of fifteen children. Such an assessment criterion might use up half of the lesson time that is available to a teacher. Instead, daily objectives might best be measured by one-shot questioning (one-out-of-one trials correct). Children who do not pass that criterion might then be further questioned on that day or the next day until they reach the one/one criterion consistently. This is not to discourage teachers from using criterion measures such as nine-out-of-ten correct, for such large behavior samples are often important in areas such as arithmetic accuracy and persistence. A teacher quite easily could collect a sample of a child's performance on the first ten problems given to the youngster each day and use nine-out-of-ten correct criterion as a guide to decide whether a child should be given entrance to the next level of instruction. Daily collection of such written products by children, along with the use of the nine-out-of-ten correct criterion could become part of a daily routine.

The final aspect to be considered here concerns the writing of objectives for group lessons. Although the same lesson might be taught to several children, there can be diversity in the behavioral objectives so that particular needs of individual children can be met. Such planning is especially important in remediation situations and in special education classrooms in which there is heterogeneity among children. For example, in a preschool story time for an entire group, several behavioral objectives could be planned. Objectives for some children might focus on leading the group in song; for other children objectives might involve labeling pictures. Some would be focused primarily on listening to the storyteller, and others would be involved in activities that essentially extended the story to a new situation or to another type of conclusion. Group lessons, then, should include levels of behavioral objectives that are appropriate to the performance levels of all group members.

Methods of Instruction

Teaching methods are closely related to teaching materials; thus a number of the considerations presented here are equally relevant to the evaluation of teaching materials. There may be times, however, when a teacher may wish to evaluate methods and materials independently. Therefore, we will treat each of these areas somewhat separately in this chapter.

Before enumerating some of the major guidelines that seem applicable to evaluate teaching methods, it might be appropriate to consider some of the major roles of a teacher. Following this brief discussion, we will focus on procedures for evaluating methods used by a teacher in the performance of these various roles. In a very general sense, the five major teacher roles are:

1. Structuring the learning environment.

2. Choosing and writing specific behavioral objectives that reflect the task analyses of the various curricula areas.

3. Choosing specific teaching techniques to assist children in accomplishing the behavioral objectives.

4. Systematically and appropriately reacting to student responses, behaviors, and performance.

5. Evaluating the learning environment and the learners' performance.

Structuring the Learning Environment

This section will focus on the environmental structuring that teachers can employ within a classroom setting such as assigning children to instructional groups, selecting seating arrangements, and designing task and interest centers. Other aspects of classroom structuring, which are primarily of an architectural nature, are discussed in a later chapter.

Grouping.   The assignment of children to instructional groups is usually done on the basis of certain assessment information. Children who achieve similar scores are frequently grouped together for instruction. Using achievement-test scores as the basis for grouping children into relatively homogeneous groups has a long history. The effectiveness of grouping children according to this criterion, however, has some limitations. A child who is having difficulty with a skill may learn better if grouped heterogeneously with children who are already competent in that skill, since the slower child in a homogeneous group may well learn to imitate or model the inept behavior of others. A child who has a particular difficulty in math would probably become frustrated if assigned to an advanced group. However, speech and social skills might well be taught more effectively if the children who are having problems are grouped with the children who do not exhibit those particular difficulties.

A child with a speech problem, for example, could be constantly surrounded by correct speech models and begin to imitate them. In a case such as this better models often result in better learning. By contrast, if the youngster had been assigned to a homogeneous group in which all other children had a similar speech disorder, the potential for changing that child's behavior through modeling would be lost. The youngster would have little opportunity to observe appropriate speech behavior in peers whom he/she views as having a certain status in the peer group. Instructional groups, then, should be constituted on a heterogeneous or homogeneous basis according to the characteristics of the children and the particular skills to be taught. In certain instances, heterogeneous grouping is more appropriate than homogeneous; in other instances the reverse is true.

Once instructional groups have been formed, teachers either select or allow students to select seating arrangements. This may not appear to be a highly important decision; however, student participation in class is directly related to group size and to proximity to the teacher (Adams & Biddle, 1970). Children tend to participate more when groups are smaller and when they are located physically closer to the teacher. In typical classrooms that are arranged in rows, the children sitting in the front and center will participate more frequently and with greater enthusiasm. To encourage class participation, the teacher should endeavor to place unresponsive children in the front or select a semicircular arrangement so that the teacher and the children are in reasonably close proximity. Other seating plans may involve placing children near peers in order to implement the modeling concepts which were mentioned earlier.

In considering the design of task and interest centers, the focus should be on two purposes of such designs, namely, (1) to prompt children in such a way that will maximize the probability of their engaging in certain behaviors, and (2) to facilitate both the acquisition and the generalization of certain desired behaviors.

Prompting Desired Behaviors.   The technique of prompting behaviors has been used successfully to teach a wide range of behaviors including discrimination tasks (Whaley, Weet, Hart, & Malott, 1967, pp. 153–155), academic tasks (Becker, Engelmann, & Thomas, 1971) and toileting tasks (Mahoney, 1971). In arranging and decorating areas of the classroom the teacher can facilitate learning and skill development by building-in certain behavioral prompts. For example, color-coding areas of the room to help students discriminate between task areas and free-play areas is a technique that is often used with younger children. The colors act as prompts to indicate which areas of the classroom are to be devoted exclusively for work and which areas are for play. Classroom rules also can be posted as prompts for appropriate behavior. Procedures within certain learning centers can be posted as prompts for which behaviors are acceptable. Carpeting in an area can indicate that the area is for relaxation, whereas, a tiled area provides a prompt for children to sit in seats. The teacher can use colors, floor coverings, bulletin boards, furniture, and the physical arrangement of the classroom as prompts to signal that particular behaviors are appropriate for certain areas of the room.

Acquiring and Generalizing Behaviors.   A word should be said about the difference between the acquisition and the generalization of behaviors. When a child accomplishes a particular behavioral objective (for example, on spelling tests the youngster can spell words from the Grade Three speller with 90 percent accuracy), the child has acquired that behavior. We do not know, however, if the youngster will be able to spell the words a year or more later, and we do not know if the child can spell the words on the list correctly in writing letters, in reports, or in spelling bees. All we know is that the child has acquired the spelling behavior that is specified in the criterion for the behavioral objective. We do not know if the behavior has generalized so that it can occur accurately in other situations and at other times. Behaviors do not generalize naturally (Kazdin, 1975), and, thus, generalization should become an intentional part of educational planning within the classroom.

Classrooms are frequently arranged to facilitate *either* acquisition or generalization of behaviors. The typical highly structured classroom in which students are constantly working at their desks or paying attention to the teacher is much more oriented toward the acquisition of behaviors than it is toward generalization. On the other hand, a classroom that is generally viewed as *open,* one that lacks structure, probably facilitates generalization of behaviors much more than acquisition.

The ideal classroom would be oriented and structured to facilitate both initial acquisition as well as application of behaviors. To do this, the teacher could plan one or more learning centers that are low in distractability in which children could be taught new behaviors within an environment that is especially conducive to holding their attention and to persistence. Other learning centers could be planned so that acquired skills could be practiced under new and varied circumstances. For example, after a child has acquired the skill of locating words in an alphabetized list, record titles could be posted and organized alphabetically in the music interest center. An encyclopedia could be placed in the science area with an assignment to locate information about certain animals. These generalization areas might represent an overall curricular structure and include art, language, science, and math centers. They may also be free-choice, inquiry areas where children could go when other work is complete. A classroom could have one acquisition area and one generalization area, or it might have several of both. The important point is that the classroom should be structured so that it facilitates both the acquisition and the application and generalization of skills already learned.

Choosing and Writing Specific Behavioral Objectives

It is a teacher's responsibility to select behavioral objectives from the curriculum. It is of utmost importance that objectives be chosen from across all curricular areas, science, social studies, math, and so on, and that objectives sample the various skill levels within each curricular area. For example, within a curricular area designated as "problem solving," specific behavioral objectives should be written at a role-learning level as well as, at the other end of the spectrum, at the guided-discovery level. There should be both breadth (across major curricular areas) and depth (levels within curricular areas) in the choice of objectives.

Some attention has been given to the specifics involved in writing behavioral objectives in previous sections of this chapter. This is an important first step in every teacher's weekly lesson planning. To reiterate, behavioral objectives should include a statement of an observable behavior, the situation under which it should occur, and the criterion which is to be accepted for determining that the behavior has been acquired. It is important to consider carefully the criteria that will be used for accepting the student's performance. By all means, an important consideration is that the criteria be realistic. Some examples might be helpful here. In teaching an oral language lesson to a group of eight children, it is unreasonable to write the following objective, "The children will complete sentences by correctly supplying the past tense of a verb, four-out-of-five times." In order to satisfy the criterion of four-out-of-five times, the teacher must plan to ask children to complete sentences orally just to check on their learning. In this case, it would involve checking on a total of forty verbally expressed sentences (five for each of the eight students). Of course, this kind of testing requires a tremendous amount of time in addition to that required to actually teach the objective. The teacher might better select the criterion of two-out-of-two times and plan to retest or reteach just those children who do not pass that particular criterion level. Also, when teaching a heterogeneous group, it is often unrealistic to ask all children to pass a behavioral objective at the same criterion level.

Insisting that a child continue to do only addition problems until a certain rate and percentage of correctness have been demonstrated can also be detrimental. A child in this situation could become bored with the same task day after day, could learn to dislike arithmetic class, could well develop a low concept of him/herself in terms of learning other math skills, and could generalize dislike for math to other school-subject areas. It might be better in this case to set a lower performance criterion for that youngster, to go on teaching new tasks, and periodically to spiral back to the first task with a slightly higher criterion level. Again, that criterion must be reasonable and realistic.

Thus far, we have mentioned two ways by which the teacher can evaluate the writing of specific objectives for lesson plans, namely, (1) looking for breadth and depth in the sampling of the curricula, and (2) looking at objectives in terms of their reasonableness and realistic character. It is of equal concern that the teacher consider the implications of the difference between acquisition and generalization of objectives. Earlier it was pointed out that behaviors do not naturally generalize to other times and situations, and that teachers must plan and intentionally teach for generalization in children. Looking at the content of lesson plans, then, teachers should be careful to determine the extent to which there are acquisition objectives, maintenance objectives and transfer objectives included in the overall curriculum. To define these terms again, concentrate on the following types of objectives.

1. **Acquisition objectives** are those in which children learn new skills.

2. **Maintenance objectives** are those in which children are given opportunity to review and recall previously learned skills.

3. **Transfer objectives** are those in which children are provided with opportunities to practice acquired skills with different people, in different locations, with different objects, and/or with different directions.

These three types of objectives should be planned and intentionally taught each week.

Incidental Learning.   Another area related to evaluating behavioral objectives has to do with *incidental learning*. While planned behavioral objectives are extremely important and should occupy most of the teaching day, children also should learn incidentally. This is not to suggest that the teacher necessarily can depend on children to learn important objectives without direct instruction. However, research does show that even very young children are capable of incidental learning (Hagen, 1967). Moreover, young children have been trained to attend selectively to both visual and auditory (Maccoby, 1967, pp. 99–125) aspects of the environment. Incidental learning can be planned just as high-level inquiry skills are capable of objectivication. To encourage incidental learning, teachers can arrange for interesting experiences to occur and reinforce learning related to those experiences. For example, recalling specific vocabulary or sequences of events after having watched the film "The Red Balloon" is illustrative of activities that relate directly to the area of incidental learning. In all cases involving incidental learning, objectives might better be written as general outcomes rather than as specific student behaviors expected from the youngsters. It is equally important to recall that all learning need not occur in school, and this has a special relevance for incidental learning. When students are motivated, teachers can encourage them to do projects, observations, and reading after school hours.

Choosing Specific Teaching Techniques

In evaluating a teacher's choice of methodologies, we can look for scientifically based teaching techniques, the extent to which the teacher is flexible in using these techniques, and the teacher's skill in engineering as much teaching and learning as possible throughout the school day.

A tremendous acceleration has taken place in reports of scientific studies of behavior that have been translated into a "scientific technology of teaching" (Becker et al., 1971; Gardner, 1974; Whaley & Malott, 1971). Teachers are becoming progressively more conversant with and skilled in using data-supported instructional technologies such as those exemplified in the concepts of shaping, prompting, and chaining. These techniques have been used in dealing effectively with children who exhibit major problems in social areas, in the academics, and in speech and communication competencies. As psychologists and educational researchers work more and more in applied situations, such as in the classroom, it is vital that teachers keep informed of the results of the various instructional methodologies that emerge from these research efforts. A number of key questions must be considered in evaluating teaching practices. Two of the most important are: Can the practices which the teacher selects for use in the classroom be supported by data? Do the teaching practices reflect currency in terms of effectiveness?

After determining the extent to which there is a scientific basis for a teacher's choice of methods, we can look at the skill with which the teacher uses a variety of these methods. There are two reasons for a teacher to develop a broad repertoire of methodologies. First, this should make the teacher more skilled in instructing youngsters in a wide range of skills in multiple-subject areas. Secondly, children tend to acquire learning styles and adopt the attitudes of those who have served as teachers and mentors. Rosen and D'Andrade (1959) found that particular child-rearing practices are specifically related to independence and achievement-behaviors in children. Educators have great influence over the abilities and flexibility in learning strategies that are adopted by children as a result of the approaches that are used in the instructional process. For example, a teacher might teach certain rote learnings (such as a word list) by having children remember the first letter of each word or by making up a jingle. If the jingle is successful as a memory aid or mnemonic device, the children are likely to use that very technique on an independent basis. Similarly, a teacher might use a complex behavior chain by having children practice one step at a time. The children might be taught a complex mechanical task by presenting them with written prompts and gradually fading them out as the youngsters gain progressively higher levels of skill in accomplishing the task. In all of these cases, the teacher is not only teaching a particular task but also modeling a method for learning such tasks. In this way, children are able to learn a method for learning as well as the skills that are indigenous to a task.

Another way in which a teacher can maximize learning is by using certain students as teachers. Peer teaching has been successful in assisting in the management of heterogeneous classrooms in which children have learning problems (Surratt, Ulrich, & Hawkins, 1969). In classrooms where peer tutoring is used, both the tutor and the tutored child benefit. The tutor practices maintenance and transfer behaviors; whereas, the tutored child works primarily on the acquisition of behaviors and skills. By providing a classroom situation in which everyone potentially can be a teacher, children have many opportunities to learn. In such situations, children usually exhibit a high level of motivation to accomplish tasks because such accomplishment could lead to their becoming teachers.

Finally, in evaluating teaching methodology, we can look at how much teaching actually occurs during the day. Do teachers plan and teach lessons and objectives that cover the entire day, or do they use a great deal of filler activities throughout the day? Teachers can and do teach the entire day, whether or not they have planned to, because they constantly serve as models for the youngsters. If teachers plan several filler activities each day, there is high likelihood that they are teaching children a way of working that involves taking innumerable breaks. On the other hand, if teachers allow children to sometimes take breaks or recesses after having completed certain amounts of work, teachers are demonstrating to the youngsters the concept that work comes first and then comes play. Additionally, teachers who come to school each day well prepared and enthusiastic are modeling desirable on-the-job behaviors. By planning and teaching objectives throughout the day and by constantly considering the forceful modeling impact that the teacher has on the children, a teacher can greatly influence how children learn.

Responding to Student Behaviors

Behavior is influenced by its consequences. The behaviors that are followed by reinforcers will increase in frequency, whereas behaviors followed by extinction or punishment eventually decrease in frequency. The appropriate arrangement of consequences for behaviors by students is a very important part of teaching. In essence, the teacher is a consequator of student behaviors; as such, we can assess the teacher's skills in delivering consequences, in analyzing student behaviors prior to consequation, and in incorporating consequences into the educational program.

There are a number of basic skills that teachers should have to effectively consequate student behaviors. For example, there is need for teachers to be skilled in the various technologies of positive reinforcement, extinction, punishment, and negative reinforcement.

Positive reinforcement is used to increase the frequency of behaviors. The teacher arranges to have something pleasant or rewarding presented to the student following certain appropriate behaviors.

Punishment is used to decrease the frequency of behavior. In this case, the teacher arranges to have something unpleasant or aversive follow certain undesired student behaviors.

Extinction, too, is used to decrease the frequency of behaviors. In this case the teacher arranges to withhold all previous reinforcement after a child has exhibited a certain behavior. With no reinforcement at all, the behavior first tends to increase (this is called the "try harder phenomenon") and then eventually decreases to the point of extinction.

Negative reinforcement refers to the strengthening of behavior through the removal of an aversive stimulus. Giving a child an easier assignment when he/she is fussing about schoolwork will remove the fussing. This will probably strengthen the *teacher's* behavior of giving easier assignments (negative reinforcement). At the same time, this event will positively reinforce the child's fussing. When you or a child behave to avoid something, *negative* reinforcement is in action.

In addition to understanding these very basic principles, teachers must know how to use them in the classroom. Various scientists in the area of contingency management have demonstrated the effectiveness of extinction (Madsen, Becker, & Thomas, 1968), punishment (O'Leary, Kaufman, Kass, & Drabman, 1970), and intrinsic reinforcers (McKenzie, Clark, Wolf, Kothera, & Benson, 1968) in changing the behaviors of school-aged children. To utilize these techniques, teachers should know the specific events and activities that are rewarding and those that are punishing to their students. They should also be skilled at delivering the consequences following a certain behavior manifestation in a quick and consistent fashion. They should also be alert to the desirability of moving from contrived (candy) to more natural ("Good job, Pat") reinforcers.

Deciding when to deliver which consequence is complex, yet it is inextricably related to the success a teacher can expect in implementing virtually all methodologies. The decision-making process that relates to the problem of when to use which consequence goes something like this:

1.   Categorize whether the student's behavior should be:
     a. Increased.
     b. Decreased.
     c. Maintained at its present level of frequency and/or intensity.

2.   Decide whether to consequate the behavior.

3.   If the decision is to consequate, decide on a consequence that is based on previous experience with that child.

4.   When the child manifests the behavior, deliver the consequence as quickly as possible.

5.   Observe the subsequent behavior of the child and decide the extent to which the consequence has been useful. Ask, "Did the consequence have the expected effect on the behavior?"

6.   If there was no change in the child's behavior as a result of the consequatation, analyze the situation again in terms of the child's reward preferences, and then choose a different consequence.

Teachers may know very well the basic skills of positive reinforcement, punishment, and extinction but may not be making proper decisions as to when or how to use these techniques. For example, a teacher may choose a punishment procedure (such as sending the child to a time-out seat) to consequate a child's talking-out behavior. The child, however, may continue to talk out daily. This leads the teacher to decide that the time-out seat did not function as a punisher for that child. In fact, the teacher observes that sending the child to the time-out seat appeared to reinforce the behavior, that is, make it occur again and again with increasing frequency. The teacher, then, suspects that the attention given to the child by the time-out procedure in and of itself may have been reinforcing. The teacher then plans to ignore the talking-out behavior and will give the child attention when the youngster is quiet and raising his/her hand to be recognized. The teacher solved the problem by giving careful attention to the effects of the original consequence. The problem initially was not that the teacher was not skilled in using time-out, but that time-out was not an appropriate consequence for that child and for that particular behavior. The actual use of consequences, then, should involve the decision-making process just described.

Consequences should always be chosen so that they are as natural as possible. Drastic consequences such as severe punishment should be used *only* when all else has failed and *only* when its use has been approved through proper channels (Braun, 1975). Every attempt should be made to try to wean children from primary use of contrived consequences (such as candy or trinkets) to a more natural kind of reward system.

On the assumption that the teacher has developed the various skills of consequating behavior and is able to apply them correctly in appropriate situations, we can now ask what educational benefits this use of consequence has for the students. How are consequences incorporated into the educational program? Of course, a very important educational benefit occurs when the inappropriate behaviors are decreased and the desired behaviors are increased. However, beyond this children learn many things by participating in classroom consequences. We often imitate patterns of consequating behavior in dealing with ourselves (Bandura & Kupers, 1964) and with others (Sarason & Glanzer, 1969). Children learn to punish others; they learn to reward others. They learn to be calm and kind by observing how the teachers react toward the behavior of others, that is, how the teachers consequate behavior. We might evaluate a teacher's behavior as a consequator by asking if the teacher models desirable behaviors in this area for the children to learn.

In addition to these patterns of consequating behavior, we can also look at the content of the consequences, that is, what the teacher uses as rewards and punishers. In choosing rewards and punishers, teachers make statements about their own values and feelings about certain events. For example, the teacher who punishes youngsters by giving them extra homework is saying that schoolwork is essentially aversive. The teacher who constantly uses candy and food as reinforcers is teaching children to reward themselves and others with food. The teacher who persists in rewarding children with plastic, breakable toys may be modeling poor purchasing behavior. The careful selection of rewards and punishers can teach children worthwhile ways for consequating behavior.

In schools where time-out is used as a punishment, we often hear of children who independently go to their rooms to be alone after they have acted inappropriately or when they begin to act inappropriately. Such children have learned to manage their own behavior—to substitute one behavior (going to the room) for another less desirable one (fighting with siblings). By carefully choosing a punishing consequence, the teacher gives the child a technique the youngster can use outside of the school.

Finally, a word regarding positive reinforcers. We can teach children to work for long-term rewards, to work for the sake of doing something correctly, to please themselves and others, and to enjoy crafts and hobbies. Of course, we must start where the child is presently functioning in terms of reinforcement. Children are not naturally rewarded by long-term events or by intrinsic reinforcement. We can, however, move them in the direction of reinforcement by higher-level rewards through a series of successive approximations.

Evaluating the Learning Environment and the Learners

In attempting to assess educational efforts, we could evaluate the learners' behaviors and the learners' environment. The predominant position taken in this text is that the environment greatly influences the behavior of learners and that by evaluating and improving the environment, behavior of learners will change. It is, indeed, part of the teacher's role as an evaluator to assess the characteristics of the learning environment; however, this could be a lengthy task. We suggest that such an evaluation of the total environment be made twice a year—perhaps at the beginning and toward the end of the school year. When faced with particular problems at other times, it is quite logical that the teacher might want to do a cross-sectional analysis.

In addition to evaluating the learning environment, the teacher should frequently assess the performance of the learners themselves. In the first instance, the student should be located within the curriculum in terms of the specific task being focused upon. There are several techniques for doing this. Standardized tests that are directly related to the curricular targets can be used when appropriate; informal, curriculum-based survey tests can also be administered. In addition, teachers can make observational judgments concerning student placement or teachers can interview students or their parents.

Record Keeping.   After the students have been located within the curriculum and instruction has taken place, records of this progress should be kept on a reasonably continuous basis. Since the teacher might be interested both in the quantity and quality of the student's progress, keeping a record of the following information for each curricular objective would be helpful: date that the instruction began, date that the objective was accomplished, and the performance level at the completion or check-off time (the percent of accuracy). Such data can be listed in three columns opposite the objectives on a curriculum sheet, and the teacher would thus be reminded to record this kind of information on a regular basis. By referring to the curricular targets, the teacher could report what the child has learned and what criterion as well as how quickly. This kind of information makes an excellent base for progress reports and permanent records.

Teachers may prefer to do such record keeping as frequently as each week or as infrequently as once a month. Recording less often than monthly, however, would not be so accurate in providing information on student learning rates. For example, a student may have accomplished an objective in two weeks but not have it checked off for three months.

Student Involvement.   Another beneficial evaluative activity involves getting the student intimately associated with the evaluation process itself. Such student evaluation can occur at two levels. The student can be engaged in collecting data on his/her own behaviors, and the student can participate in evaluating personal attitudes toward the curricular content, teaching strategies, and his/her own personal progress. Such information communicates to students a concern which the teacher has for their opinions. It also communicates to the teacher each student's affective reactions to the learning environment.

Communicating Results.   The final evaluation activity involves communicating results to others. Any variety of persons might be interested in the evaluation results. Certainly the students themselves should be kept informed of how things are going in school. Parents are also an important group with whom the schools want to communicate data. Of course, most schools require periodic progress reports to parents, but it might also be effective to send reports home when children have completed specific objectives. And this way parents can reinforce the child's accomplishments soon after progress has been made. When accomplishments are not acknowledged until report card day, children often forget why they received certain marks. Certainly community support of the schools and of its students can be strengthened by sharing information, within reasonable limits of privacy, on the various successes within the schools. One can see from this discussion of evaluation, this progress should be an ongoing, regularly scheduled and planned event in the teacher's routine.

Instructional Materials

The evaluation of instructional materials should be a matter of concern throughout the school year. It is important that both the strengths and weaknesses of the current library of materials be assessed to plan for future purchases. Teachers also need to evaluate newly advertised and developed products for possible purchase and use in the classroom, and a frequent assessment must be made of the suitability of instructional materials for particular children.

There are two dimensions with which the teacher should be especially concerned in evaluating instructional materials. First, the examination of the technical aspects of the material should be given consideration. Whether their design is consistent with learning principles and technology, whether they are sufficiently validated, and the degree to which data are published concerning their efficacy should be considered. Second, the practical aspects of the material should be examined. These include the cost-benefit ratios, the physical robustness of the materials, and the extent to which it is difficult to transport the materials from one classroom to another. The subsequent discussion will relate primarily to these two major factors.

It was mentioned earlier that the variables relevant to the evaluation of teaching methods are also, in substance, relevant to the evaluation of teaching materials. The suggestions mentioned in the sections devoted to the behavioral objectives, teaching techniques, and consequating behaviors are especially pertinent to this discussion. We now want to turn our attention to a discussion of teacher materials.

Technical Considerations

A great deal can be learned about instructional materials merely by examining information and documents which publishers direct toward the teacher—the teacher's guide, the record-keeping materials related to the instructional material, and the program tests. Some attributes to consider in these materials are the breakdowns of the subject matter, the statements of the program and lessons, the suggestions for teaching strategies, and the evaluation and procedures in field-testing information that is provided. "Breaking down" the subject matter refers to the extent to which the main-content matter in a discipline has been analyzed into smaller components. Such analyses lead to a more precise and thorough coverage of the content area. And such analyses make teaching and learning immeasurably easier because large tasks are broken down into smaller, more manageable skills. Teachers can recognize programs and materials that are based on a task-analysis philosophy and format because they refer to component skills such as *task specific attention, specific information, discrimination, operations,* and *sequences.* In instructional materials which purport to teach broad content areas (for example, mathematics or social studies) a task-analysis approach should be evident even in the table of contents. Indeed, even in materials that are designed to teach relatively small tasks such as labeling likenesses and differences, some attempt should be made to show how that task is an important component of the overall curriculum or of a specific subject area. When this is done, a teacher can more easily decide how materials fit into the overall classroom program. A task-analysis approach can be detected by looking for a breakdown of component tasks in the scope and sequence charts that accompany most instructional materials, in the program-objectives lists that are frequently included, and in the teacher's guidebook.

In addition to looking for the extent to which a task analysis has been performed within the subject area, it is important to examine the content of the program objectives. First, you ought to question whether the objectives or their descriptions refer to specific behaviors that can be readily observed. Moreover, the extent to which the individual lessons are preceded by statements of behavioral objectives for those lessons must be ascertained. Material not related to specific objectives probably does not help students learn or teachers focus on specific behaviors. Next, you should examine the teaching strategies that are suggested by the teacher's guidebook. Ask: Are the strategies supported by data? Do they include specific examples? Is there a variety in the techniques suggested or might they well become tedious for children? You might also determine if the techniques seem applicable for your particular situation as well as for others.

It is most urgent to look for field testing and evaluation information as you consider instructional materials. There are two key questions to ask in this regard: Does the information that is presented validate the objectives that are stated by the materials designer? Is there a history of the materials or program being reliably successful? It is important for teachers to look for components such as task ladders of program skills in which to place individual children. Evaluation materials or procedures should be provided for teachers so that program tests are imbedded in the materials at various levels of difficulty. Techniques for analyzing specific areas should be included so that remediation can begin at a precise level.

Thus far we have been discussing technical aspects of teacher-directed materials. Now let us look at student materials. It is important for the teacher to look for evidence that many of the teaching strategies we have previously discussed have been incorporated into the materials. Examine how the content material is taught. Determine if the programming techniques of shaping, chaining, and fading of prompts are contained within those materials. Are reinforcers built into the materials to allow for immediate reward of success? Are there opportunities for the youngster to have immediate feedback of responses? Are the reinforcers embedded within the tasks so that they are interesting and appropriate for the age of the children using the materials? Related to this, determine if the materials are appropriate to the skill levels of particular children. Ample opportunity should be provided within the materials for repeated practice, maintenance and transfer of skills, and take-home exercises. A key matter is whether or not the materials lead the student to become an autonomous learner rather than teacher directed.

Practical Considerations

In addition to these technical considerations, there are a host of practical considerations the teacher must weigh in evaluating instructional materials. Of course, many of these considerations are situation specific, and it would be virtually impossible to include in this discussion all of the variables that are significant to any particular situation. However, here are some of the generic ones. First, how useful are the materials? Can they be used for several children, for significant parts of the curriculum, and for more thorough learning? Second, are the materials time-saving? Will children learn more efficiently? Will teachers need less planning and record-keeping? What about the amount of time the teachers must devote to the preparation with the materials? Consider whether the price is compatible with the degree of usefulness and efficiency of the materials.

Factors to consider in addition to the actual price are the durability of the materials, the yearly costs of consumable parts, the price of training teachers to use the materials, and the maintenance required for any of the mechanical parts of an instructional device. Are there important, practical considerations in evaluating materials? Are there extents to which there are sex role or ethnic stereotypes? What is the practicality of the materials for certain types of handicapped students? To what extent do the materials represent a well-balanced curriculum?

Although typically teachers evaluate new materials, it is equally important to assess the environment in terms of the existing materials used. After conducting such an environmental assessment of materials, teachers can be in a better position to select any new ones that will help to balance or complement the ones that are already being used in the classroom.

ASSESSMENT CHECKLIST: CURRICULUM, METHODS, AND MATERIALS

Components	Question	Yes	No	Undecided

A. Curriculum

1. Are the needs of society evident as a source of curricular objectives? _____ _____ _____

2. Is the child a source of curricular objectives? _____ _____ _____

3. Are subject-matter specialists a source of curricular objectives? _____ _____ _____

4. Are there hierarchies of skills within the curriculum? _____ _____ _____

5. Do objectives shape toward more difficult tasks? _____ _____ _____

6. Does the curriculum spiral? _____ _____ _____

7. Is the curriculum useful for planning objectives? _____ _____ _____

8. Is the curriculum useful for recording achievement? _____ _____ _____

9. Do curricular objectives include high-level as well as rote-level skills? _____ _____ _____

10. Does the curriculum sample a broad base of behaviors— across the three taxonomies? _____ _____ _____

Components	Question	Yes	No	Undecided
	11. Do the specific behavioral objectives specify the topography of the behavior?	———	———	———
	12. Can the criteria measures in the objectives be taken practically?	———	———	———
	13. Are behavioral objectives for group lessons applicable for the range of children within the group?	———	———	———
	ENTER NUMBER OF QUESTIONS ANSWERED YES	☐		

B. Instructional Methods

Components	Question	Yes	No	Undecided
1. Learning Environment	14. Are both homogeneous and heterogenous grouping used to enhance learning through modeling?	———	———	———
	15. Are instructional groups small enough so that all children have adequate access to the teacher?	———	———	———
	16. Are modeling effects considered in planning seating arrangements?	———	———	———
	17. Are environmental prompts used to assist children in discriminating what behaviors are expected of them?	———	———	———

Components	Question	Yes	No	Undecided
	18. Are areas of the classroom structured to facilitate acquisition of behaviors?	_____	_____	_____
	19. Are areas of the classroom structured to facilitate generalization of behaviors?	_____	_____	_____
	ENTER NUMBER OF QUES-TIONS ANSWERED YES	☐		
2. Selecting Objectives	20. Are acquisition objectives included in lesson plans?	_____	_____	_____
	21. Are maintenance objectives included in lesson plans?	_____	_____	_____
	22. Are transfer objectives included in lesson plans?	_____	_____	_____
	23. Are opportunities for in-cidental learning included as part of lesson plans?	_____	_____	_____
	24. Are criterion measures realistic for individual children?	_____	_____	_____
	ENTER NUMBER OF QUES-TIONS ANSWERED YES	☐		
3. Teaching Methods	25. Does the teacher use methods that are supported by empirical evidence?	_____	_____	_____

Components	Question	Yes	No	Undecided
	26. Does the teacher keep informed of and use current, empirically supported methods?	_____	_____	_____
	27. Does the teacher use a variety of teaching methods?	_____	_____	_____
	28. Does the teacher use model behaviors that he/she wishes to teach the children?	_____	_____	_____
	29. Is peer-tutoring used to maximize learning?	_____	_____	_____
	ENTER NUMBER OF QUESTIONS ANSWERED YES	☐		
4. Consequating Methods	30. Can teachers list rewards and punishments that are successful with individual students?	_____	_____	_____
	31. Are consequences delivered consistently?	_____	_____	_____
	32. Are consequences delivered quickly?	_____	_____	_____
	33. Do consequation techniques vary from contrived to natural?	_____	_____	_____
	34. Are consequation techniques experimentally determined for individual children?	_____	_____	_____

Components	Question	Yes	No	Undecided
	35. Are consequences used by the teacher ones that could also be appropriately used by children?	____	____	____
	36. Is an attempt made to move children from contrived to natural consequation techniques?	____	____	____
	ENTER NUMBER OF QUESTIONS ANSWERED YES	☐		
5. Evaluating Instruction	37. Does the teacher evaluate the environment?	____	____	____
	38. Are learners initially located on instructional task ladders (curriculums)?	____	____	____
	39. Is a learner progress regularly recorded on task ladders?	____	____	____
	40. Do students participate in evaluation by assisting in observing and recording behaviors?	____	____	____
	41. Do students participate in evaluation through attitudinal surveys?	____	____	____
	42. Are childrens' achievements communicated to parents?	____	____	____

Components	Question	Yes	No	Undecided
	43. Are childrens' achievements communicated to children themselves?	——	——	——
	44. Are childrens' achievements communicated to others in the community?	——	——	——
	45. Are achievements reported as soon as possible after their occurences, not just at report periods?	——	——	——
	ENTER NUMBER OF QUES-TIONS ANSWERED YES			

C. Materials

Components	Question	Yes	No	Undecided
1. Commercial Materials	46. Do materials use methods that are supported by empirical evidence?	——	——	——
	47. Do the materials use current validated methods?	——	——	——
	48. Are materials useful for needs of the particular class?	——	——	——
	49. Are materials relevant to the curricular objectives?	——	——	——
	50. Will the materials assist the teacher by saving him/her time?	——	——	——

Components	Questions	Yes	No	Undecided
	51. Are the costs and usefulness of materials balanced?	_____	_____	_____
	ENTER NUMBER OF QUES-TIONS ANSWERED YES	☐		
2. Teacher Materials	52. Are objectives task-analyzed?	_____	_____	_____
	53. Are program and lesson objectives listed?	_____	_____	_____
	54. Are program and lesson objectives specific and teachable?	_____	_____	_____
	55. Are evaluation procedures suggested for the materials?	_____	_____	_____
	56. Are in-programmed mate-rials, in-program assess-ments, and diagnosis included?	_____	_____	_____
	57. Are validation and field-testing information given?	_____	_____	_____
	58. Are specific suggestions for strategies included?	_____	_____	_____
	59. Are strategies applicable for the situation?	_____	_____	_____
	60. Are strategies suggested for the generalization as well as			

Components	Questions	Yes	No	Undecided
	acquisition of the behaviors taught?	_____	_____	_____
	61. Are strategies related to principles of programming?	_____	_____	_____
	ENTER NUMBER OF QUES-TIONS ANSWERED YES	☐		
3. Student Materials	62. Does the program use task-imbedded reinforcers?	_____	_____	_____
	63. Can the materials be used autonomously?	_____	_____	_____
	64. Are reinforcers and/or feedback built into the program?	_____	_____	_____
	65. Are varied and effective learning methods used?	_____	_____	_____
	ENTER NUMBER OF QUES-TIONS ANSWERED YES	☐		

Summary Section

A. Curriculum (questions 1-13)   _____

B. Instructional Methods

  1. Learning Environment (questions 14-19)   _____

  2. Selecting Objectives (questions 20-24)

3. Teaching Methods (questions 25-29)   _____

4. Consequating Methods (questions 30-36)   _____

5. Evaluating Instruction (questions 37-45)   _____

Subtotal: Instructional Methods   _____

C. Instructional Materials

1. Commercial Materials (questions 46-51)   _____

2. Teacher Materials (questions 52-61)   _____

3. Student Materials (questions 62-65)   _____

Subtotal: Materials   _____

TOTAL INSTRUCTIONAL ENVIRONMENTAL SCORE   =========

ENVIRONMENTAL PROFILE: CURRICULUM, METHODS, AND MATERIALS

Components   *Scores: Number of Questions Answered Yes*

1 2 3 4 5 6 7 8 9 10 11 12 13 14 15

A. Curriculum: Curriculum

B. Methods: Learning Environment

Selecting Objectives

Teaching Methods

Consequating Methods

Evaluating Instruction

C. Materials: Commercial Materials

Teacher Materials

Student Materials

4

Evaluating the Social Environment

It is difficult to overestimate the importance of the social environment in which children learn. The types of relationships that they form with teachers and classmates fundamentally affect not only academic performance but, more importantly, their growth as total individuals. Daily experiences as class members signficantly influence children's feelings about themselves, their attitudes toward others, and the social patterns of behavior that they will ultimately adopt. It is critical, therefore, that each teacher keep well informed in this area. Rather than simply react to problems as they arise, sensitive and understanding teachers can prevent many difficulties and provide opportunities for optimum social growth. Teachers who are aware of the social climate in the classroom are better prepared to identify those children who need specialized professional help.

To assist teachers in creating a wholesome social climate, this chapter focuses on three separate factors that contribute heavily to the process: teacher influence, peer influence, and curriculum influence. Several informal assessment techniques are suggested that, when used as described, should allow the teacher to objectively evaluate the critical element of teacher behavior. Also of equal importance is the peer culture of the classroom; assessment techniques for studying this second factor are also described. While peer pressures can often be problematic and difficult to influence, teacher awareness of student norms and values is essential to open communication. Third, the curriculum used in the classroom can hinder or facilitate social growth. This chapter gives suggestions to assist teachers in determining how positive an impact their current approach is having and what modifications might be made to improve it. Throughout the chapter emphasis is placed on practical, uncomplicated assessment techniques that yield usable information to promote a healthy social environment in the classroom.

Teacher Influence

Anyone who has had the opportunity to visit a number of different classrooms and observe the various levels of activity and student-teacher interaction that are taking place is surely aware of the very significant differences that typically exist. Physical settings play a part and the children in the class are obviously a factor, but even when these elements are essentially the same, the difference is still very real. The atmosphere depends on the teacher. Of all the factors that contribute to the social environment in which children are educated, the teacher is by far the most decisive. The teacher's attitude toward children and education determines to a very real degree how children perceive school, themselves, and each other—and how much progress they actually make. Teachers can make learning pleasant or punishing; they can create motivation or fear; they can produce excited anticipation or dread. A teacher's personal style and approach, more than anything else, create the climate and mood which will characterize the classroom.

The tremendous impact of teacher behavior in the classroom has been clearly supported by a spate of recent studies. For example, systematic changes in the teacher's use of attention, approval, and praise have been shown to result in predictable changes in student behavior. With elementary school children (Hall, Lund, & Jackson, 1968) and with high school students (McAllister, Stackowiak, Baer, & Canderman, 1969), the contingent use of teacher attention has produced desirable changes in student performance. At the same time, the removal of such social reinforcement in the presence of inappropriate student activity has eliminated numerous classroom problems (Hart et al., 1974). Such studies dramatically illustrate the causal relationships that exist between teacher and student behavior.

In light of the critical role played by teachers, it is obviously necessary that they frequently evaluate their own performance and the impact their behavior is having on the social development of the students. No doubt most teachers do this in one way or another. More often than not, they reflect on the occurrences of the day, relive the successes, and voice concern over their possible mistakes. Nevertheless, it is difficult to objectively assess our own behavior; to see ourselves as others do. This is especially true in the classroom where the interaction between teacher and students is so complex. Personal biases and emotions often can overshadow the subtle variables that affect all levels of human interaction. Teachers are all too quick to assume that a child's inappropriate behavior must be the result of problems at home or due to immaturity. Teachers need to realize that these behaviors are, at least partially, a consequence of their own actions.

Critical Dimensions of Teacher Behavior

While total objectivity in self-evaluation is impossible, this section examines a number of informal procedures that can be used by teachers to evaluate their impact on the students and to identify discrepancies between intended objectives and actual practice. Any such attempt must take into account several critical areas of teacher behavior that are conducive, if not prerequisite, to a healthy social environment in the classroom.

Positive-Negative. Human behavior is contagious. When people are in good moods, their cheerful and happy behavior usually will have a ripple effect. Those around them usually begin to show at least some of the same feelings. This phenomenon is a form of *modeling* or demonstration and is especially relevant when examining the effects of teacher behavior. Teachers' status and power in the classroom increase the probability that their behavior will be modeled by the children (Bandura, 1971 pp. 653–708). It is critical, therefore, that teachers be positive and enthusiastic whenever possible. While, quite naturally, everyone has some bad days, it can be devastating when they outnumber the good. A continuing pattern of negative teacher attitudes and behavior will inevitably affect the children in many unfortunate ways, such as student passivity, withdrawal, and fear.

A major part of the teacher's general outlook concerns the teacher's expectations for student academic achievement and social behavior. There is evidence that what a teacher expects to happen generally does, whether with an individual child or with an entire class (Rosenthal & Jacobsen, 1975). If a teacher is negatively biased by low IQ scores or personal perceptions, the concomitant low expectations may result in a student's self-fulfilling the prophecy. Cued by the teacher's comments, criticisms, and lowered standards, the student as well as his/her classmates may soon show the same negative opinions. When this happens, learning or social development cannot be encouraged. By contrast, the student whose teacher exudes optimism and challenges him/her to perform well should enjoy much success.

Positive attitudes and expectations must be combined with positive reinforcement. Liberal amounts of praise, support, and encouragement are found in every good classroom. By emphasizing children's good points, the teacher can build their confidence and desire to tackle more diffcult activities. Failure to use such encouragement is a mistake teachers cannot afford to make. The development of a healthy social interaction in the classroom has never been accomplished through criticism and ridicule.

Planned-Haphazard. To promote the participation of every child in the learning experience, the teacher must continuously plan, evaluate, and modify the daily educational program. To promote learning, all materials should be readily accessible, guidelines and limitations should be clearly spelled out, and the duties and responsibilities of the children should be clearly delineated (Klienfeld, 1963). After assessing individual differences, the teacher must use the information gained to select materials and imaginative activities that will stimulate thinking and enhance learning. Lack of such preparation will result in distrust, frustration, and failure for the children. These, in turn, can produce many undesirable social behaviors and prevent healthy social and emotional growth.

There is no one best way of teaching for all students or even for one student in all subjects. It is the responsibility of teachers, therefore, to identify the approach that is best suited to their educational objectives and to the abilities of the students. Discussions such as those concerning the advantages and disadvantages of open versus structured teaching styles are meaningless, unless they are related to these important variables. Emphasis must be given to the development of basic skills, that is, reading, writing, and arithmetic. They are the fundamental prerequisite to mastery of other areas. With this in mind, the teacher must realize that teaching styles which produce high levels of student morale or satisfaction do not necessarily result in the highest levels of learning (Boocock, 1973).

Regardless of the approach used, teachers must remain keenly aware of the effect their own behavior has on that of the children. The literature is replete with examples of how teachers have inadvertently reinforced inappropriate social behavior. Teachers need to realize that many disruptive behaviors can be modified by controlling their own responses to them. Similarly, systematic changes in teacher-behavior that is directed toward desirable classroom activity will increase its frequency and duration (Thomas, Becker, & Armstrong, 1970).

Flexible-Rigid.   With teaching, as with any profession, excellence demands continued growth and a willingness to change as the situation warrants. Each year brings new students and new problems. They come from a rapidly changing social environment and are characterized best by their diversity. Teachers who rely rigidly on an instructional methodology and an educational philosophy acquired years earlier are usually ineffective in the classroom. While some react to the students with disillusionment, most teachers quickly learn to deal with students on a trial-and-error basis. Learning from their failures as well as from their successes develops an openness to change that is one of a teacher's most valuable assets.

With colleagues, this open attitude should be reflected in the teacher's active search for new ideas and suggestions that will improve his/her own performance. Teachers should be willing to call in resource persons to discuss and explain techniques and principles with which they are unfamiliar. With students, they should readily admit that they do not know everything and that they can learn from the children just as the children can learn from them. By listening to their students and having the flexibility and security to incorporate some of the students' ideas into the daily routine, teachers can promote a high level of interest and participation in the classroom.

Consistent-Inconsistent.   Regardless of the age of the students or the type of educational program employed, it is of paramount importance that teachers be consistent in their interaction with both individual children and the group as a whole. This can be accomplished by clearly specifying the rules or standards for classroom behavior, as well as the consequences for noncompliance. If adhered to consistently, these guidelines can avoid the numerous social problems that otherwise erupt when teachers make frequent, arbitrary, or contradictory changes in the expected behavior code. Changes such as these can be expected to produce numerous misunderstand-ings, a wide range of "testing" behaviors, and considerable bitterness from the students.

The development of a healthy social environment in the classroom depends largely on the ability of teachers to gain the willing compliance and participation of the pupils. They must achieve this through a process of social exchange. Through affection and sincere concern they must prove to the students that they are working in their best interests; such action will thereby legitimize the power they exert. This process, however, can only be effective when that power is applied consistently from day to day and child to child. If and when the fairness of a teacher's behavior is adulterated by such inconsistences as frequent mood swings or favoritism, an atmo-sphere conducive to social growth cannot be maintained.

Understanding-Intolerant. Considering the cultural diversity that typifies so many classrooms today, it is likely that teachers very frequently will be products of environments quite different from those in which a few or even a majority of their students live. Teachers must be keenly aware of these differences and be sensitive to the conflicts or misunderstandings that can result from them. The cultural stereotypes and prejudices that can be lethal in the classroom usually stem from ignorance. Whether expressed openly in the teacher's words or actions, or more subtly in the teacher's lowered expectations for performance, such intolerance for diversity affects any child who differs from the norm—racially, socially, or mentally. By gathering information from a number of sources, whether in the school, the community, or the child's own home, interested teachers can gain a better understanding of these dif-ferences and use this knowledge to design a relevant program. They must be patient with differences and nonjudgmental. They must likewise avoid any form of moraliz-ing and not try to impose their own values and attitudes on the group. If accomplished, this open, accepting atmosphere will provide the optimum setting for the social, as well as academic, growth of the entire class. At the same time it will provide all the children with a model of understanding too often absent in their world.

Assessment Instruments and Techniques

There is no single assessment device that alone can provide an accurate picture of a teacher's behavior in the classroom. A variety of methods, both subjective and objec-tive, must be employed to study all of the critical dimension of performance just discussed.

While numerous approaches have been described in the literature, their prac-ticality for self-evaluation by classroom teachers is often questionable. Complex, time-consuming, and sometimes abstract, their relevance for controlled research is probably far greater. In line with the informal assessment envisioned in this book, therefore, the approaches suggested in this section require little or no training and are easy to adminster and interpret. Despite their simplicity, we believe that if they are used in combinations, they will provide information needed to identify the strengths and weaknesses in their performance and data needed to suggest specific targets for change.

Teacher-Attention Scale.   A teacher-attention scale is a very simple device intended to assist teachers in determining how effectively they employ social reinforcement in their interactions with the students. How frequently do they praise and encourage students? Do they tend to overlook desirable behavior and attend to inappropriate activity? Is aversive control depended on too heavily? These are the type of questions this tool can help the teacher answer.

A teacher-attention scale, as illustrated below, categorizes the social, verbal, and nonverbal responses of the teacher into three categories.

Reinforcing Actions (Positive, pleasant)	**Punishing Actions** (Aversive, unpleasant)	**Extinguishing Actions** (Ignoring, overlooking)
Supportive encouraging re-marks	Deliberately not answer-ing a question	Criticism
Expressing satisfaction/pleasure	Looking away	Ridicule
Smiling at student	Turning back to child	Verbal reprimands
Physical signs of affec-tion (pat on the back, a hug)	Leaving an area of the room	Facial expressions indi-dicating disapproval (frowns, scowls)
Acknowledging use of student's idea	Redirecting attention to another child	Body movement indicating hostility, dislike, irritation
Verbal praise		

The teacher behaviors are related to two general categories of student behavior: appropriate and inappropriate. While the definition of what is appropriate or inappropriate depends largely on the teacher, the circumstances, and the type of students, these examples are typical.

Appropriate Student Behavior	**Inappropriate Student Behavior**
Working quietly at seat	Talking loudly
Cooperating with a peer	Calling others names
Raising hand to ask a question	Running in the building
Participating in class activities	Daydreaming
Finishing assignments	Refusing to do assigned work

The teacher-attention scale is easy to administer. Using the table in Figure 6, the teacher records the number of reinforcing, punishing, and extinguishing actions directed toward appropriate and inappropriate student behavior in a given time period. During periods of relative inactivity, such as times when the students are assigned in-seat work, the teacher can maintain a fairly accurate record of all such behaviors (see Figure 6). During regular instruction or other group activities, however, this would be impractical. Self-monitoring during these periods would have to be limited to a single category, such as the number of times reinforcing actions were directed toward appropriate student behaviors and the number of times they followed inappropriate activity. A wrist counter can greatly facilitate the recording procedure. Data collection requires little effort; however, the teacher must remember to press the counter or to record a mark for each occurrence.

FIGURE 6   A.   Record of Teacher and Student Behavior

Teacher Behavior

		Reinforcing Actions	Punishing Actions	Extinguishing Actions
Student Behavior	Appropriate	ĬĤ ĬĤ I		III
	Inappropriate	I	I	ĬĤ I

While such self-collected data must be less than totally objective, it can be gathered at any time without the assistance of anyone else.

The same procedure, no doubt, can be enhanced if a neutral observer is used. A fellow teacher or an aide, if available for a half an hour each day for a week, could obtain a more complete and objective record of teacher attention in the classroom. Using video tapes also would be a possibility. After a period is recorded, the teacher or someone else could review the tape and score the use of attention as before.

The interpretation of these data is as uncomplicated as the procedure for recording them. With a few qualifications, the table in Figure 7 presents what most would agree to be the best use of the very potent social reinforcer, teacher attention. As can be seen, the emphasis has been placed on positive social interaction. Clearly, however, the reinforcing actions must be sincere and must be interpreted that way by the students. Any positive comment made habitually and repeatedly will result in a large count of reinforcing actions, but will not reflect the actual quality and degree of the social reinforcement used.

Of course, the teacher should avoid reinforcing inappropriate student behavior or punishing and extinguishing appropriate activity. It is also desirable to use as little punishment as possible, although there will be occasions when strong disciplinary action is warranted. The number of extinguishing actions recorded will depend on the amount of inappropriate student behavior, but such actions should decrease

FIGURE 7   B.   Record of Teacher and Student Behavior

Teacher Behavior

		Reinforcing Actions	Punishing Actions	Extinguishing Actions
Student Behavior	Appropriate	High number desirable	No occurrences optimum	No occurrences optimum
	Inappropriate	No occurrences optimum	No occurrences optimum. Use sparingly when needed.	Number depends on student behavior. Use when needed.

over time if used consistently and in combination with frequent positive reinforcement.

Flanders' Interaction Analysis Model.   Flanders (1963) has suggested that there is a relationship between certain patterns of teacher verbal behavior and student learning and participation. The critical factor, according to Flanders, is the degree of freedom that teachers allow the students. If teachers are direct, basing their interaction with the class on a continuing series of lectures, instructions, and corrections, it is believed such an approach is less than optimum for learning and social growth. A more open, accepting approach should facilitate pupil-teacher interaction and greater involvement among the students themselves.

Based on this idea, Flanders developed a system for observing and interpreting the verbal interaction between teacher and pupils. Described in *Interaction Analysis in the classroom: A manual for observers* (Flanders, 1964), the technique requires a trained observer and a commitment to detail. In some situations, when assistance is available for evaluation of teaching effectiveness, it could provide a great deal of valuable information. In most cases, however, the system, as originally conceived, would be difficult to employ.

Every teacher, on the other hand, could benefit from a somewhat simplified version of the Flanders technique. Using a tape recorder would eliminate the necessity of an observer. Recordings made during the day could be replayed and interpreted by the teacher at a later time. Using the ten different categories of teacher and student statements, summarized in Table 2, the teacher would decide which one best represents the verbal interaction in each interval of observation and then record its corresponding category number (1–10). Recording in this way at three-second intervals, the teacher can identify the predominant patterns of student-teacher interaction taking place.

Before scoring the tapes, the teacher should prepare himself/herself by memorizing the numbers of the categories. The teacher should also remember, in making subtle distinctions between categories, to lean in the direction of the pattern of verbal behavior that has dominated the particular period covered by the tape. As in any assessment procedure, personal biases or expectations must not color the results.

The use of this assessment device can provide teachers with a fairly good description of the verbal interaction taking place in their classrooms and help them answer several important questions. For what percentage of the time are they talking? Do they use more praise than criticism? Do the students initiate much of the conversation, or do they simply respond predictably to the requests of the teacher? These and other questions can be studied by comparing the frequency with which each of the categories in Table 2 has been recorded. While not as thorough or objective as the traditional Flanders procedure, it can sensitize teachers to these very important aspects of the social climate of their classrooms.

Student Questionnaires.   Any evaluation of the teacher's performance and impact on the social environment of the classroom would be incomplete without some measure of the students' perception of the teacher. In fact, if this can be accurately obtained, it may be the most valid indicator of the effectiveness of the

TABLE 2   Categories for interaction analysis, 1959

TEACHER TALK	**INDIRECT INFLUENCE**	1.* ACCEPTS FEELING: accepts and clarifies the tone of feeling of the students in an unthreatening manner. Feelings may be positive or negative. Predicting or recalling feelings are included.
		2.* PRAISES OR ENCOURAGES: praises or encourages student action or behavior. Jokes that release tension, but not at the expense of another individual, nodding head or saying "um hm?" or "go on" are included.
		3.* ACCEPTS OR USES IDEAS OF STUDENT: clarifying, building, or developing ideas suggested by a student. As teacher brings more of his own ideas into play, shift to category 5.
	DIRECT INFLUENCE	4.* ASKS QUESTIONS: asking a question about content or procedure with the intent that a student answer.
		5.* LECTURING: giving facts or opinions about content or procedure; expressing his own ideas, asking rhetorical questions.
		6.* GIVING DIRECTIONS: directions, commands, or orders which students are expected to comply with.
		7.* CRITICIZING OR JUSTIFYING AUTHORITY: statements intended to change student behavior from unacceptable to acceptable pattern; bawling someone out; stating why the teacher is doing what he is doing; extreme self-reference.
STUDENT TALK		8.* STUDENT TALK—RESPONSE: talk by students in response to teacher. Teacher initiates the contact or solicits student statement.
		9.* STUDENT TALK—INITIATION: talk initiated by students. If "calling on" student is only to indicate who may talk next, observer must decide whether student wanted to talk.
SILENCE		10.* SILENCE OR CONFUSION: pauses, short periods of silence and periods of confusion in which communication cannot be understood by the observer.

*There is NO scale implied by these numbers. Each number is classificatory, designating a particular kind of communication event. To write numbers down during observation is merely to identify and enumerate communication events, not to judge them.

Source: Flanders, N.A. *Teacher influence, pupil attitudes, and achievement.* Washington, D.C.: U.S. Department of Health, Education and Welfare. p. 20.

teacher. Nevertheless, there are problems with this area of assessment. We cannot always assume that what children put down on questionnaires is what they really feel. They may simply be responding in a way they think would please the teacher or in a way that corresponds with their friends' feelings. They may also fear reprisals from the teacher if they are negative in what they say.

Despite these problems, the teacher must tap this very valuable source of information. To do this, a number of devices and procedures can be used. The two presented in Figures 8 and 9 are probably the most common types. While they illustrate the general content and structure that can be used, teachers must devise questions that can be read and understood by their students. The questions should examine those aspects of the classroom that the teacher considers most relevant. The teacher also must take steps to minimize the problems noted earlier. Above all, anonymity must be stressed. Students should not be asked to fill in their names, and the collection of the questionnaires should be handled to prevent the teacher's knowing who wrote which paper.

The questionnaire in Figure 8 uses a true-false format that is easy and quick for students to answer. It can be used to measure children's attitudes toward the teacher and the school and can help to identify those practices that help or hinder their development. When using this approach, it is important to disregard those questionnaires that were filled out thoughtlessly or automatically, that is, with all questions marked *true* or *false*. This can be done by including questions that would be contradictory if all are marked *true*. In Figure 8 for example, answers of *true* on questions 10 and 11 would be contradicted by answers of *true* for 26 and 28. When such is the case, it should be obvious to the teacher that the student replied without thinking and that particular questionnaire should be disregarded.

A second type of questionnaire that teachers frequently use with their students is the sentence-completion approach (see Figure 9). While this form requires more time and ability on the part of the students, it can provide very meaningful information not obtainable through more direct instruments, such as the true-and-false device. Using open-ended sentence stems, this questionnaire allows students to respond in their own unique, personal, and often surprising manner.

It is very important, in administering this instrument, to emphasize to the students that it is not a test. Teachers should encourage them to respond the way

Regular evaluation of the classroom society will help
the teacher establish goals for each student.

FIGURE 8   *True-False Student Questionnaire*

This questionnaire was made up to help your teacher find out what things he/she does well and what else he/she might do to help you learn. Read each of these sentences carefully. If you think that the sentence is true, circle Ⓣ. If you think that the sentence is false, circle Ⓕ.

True	False		
T	F	1.	My teacher helps me to do my best work.
T	F	2.	It is easy and fun to learn in this classroom.
T	F	3.	I pay attention in this classroom.
T	F	4.	The teacher knows when we are bored.
T	F	5.	At night I often think about things we learned in school.
T	F	6.	My teacher likes us to ask questions.
T	F	7.	When I don't understand something, my teacher explains it to me.
T	F	8.	When I do a good job, my teacher is very pleased.
T	F	9.	I am able to keep up with my assignments.
T	F	10.	When I disagree with my teacher, he/she listens to me.
T	F	11.	My teacher likes me.
T	F	12.	I usually know what my teacher wants me to do.
T	F	13.	I am usually interested in the subjects we study.
T	F	14.	My teacher talks all the time.
T	F	15.	Our exams are fair.
T	F	16.	Assignments are clear and easy to understand.
T	F	17.	Our teacher allows us to help each other.
T	F	18.	You have to get permission to do anything in our class.
T	F	19.	My teacher has a "pet" in our class.
T	F	20.	I like to come to school.
T	F	21.	My teacher always seems to know what he/she is doing.
T	F	22.	I'm never sure when my teacher will get angry with me.
T	F	23.	Some of the students in my class are not liked by my teacher.
T	F	24.	My teacher thinks I do good work.
T	F	25.	Sometimes my teacher says unkind things to me.
T	F	26.	My teacher doesn't like me.
T	F	27.	My friends and I have fun in our class.
T	F	28.	Our teacher doesn't like us to disagree with him/her.
T	F	29.	My teacher is usually in a good mood.
T	F	30.	I like my teacher.

they really feel and not to worry about right or wrong answers. In addition, they should make sure the students understand that the teacher is the only one who will read their papers. Before students begin, several sample sentences should be completed to illustrate how they are to respond.

FIGURE 9   *Sentence-Completion Student Questionnaire*

1. I learn best if_____

2. I am happiest when my teacher _____

3. In this class, working with others is _____

4. My teacher thinks I am _____

5. When I ask questions, my teacher _____

6. When I am discouraged, my teacher _____

7. This class is _____

8. The thing I like best about my teacher is _____

9. When I do a good job, my teacher _____

10. The thing I like least about this class is _____

11. If only my teacher _____

12. The thing I like most about this class is _____

The sentence-completion questionnaire in Figure 9 is not appropriate for every classroom. Its applicability depends on the age and ability of the students and the classroom situation. Nevertheless, this form can serve as an example that teachers can use to develop something especially suited for them. Since there is no set scoring system, items can be easily added or deleted.

Teachers can supplement the information obtained in these forms by simply observing student behavior with specific questions in mind. For example, they may wonder how to increase active student participation and social exchange in the classroom. If so, it would be profitable to note carefully the setting, activity, and their own behavior during times when students are interested, enthusiastic, and asking many questions. While very informal, such examination of the daily routine can help teachers identify those aspects of their approach and program that generate desirable activity. A similar study of the environment can be made when the children become bored, fidgety, or "act out." Such studies are worth the time and effort if they will help teachers avoid the blind, unquestioning use of the same old routines and the deadening effects they can have on the social environment of the classroom.

Implications and Suggestions for Change

All too often, in education, assessment becomes an end in itself, rather than a method to identify and promote more effective programs. Various tests and measures are administered, yielding impressive amounts of data, and all concerned feel that an important and necessary process has been completed. For one reason or another, however, the information obtained does not result in any substantial change in the program. In all the sections in this chapter, therefore, suggestions are made to encourage the meaningful use of the data collected.

All the assessment techniques described in this section thus far have dealt, directly or indirectly, with teacher behaviors. Areas of weakness identified by these procedures, therefore, should result in some form of a behavior-change program. A teacher's general resolve to improve is not enough. It would be far more effective for teachers to identify specific behavior targets for themselves, much as they do for their students. They would then chart the target behavior and implement strategies to increase or decrease its frequency, whichever is appropriate. If, for example, the teacher-attention scale and the student questionnaires indicated that the teacher did not praise or encourage students enough, he/she could focus on this specific problem. A daily record could be kept on the number of positive statements directed toward the children. A golf counter could be used, or the students themselves could be asked to record the number of times the teacher said something nice to them. Frequently, such feedback by itself can produce positive changes, but progress could be further enhanced by using prompts. Teachers could keep a varied list of positive words and phrases in a prominent place on their desks as a reminder, as well as an aid, to give meaningful praise. While initially awkward, such verbal behavior becomes much more natural and spontaneous with practice.

In addition to developing specific behavior-change goals and programs, the teacher could share the results of the self-evaluation with fellow professionals and solicit their suggestions. This is especially effective if the teacher first narrows the focus to specific areas that most need improvement.

Much help can also be obtained from professional journals and books. Books on classroom games and activities can assist teachers in stimulating student interest if this is lacking. Journal articles that report new and innovative teaching styles can often yield ideas which can be modified or adapted by teachers to enhance and invigorate their own approaches.

Peer-Group Influence

In studying school-age children and the social environment of their classrooms, it would be difficult to overestimate the influence exerted on them by their peers. Interacting with them daily in a variety of activities and settings, the children learn to see themselves as leaders, followers, fringers, or isolates. When accepted and liked by their peers, children gain confidence and self-assurance and indeed perform better on academic tasks (Spaulding, 1964). Uncertain or partial acceptance, on the other hand, can produce anxiety and self-doubt. When students are totally rejected, they may experience genuine trauma and act out aggressively or withdraw into apathy or fantasy (Goldenson, 1970).

The degree to which children are affected by their peers depends on many factors, including age, background, and race. Elementary age and younger students, for example, tend not to form strong peer-group values (Shinn, 1972). At this level of maturity, home and adult praise are still more important than peer approval. As a child approaches midadolescence, however, the influence of the peer group grows dramatically. Peers have also been shown to assert more influence over classmates from lower socioeconomic levels (Tasseigne, 1975). Whereas children from stable family situations show less need to conform (Rice, 1975), the inadequate home life frequently found in lower class areas can insure broad and pervasive peer influence. In such cases, peer acceptance may be all important to youngsters at that particular time in their lives. Considering the minimal value typically attributed to school-related achievement by children from low socioeconomic backgrounds, it is more than likely that attitudes and behaviors not conducive to learning will be reinforced.

According to Winkler (1975) the effect of peer-group composition, especially in the area of academic achievement, can also depend on the race of the child. He states that if black youngsters move from a largely black school to a mostly white school, they may be affected adversely in two ways: (1) the new and tougher academic standards they will probably face may discourage their efforts and likelihood for success, and (2) they may feel socially threatened and avoid trying so as not to appear competitive with white classmates.

Considering the crucial impact that children's peers can have on their social and academic development, teachers must become as knowledgeable as possible about this component of the classroom social environment. While teacher control of peer influence is often very difficult to achieve, especially with adolescent groups, there are things that a teacher can do to increase the chances for healthy social interaction among the children in the classroom. Any attempt to so guide peer-group activity and thinking must, however, be based on an awareness of two key factors. These factors must be the focus of careful evaluation before effective intervention can be planned.

Peer Norms and Values

In every school classroom, where children learn and play together daily, an extensive system of norms, expectations and values quickly develops. As with all social groups, this system stipulates what will be accepted and admired in every common area of behavior. Dress codes and the adherence to an ever-changing series of fads, provides an obvious illustration. Patterns of speech, with the various in-vogue slang expressions, also are typically present. Of more significance, however, is the impact peer norms can have on the academic achievement and social behavior of the students. Children want to be popular and accepted by their peers. If they perceive, therefore, that such activities as getting good grades, participating in class, or cooperating with the teacher are unacceptable, most likely they will avoid them and conform to the group's standard of behavior. Conversely, peer reinforcement for these and other behaviors can be tremendously effective in motivating individual students.

In a related study, Tannenbaum (1959) asked more than 600 students to rate the social acceptability of eight hypothetical classmates. The ranking in acceptability was as follows:

Student   Social Acceptability

1. Brilliant, nonstudious, athletic.
2. Average, nonstudious, athletic.
3. Average, studious, athletic.
4. Brilliant, studious, athletic.
5. Brilliant, nonstudious, nonathletic.
6. Average, nonstudious, nonathletic.
7. Average, studious, nonathletic.
8. Brilliant, studious, nonathletic.

Whether or not these rankings are typical is not important. They simply illustrate the type of stereotyping that exists in every peer group. Teachers must know, in advance, what their students' beliefs are and whether they conflict with or support their own.

In addition to the behavioral norms just discussed, each peer group develops and maintains a set of attitudes, values, and perceptions that colors the way the children see others. There are often stereotypes of authority figures and, accurate or not, they can have a very real effect on the relationships children have with such people. Group thinking similarly influences children's perceptions of their home, school, social class, and race. Quite often the peer group maintains the prejudices and biases modeled from their parents.

How much a teacher can influence peer-group thinking depends on many things, but in any case to try will be challenging. As Calvert (1975) states, "in the face of peer-group norms which conflict with the official norms, teachers are virtually powerless, and one of the most serious problems of today's school can be conceptualized as the resolution of the conflict between this rival set of norms" (p. 76). Nevertheless, there are actions sensitive teachers can take if they understand the peer culture of their classroom.

Peer Roles and Relationships

The peer group in every classroom, no matter how large or small, has some degree of organization. For example, it has leaders who attain their popularity and status through actions and attributes considered important by the group. In such roles, peer-group leaders frequently are instrumental in determining group activity, initiating the acceptance of new members, establishing a cooperative or antagonistic attitude toward the teacher, and deciding numerous other questions that confront the group. Quite obviously, where there are leaders there are also followers. Many children accept these roles and the implicit expectations for behavior that accompany them. Even among the followers a pecking order often exists, and some youngsters are continuously to be found on the fringe of activity. According to Weigand (1972), these various roles become fixed early in the school year, and the status quo tends to be maintained.

In a classroom cliques and subgroups commonly exist within the overall peer group. This is especially true in schools where the student body is socially and economically heterogenous. Formed on the basis of personality types, geographical location, or common problems or goals, these subgroups often manifest their own behavioral code and follow their own leaders.

Teachers must identify student leaders and understand classroom alliances if they are to be effective in promoting a healthy social climate. As Fox, Luszki, and Schmuck (1966) point out, hopefully the teacher will discover a diffuse pattern of friendships, in which each student is "most liked" by some other member of the class. On the other hand, they point out that in "a narrowly focused pattern of friendships, in which one subgroup or pupils is not popular, another subgroup is most unpopular, and the rest of the pupils have few if any friends, many pupils tend to have negative feelings towards themselves, perceive school unfavorably and make poor use of their potentials" (p. 23).

Assessment Instruments and Techniques

While probably not so difficult or so emotionally involving as the teacher self-assessment discussed earlier, the objective evaluation of the peer culture is a challenge for the teacher. This is due, in large part, to the discrepancy between the teacher's and the student's perception of peer behavior (Yarrow & Campbell, 1963). When we consider the limitless parent/child conflicts blamed on the generation gap, it is easy to understand how the age factor, in combination with value and sometimes sex differences, can lead to a teacher's misinterpretation of peer-group behavior. Quite obviously, a white, middle-class female teacher in a predominately black inner city school would require tremendous skill, experience, and luck to perceive accurately the attitudes and social behavior of the boys—or for that matter—of the girls in the room. While most teaching situations are not so challenging, it is imperative that teachers be cognizant of value discrepancies and study their students' social behavior with open and understanding minds.

Questionnaires on Classroom Norms.   It is questionable whether teachers ever fully understand peer-group norms and attitudes. Any attempt to identify them and assess their impact on classroom social behavior is compounded not only by their own values, but also by the diversity of values among the students themselves. In fact, it is questionable whether individual students correctly perceive these standards of behavior. Nevertheless, teachers can use a rather simple procedure that involves two questionnaires to help them learn about this important aspect of the student's social environment. Developed by Fox et al. (1966), one question-naire (Figure 10) studies the student's perception of how the class feels about different items, and the second questionnaire (Figure 11) examines the child's personal feelings about the same things. While not appropriate for every classroom setting, the procedure does provide a prototype that can easily be modified to better suit particular situations. Questions, such as those listed here, could be used with the same format to study numerous areas of student thinking.

1.   It is good to do well in school work and to get as high grades as possible.

2.   It is good to tell the teacher if one student is hurting or fighting with another student.

3.   It is okay to cheat if you are only giving answers to a friend.

4.   It is best if you study just enough to pass.

5.   It is good to sit in the front of the class.

6.   It is okay to work alone sometimes on things that you are interested in.

7.   It is best if you are in good with the teacher.

8.   It is good to participate after school in clubs and other activities.

Whatever questions are ultimately included, using these two forms can provide a very interesting picture of group and individual norms. As suggested by Fox et al. (1966), a meaningful interpretation of these data can best be accomplished by examining the consequences and discrepancies among the different measures. To do this, the teacher should follow these steps:

1.   Tabulate the collective results in the class norms questionnaire (Form A); note the frequency with which each response was checked. This distribution repre-sents the perceived classroom norms.

2.   Tabulate the collective results on the personal norms questionnaire (Form B). By comparing this distribution with that obtained on Form A; estimate the degree of consequence between perceived norms and individual standards. If the two correspond closely, then there is probably open, effective communication among students. If, however, there is a substantial discrepancy, the perceived norm is not real. Strategies to promote greater social interaction must then be developed.

3.   Compare one student's responses on Form A to the distribution of re-sponses made by the rest of the class. A discrepancy between the student's percep-

FIGURE 10   Form A.   Questionnaire on class norms

Date _____

Your number _____

Class _____

How This Class Feels

School classes are quite different from one another in how pupils think and feel about school work, about one another, and about teachers. How do you think your classmates feel about the following things? Put a check √ in one of the boxes under "How Many Feel This Way?" for each of the statements below. *There are no right or wrong answers.*

How Many Feel This Way?

	Almost all	Many	About half	Some	Only a few
1. It is good to take part as much as possible in classroom work.	☐	☐	☐	☐	☐
2. Asking the teacher for help is a good thing to do.	☐	☐	☐	☐	☐
3. It is good to help other pupils with their school-work except during tests.	☐	☐	☐	☐	☐
4. Schoolwork is more often "fun" than it is "not fun."	☐	☐	☐	☐	☐
5. Our teacher really understands how pupils feel.	☐	☐	☐	☐	☐

Source: From *Diagnosing Classroom Learning Environments,* p. 42, by Robert Fox, Margaret Barron Luszki, & Richard Schmuch. Copyright © 1966, Science Research Associates, Inc., Chicago, Illinois, 1966. Reprinted by permission of the publisher.

tion of the norms and the actual consensus may indicate at least a partial isolation from the group.

4.   Finally compare one child's responses on Form A to those made by the same child on Form B. There may be a difference between what the child per-

FIGURE 11   Form B.   Questionnaire on personal norms

Date _____

Your number _____

Class _____

How Do You Feel About These Things?

Put a check √ in the box that tells how you feel about each of the statements below. *There are no right or wrong answers.*

	I agree almost always	I agree more than I disagree	I agree as often as I disagree	I disagree more than I agree	I disagree almost always
1. It is good to take part as much as possible in classroom work.	☐	☐	☐	☐	☐
2. Asking the teacher for help is a good thing to do.	☐	☐	☐	☐	☐
3. It is good to help other pupils with their school-work except during tests.	☐	☐	☐	☐	☐
4. Schoolwork is more often "fun" than it is "not fun."	☐	☐	☐	☐	☐
5. Our teacher really understands how pupils feel.	☐	☐	☐	☐	☐

Source: From *Diagnosing Classroom Learning Environments,* p. 43, by Robert Fox, Margaret Barron Luszki, & Richard Schmuch. Copyright © 1966, Science Research Associates, Inc., Chicago, Illinois, 1966. Reprinted by permission of the publisher.

ceives as the classroom norms and his own personal standards. When this is the case, it may indicate feelings of alienation or a conscious awareness of being different from the rest of the children.

Additional understanding can be achieved if the teacher responds to Form B before administering it to the children. Comparing the distribution of student responses on Form B with his/her own can indicate discrepancies between them. If the teacher's perception differs significantly from the consensus of student responses, then there is apparent breakdown in teacher-child communication. The teacher must take steps to convey more effectively his/her opinions and expectations to the class.

Sociometric Devices.   To study the organizational structure of the classroom and the network of peer interrelationships, the teacher must use a sociometric device. There are many different kinds, but all ask the child to choose from one to three children with whom he/she would like to sit, work, eat, and play. Originally developed by Moreno (1953), this form of peer rating is believed to offer the most accurate and dependable rating procedure (Fishe & Cox, 1960; Hollander, 1965; Reynolds, 1966).

The questions and format used again depend on the age and ability of the children. In all cases, however, it is preferable to word them in a positive way. "Who would you most like to have sitting next to you?" is more appropriate than "Who would you least like to have sitting next to you?" While both types of questions are frequently included on sociometric instruments, the negative form can focus unnecessary attention on the less popular members of the class. The negative approach may stimulate the curiosity of the students to subsequently compare notes and confirm their choices of least-desirable classmates. As noted by Adams (1964), it is also possible that the inclusion of questions worded this way may convince children that the teacher understands and accepts their rejection of particular classmates.

In developing an appropriate sociometric test teachers can make up their own items or possibly select questions from the following list.

1.   Who would you like to play with the most after school?
2.   Who would you most like to have on your baseball team?
3.   With whom do you best like to eat lunch?
4.   To whom would you most likely tell a secret?
5.   In our classroom, who would you most like to have sitting near you?
6.   Who would you best like to be captain of your basketball team?
7.   With which students would you most enjoy studying?
8.   Who would you most like to have stay overnight at your home?
9.   Who are your best friends in this classroom?
10.   Who are the most popular students in the class?

Three or four questions are typically sufficient, unless the teacher wishes to closely examine the effect of different settings and activities on the overall pattern of social interaction. In this case, questions specific to particular settings (the playground, shop, cafeteria) or activities (art, music, physical education, reading group) would be included. The questions selected can be presented in a variety of formats, but the one used in Figure 12 is very simple and probably suitable for most classrooms.

When using this type of sociometric device, it is helpful for the teacher to give the students the names of all their classmates. Putting the names on the board or in

FIGURE 12   Sociometric questionnaire

Name _____

Date _____

My School Friends

As your teacher, I would like to find out which children in this class you would prefer to do things with. This helps me plan our daily program. Read each question carefully and write the names of three students whom you would choose. Choose anyone in this room you wish; I'm the only one who will know your choices.

A.   In our classroom who would you most like to have sitting near you?

     1. _____

     2. Who else? _____

     3. Who else? _____

B.   With which students would you most enjoy studying?

     1. _____

     2. Who else? _____

     3. Who else? _____

C.   With whom do you best like to eat lunch?

     1. _____

     2. Who else? _____

     3. Who else? _____

D.   Who would you like to play with the most after school?

     1. _____

     2. Who else? _____

     3. Who else? _____

a handout can prevent students' overlooking a friend and can assist them in spelling their choices.

For younger children, who are unable to read these questions or to respond in written form, it is necessary to administer the device orally. The teacher could read the questions to each child individually and record the child's choices. This consumes a great deal of time. A more efficient method would be to have an older student helper, from the fourth or fifth grade, administer the device. In addition to saving time, it is conceivable that the children would respond more openly and honestly to an older student than they would to the teacher.

Remember that at any age level social relationships take time to develop. The pattern reflected in a sociometric device, administered early in the year, may well differ from one given several months later. The teacher, therefore, should allow time for groups and friendships to develop before using this type of social assessment.

Sociometric devices such as the one in Figure 12 can be tabulated in a number of different ways. The easiest involves a simple tally sheet such as the one illustrated in Figure 13. The horizontal rows indicate the choices made by each child and the vertical columns show how many times each student was chosen. Although the numerals *1, 2* and *3* were used to indicate the ranking of individual choices, the tally at the bottom simply reflects an unweighted total number of choices. Weighting the choices would take additional time and probably add very little to the interpretation.

A separate tally sheet should be used for each question asked on the sociometric questionnaire. In this way, it is possible for the teacher to determine quickly whether a change in setting or activity is reflected in the pattern of social interaction.

The class represented in Figure 13 is small but, nevertheless, sufficient in size to illustrate how to tabulate and interpret children's responses on a sociometric device. At a glance, the teacher can see which children are most popular and which children are not. Receiving eight choices in a class this small clearly establishes David as a class leader. Everyone in the class has at least one person who would like to sit by him/her, except Charles. The teacher would need to give careful consideration to his location in the classroom seating arrangement.

It is sometimes helpful to depict graphically this kind of data. One of the most common procedures for doing this is the use of the target sociogram. As can be seen in Figure 14, the target consists of four circles. Following a system developed by Bronfenbrenner (1944), the placement of a child in the target is dependent on the number of choices he/she has received. When children are given three choices, as with the questionnaire in Figure 12, those students receiving more than seven choices would be placed in the center ring; those receiving between four and seven choices would go in the second ring; those with between one and three choices belong in the third ring; and children unselected by anyone else would be placed in the outer ring.

When the data are depicted this way, the teacher can easily see how narrow or diffuse the social interaction is in the classroom. It is probably optimum to have all the students fall within the second or third rings. This would reflect social balance and would indicate that every child has developed at least one liking relationship. Nevertheless, this is usually not the case. Like the peer group represented in Figure 14, which was based on the same data recorded in Figure 13, there is often at least one child who is isolated from the rest of the students. While classroom leaders are natural and are expected, those who enjoy the degree of status which David has in this classroom often do so to the exclusion of others. The teacher

FIGURE 13   Sociometric tally sheet

Date:
Question: In our classroom, who would you most like to have sitting near you?

	Andrew R.	Billy P.	Betsy J.	Charles J.	David L.	Dotty A.	Fran B.	George F.	Johnny G.	Johnny L.	Sandy O.	Susan D.
Andrew R.		2			1				3			
Billy P.					1				2	3		
Betsy J.					3						1	2
Charles J.					3			2	1			
David L.		1						3	2			
Dotty A.			1		2							3
Fran B.			1								3	2
George F.		1					2		3			
Johnny G.	3	2			1							
Johnny L.	3	2			1							
Sandy O.			2		1	3						
Susan D.			2		3						1	
Number of Times Chosen	2	5	4	0	8	2	1	2	5	1	3	3

must make an effort to point out and encourage the strengths and leadership of the other children as well.

Another way of plotting sociometric data to aid the teacher grasping its meaning is depicted in Figure 15. This is another form of sociogram which is sometimes called a *class map*. While this technique is not as practical as the target sociogram when evaluating large classrooms, it can assist a teacher who is responsible for a small group of children.

Using only the first and second choices of the students to simplify the diagram, the data from Figure 13 were plotted as a class map (Figure 15). In examining Figure 15 additional information becomes readily apparent. There is a strong mutual relationship among David, Billy, and Johnny G. The other boys have directed most of their choices toward the members of this clique, but the absence of reciprocal choices by the clique indicates an unwillingness to include them. Among the girls, Betsy is the most popular, and along with Sandy and Susan makes up another subgroup in this classroom. There is more interaction between the boys and girls than would be expected for a fifth grade, although most of it involves the

FIGURE 14   Target sociogram

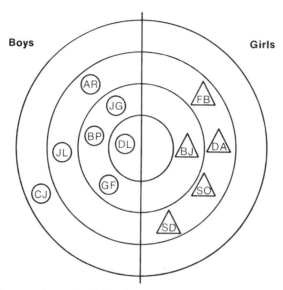

popularity of only one boy, David, with three of the girls. Interestingly enough, Fran's only positive choice came from a boy.

School children are typically very concerned about where their desks are located and whom they are sitting near. Their responses to a question about this are therefore very informative. Nevertheless, a teacher may find different patterns of interaction for different settings or activities and should separately tabulate and analyze responses to questions examining these areas.

It is interesting how enlightening sociometric techniques can be in evaluating a teacher's classroom behavior. In addition to approaches described in an earlier section that focused on self-assessment by the teacher it would be beneficial to ask, "Who in this class is most liked by the teacher?" As suggested by Hammill and Bartel (1975), teachers may very well discover that their attraction toward or biases against particular children may be clearly perceived by the rest of the class. If one or two names are repeatedly selected in answer to either of these questions, this is probably happening. On the other hand, a variety of responses would show that the teacher does not isolate children in this way.

Observation of Student Behavior.   While student questionnaires and sociometric devices are valuable tools in the assessment of peer influence and relationships, they should always be supplemented by direct, systematic observation of student behavior in the classroom. If carried out routinely, observation can provide numerous insights into the social activity of the students and can serve to check the sometimes dubious validity of the *self-report* techniques. In addition, observation can provide much needed feedback on the effectiveness and success of the strategies the teacher employs to enhance social development.

It is beyond the scope of this text to comprehensively examine all the various observation techniques and procedures that have been developed by educators and

FIGURE 15   Sociogram

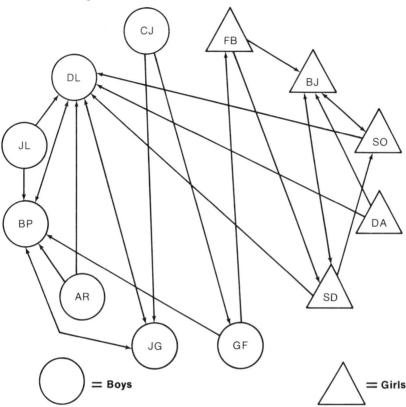

psychologists over the past two decades. If readers are unfamiliar with such terms as *baseline, frequency counts* or *internal recording,* they should refer to the many books that focus on these important techniques. One of the best is Cartwright and Cartwright, *Developing Observation Skills* (1974).

Given the complexity of peer-group interactions and the large class size which is characteristic of most educational situations today, it is obviously impossible for teachers to observe everything. Even with the help of an aide, overly ambitious schedules of observation can be frustrating and counterproductive. Teachers, therefore, must establish priorities and concentrate their observations on some aspect of the social environment.

One approach would be to observe the behavior of the student who is most in need of help or who most directly affects the social atmosphere of the classroom. By systematically observing a child who frequently annoys other students or disrupts group activities, teachers may discover an approach that could assist them in developing a more healthy social interaction. Most of the disruptive behavior actually may occur during a certain period of the day, such as in reading group or while doing in-seat work. On the other hand, the child may be acting up most often when with a particular child or group of children. Such clues may be picked up with careful observation.

In studying the social behavior of individual children, it can also be very helpful to observe the reaction of their peers immediately after they act inappropriately. As we have already discussed, inadvertent attention from the teacher can greatly strengthen such activity. Similarly, the attention a child gets from peers is a critical factor in determining behavior. Figure 16, an observation form, illustrates one child's behavior with the reaction of his peers. The undesirable behavior was a fifth grader's frequent use of swear words in class. For every audible occurrence, the time was recorded to the nearest minute. At the same time, an estimate of the peer response was made. Any laughter at all resulted in a check under the corresponding column. When there was no apparent reaction from the child's peers, this was indicated by a check in the last column. As can be seen, this child's swearing consistently resulted in much peer attention.

Many times the attention that children receive from their peers for maladaptive behavior is very obvious. While the use of an observation form in such situations may be unnecessary, it can provide a baseline on peer-reaction behavior. Any attempt to extinguish the undesirable behavior of a student would have to control this very potent source of social reinforcement. Programs devised by the teacher to accomplish this could quickly be judged effective to the degree to which they have reduced the checkmarks under *laughter* and *approval*. While the ultimate test lies in the elimination of the student's behavior, this requires more time and can only result after the peer reaction is controlled.

Observation of the total class is more difficult than the procedure just described but also can help to evaluate the impact of different settings and activities on the social interaction of the students. To facilitate the process, the teacher should limit observation to one or two easily seen behaviors that reflect a positive social exchange. The teacher should use a seating chart and a simple coding procedure, and then observe the class during short periods throughout the day. The frequency of student-initiated conversation might, in this way, be compared in different settings or grouping arrangements.

In this area of classroom assessment, the teacher must not overlook the possibility of helping the students to use self-appraisal to modify and improve their social behavior. Garner (1974), working with intermediate level children, demonstrated how this might be done. The children first made a checklist of talking and listening behaviors.

Talking Behaviors	**Listening Behaviors**
Answering a teacher's question	Being attentive (looking at the speaker)
Answering a pupil's question	Being inattentive (not looking at the
Asking a question	speaker)
Offering additional information	Being disruptive (yawning, fidgeting, etc.)
Making an irrelevant contribution	
Interrupting to make a relevant comment	
Interrupting to make an irrelevant comment	

Subsequently, the class was divided into three groups, with each participating in a microteaching situation that was recorded on videotape. Each child then viewed

FIGURE 16   Behavior observation form

Name: Billy J.

Date: September 16, 19XX

Behavior: Audible use of swear words

Time of Each Occurence	Peer Reaction		
	Laughter	*Disapproval*	*No Response*
9:35	√	√	
10:15	√		
10:37	√	√	
11:06	√	√	
11:10	√		
(Lunch break)			
1:17	√		
2:32			√
2:55	√		

the replay of all three videotapes, using the checklist of behaviors to code his/her own behavior or that of one of his/her classmates. This simply involved checking the appropriate behavior each time a beep sounded every ten seconds.

After the coding sessions, the children discussed their behavior. All value judgments were avoided by the teacher, but the children made comments such as:

"I think John added a lot to the discussion."

"I didn't realize that I constantly twist my hair."

"I didn't talk at all."

"Chewing on my pencil sure looks crummy."

This experiment, which was repeated with similar success using a teacher-made checklist, strongly suggests that children at this level are capable of studying their own behavior. The discussions of what they liked and disliked in themselves, if guided sensitively by the teacher, could offer an effective strategy for both assessment and behavior change.

Implications and Suggestions for Change

The peer group in every classroom is different. Its unique composition of norms, values, and patterns of friendship depends on a wide range of factors. Each teacher, in using the various assessment techniques described in this section, will identify different problem areas. Improvement of peer relationships, in each case, will necessitate careful planning and implementation of an especially planned program. Nevertheless, there are a number of approaches that have enjoyed repeated success in this area, and at least deserve mention at this point. While each strategy discussed cannot be dealt with comprehensively, sources are cited from which teachers can get additional information and ideas for practical application.

Controlling Peer Attention.   Probably the most important thing that a teacher can accomplish with the peer group in the classroom is to promote the constructive use of peer attention. This necessarily involves two things: 1) the elimination of peer reinforcement for undesirable social behavior, and 2) the encouragement of peer acceptance of and attention for appropriate activity.

These objectives have been accomplished in a variety of ways. A group-contingency method was employed by Barrish, Saunders, and Wolf (1969) to eliminate inappropriate talking and out-of-seat behavior in a fourth grade class. They divided the class into two teams and established a point system whereby the teams could earn privileges. Points were lost when team members acted inappropriately. Such an arrangement puts pressure on all students to abide by class standards. Seeing their own self-interest at stake, their peers no longer attend to the antics of misbehaving classmates. To the contrary, they often actively discourage any activity that will result in the loss of privileges for all.

A similar study was conducted by Sherman (1973) to eliminate noisy, disruptive behavior in the cafeteria. A class-competition program was established in which the group behavior of five different classes was judged during lunch. Each day the winning class received a star, which was posted on the class chart in the cafeteria; a special plaque then was hung for the day on the outside of the classroom door.

Another approach was used by Patterson (1965) to modify the hyperactive behavior of an elementary-age child. It was explained to the class that if this child improved his behavior, he would earn candy that would be saved up until there was enough to share with the entire class. Under these conditions, students were inclined to cooperate with the teacher in ignoring the child's disruptive conduct.

These studies clearly illustrate that the teacher can exert some control over the attention and encouragement that children give to each other. There are few consequences that are more powerful than peer attention, and an imaginative teacher should be able to redirect numerous socially inappropriate behaviors by using strategies such as those discussed here. One word of caution, however, is in order. The teacher must be sure that the criteria for performance are realistic and easily attainable by the children involved. Otherwise facilitating peer pressure could quickly change to scorn or resentment if a child's failure to behave resulted in frequent loss of privileges or rewards for everyone else.

Peer Tutoring.   Another strategy that can be used to improve the social interaction of children is peer tutoring. While various arrangements can be made, this approach typically pairs a child who is strong in a particular academic subject with a student who is having difficulty in it. If the children are matched carefully and given a minimum of assistance, benefits can result not only in the academic realm but also in terms of social growth. If the peer tutors have status and are popular, it is likely that the children with whom they work will model their behavior and respond eagerly to the program.

Using the information gained from a sociometric device, such as the one presented in Figure 12, the teacher can determine which students would probably work effectively together. While it would be optimum to pair children who have indicated a preference for one another as study partners, sometimes this is impossible. The children who are isolated from the group usually are most in need of such involvement. Therefore the teacher usually must solicit the cooperation of the more mature children in the class to serve as tutors. When necessary, participation can be encouraged by using a *contingency contract.* In such a contract both children receive a mutually appealing reward when the student being tutored reaches a specified level of improvement.

When using the peer-tutoring approach, it is essential that both children clearly understand how they are to proceed. The teacher should structure the tutoring session as much as possible by establishing a set routine and by providing easy-to-use materials. Numerous peer-tutoring programs have been described in the literature (Brown, Fenrick, & Klemme, 1971; Starlin, 1971; Wagner, 1974) and reference to them can provide teachers with ideas and examples to use when implementing such programs.

Role Playing.   When it is evident from the class norms and personal norms questionnaires that one or several of the children are not accurately perceiving the attitudes and expectations of their classmates, it is often helpful to set up role-playing situations. The children are encouraged to act out brief episodes that involve problems of getting along with one another. Role playing provides a nonthreatening circumstance in which to encounter the various reactions of others and to learn appropriate ways to cope with such experiences. Even with children characterized by emotional problems, this technique has been used to establish more positive attitudes toward school and more realistic reactions to frustration.

Any number of situations can be presented through role playing. Teachers could take note of problems or conflicts that arise during class and have them reenacted later on in role-playing sessions. They also may want to introduce new situations that have not yet been encountered but which, in time, undoubtedly will arise. An excellent source of ideas for role playing is provided by Shaftel and Shaftel (1969).

Whenever using the role-playing technique, the teacher should remember the following points:

1.   Select situations that are concrete and relevant. While role playing offers an excellent way to deal with group problems, such as racial prejudice, specific, meaningful encounters should be used.

2.   Ask for volunteers to play the roles. Don't force children to role play in situations that are too upsetting to them. At the same time, avoid placing a child in his usual classroom role. The role-playing experience can become very personal and disturbing to a child placed in such a situation.

3.   Keep the role-playing sessions brief, and stop after the point has been made. If necessary, repeat particular situations several times with different children, but avoid long, drawnout encounters.

4.   Explain to the children observing a role-playing situation what they should

be watching for and ask them questions ahead of time that will help them grasp the meaning intended.

5.   Evaluate each session in an open, nonjudgmental manner. Always focus the discussion on the behavior rather than the child portraying it.

New Seating and Work Assignments.   As discussed earlier, each classroom is typically characterized by various patterns of friendship and social interaction. Sociometric data that are plotted in sociogram form can quickly reveal leaders, isolates, and subgroups as well as the existing relationships between the boys and the girls. Lack of communication and social distance can also be detected through the questionnaires described. When teachers have identified children or subgroups who only minimally participate in peer-group relationships, they should make changes in the seating and work assignments to encourage more involvement.

Rearrangements in seating plans may simply involve moving an isolated child closer to the center of the class or next to a friendly peer who is most likely to accept the isolate. If, on the other hand, whole groups of children are on the fringe of activity or in conflict with other cliques in the classroom, the teacher may want to use a seating arrangement that fully integrates the members of the different factions with each other. In any case the teacher should consider using a seating plan that promotes rather than hinders social interaction among students.

Four common seating arrangements are depicted in Figure 17. Plan A is probably the most commonly used and, unfortunately, is the least conducive to peer-group interaction. As the arrows indicate, the students face the teacher. This encourages teacher-to-student and student-to-teacher interaction and facilitates classroom control, but does little for social growth. Both plans B and C, by contrast, have the children facing each other. This stimulates student-to-student interaction and enhances class discussions and activities. Plan D, which places desks together in small groups, can be used to encourage teamwork or to foster closer relationships among students. The suitability of each of these arrangements and any other seating plans devised depends on the class size, the age and ability of the children, and the objectives of the teacher. Any plan, however, can be improved by providing space in the classroom where uninterrupted small-group activities can take place. In each of the plans depicted in Figure 17, the placement of partitions and tables for this purpose has been illustrated.

In terms of work assignments, the teacher can also stimulate social interaction between popular and accepted students and those usually relegated to the fringe of classroom activity. By selecting children for group reports, art projects, or recreational teams, the teacher can give neglected children an opportunity to participate actively. Whenever possible, the teacher should also assign duties and responsibilities to such children to further enhance their role and status in the classroom. Finally, if a rejected child has any special skill or knowledge, the teacher should think of situations in which the rejected child could share those skills with the group.

Additional Help for Isolated Children.   Frequently, when a sociometric device or a classroom questionnaire indicates that a child is isolated from or neglected by peers, this isolation can be explained quite easily. For example, the child may be new to the class, or for one reason or another, may be older than the other students.

FIGURE 17   Classroom seating plans

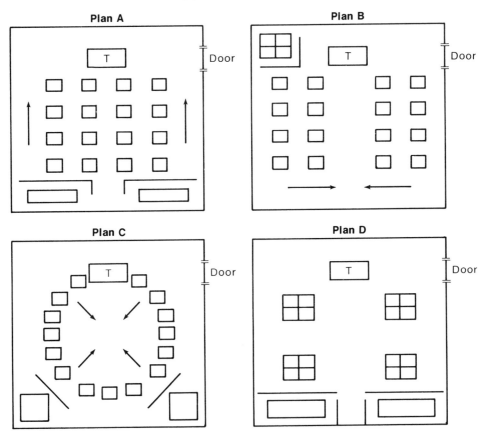

In such cases, a sensitive teacher can quicken the child's acceptance by using strategies such as those just given. There are times, however, when children are isolated or withdrawn for much more serious reasons. Some children, who are affected by serious emotional problems, act out their distress with a variety of maladaptive and disruptive behaviors. Their need for help is very apparent, and more specialized help should be sought by the teacher. Children who are withdrawn may have emotional conflicts that are just as grave as those of the acting-out child, but all too often they are overlooked. When teachers, therefore, cannot make progress in returning such children to a healthy social involvement in the class, it is critical that they make referrals to other professionals and disciplines. Teachers then will receive assistance in identifying effective ways to deal with the children's problems.

Curriculum Influence

The curriculum that teachers employ in the classroom must provide direction in terms of what is to be taught, how it is to be taught, and when it is to be taught. It must focus on stated goals, delineate procedures for accomplishing them, and offer techniques for remediating basic learning difficulties. It must attend, however, to more than academic content or teaching methodology. If selected and developed carefully, the curriculum can contribute very significantly to the social growth of the students as well.

Curricula differ tremendously in terms of several socially critical variables. As discussed by Joyce and Weil (1972), the student-teacher roles, the authority relationships in the classroom, and the norms for student behaviors that are encouraged and rewarded are all implicit or directly specified. They note that the range of leadership roles for the teacher includes acting solely as a facilitator of group activity, serving as a counselor for individual children, and acting as a taskmaster. In some cases teachers are the center of activity, arbitrarily making decisions as to the organization, focus, and pace of every endeavor. In other curricular models, a more equal relationship between the students and the teacher is called for. The expected student behavior varies accordingly, with vast differences in terms of the levels of independence and initiative required.

Faced with numerous curricular models and the tremendous diversity that characterizes them, the teacher must try to identify the optimum match between the unique academic and social needs of the students and the content and methodology inherent in each curriculum. This typically necessitates a balanced program somewhere in between an open, indirect student-oriented curriculum and one that is structured and content-oriented. As will be described, both have advantages and disadvantages. There is no single best approach, and it is usually ill-advised for a teacher to wholeheartedly embrace either in its entirety.

Structured, Content-Oriented Curriculum

In the structured, content-oriented approach, the emphasis is placed on the routine of the educational process. High priority is given to homework, good recitation, neat workbooks, and high test scores. The teacher's main role is to instruct, to present material, and the student's role is to learn it. In effect, this describes the traditional classroom, and the impact that it has on the social development of the student can be undesirable. Allman-Synder, May and Garcia (1975) have listed a number of the social conditions that sometimes coexist with this approach:

1. Environment of dominance and subordination occurs among teachers and students.
2. There is heavy reliance on authority to carry out educational functions.
3. Communication is discouraged.
4. Children are required to ignore peers.
5. Children must raise hands to be recognized.
6. Children have little freedom in selecting what they desire to learn.
7. There is strict adherence to rules.
8. There is minimized student participation and interaction.
9. Success is dependent on passivity.

10.   Feelings of submission, vulnerability, and perhaps fear in the child are created. (pp. 134–140)

Open, Student-Oriented Curriculum

In rather stark contrast, the open, student-oriented type of curriculum concentrates on establishing personal support with the students. Acting as a facilitator, advisor, or counselor in a warm relaxed atmosphere, the teacher encourages feelings of neutrality and stimulates active involvement on the part of the student not only in the learning process, but also in determining what is to be learned. Covering material or meeting academic standards is considered secondary to the development of more fundamental skills and attitudes. As Meyer (1968) reports, many of the teachers who have used this approach believe that "the presentation of subject matter itself was peripheral to the inculcation of a sense of personal worth, faith in ability to succeed, desire to learn, and certain other middle-class values which facilitate acceptance in our society." (p. 14)

When considering the social environment of the classroom, it would seem obvious that this latter approach would be a far more desirable way to instruct children. This is probably true for those students who are capable of handling the responsibility and independence required of them. For those who are not, the price of such classroom freedom can be very high. Consider, for example, the significant national drop in the SAT scores of college freshmen. Many attribute this unfortunate decline to the widespread employment of a more liberal, open, "do your own thing" curriculum in the public schools. It is important, therefore, that the teacher carefully consider all the educational objectives when evaluating or selecting a curriculum. If extensive freedom in childrens' school years results in poor academic achievement, they may not have the skills or knowledge required later for social and financial freedom.

Variables

In light of this discussion, it is clear that any assessment of the curriculum and its impact on the social environment of the classroom must be broadly based. Again, as conceived by Joyce and Weil (1972), both the instructional effects and the indirect or *nurturant* effects must be considered. In their example, intense competition for academic achievement may spur progress, but the effects of living in a competitive atmosphere may, at the same time, alienate the students from each other. The teacher must, therefore, balance instructional efficiency with the nurturant effect inherent in a curriculum.

The following variables reflect this need for balance. Regardless of the type of students a teacher is responsible for, any assessment of the curriculum impact on their social development should reflect all of these factors.

Student Achievement and Skill Development.   In most school systems teachers are provided with at least general standards of achievement desired and expected from the students. At the end of the year their performance, and implicitly their success as teachers, is usually assessed in some way. Even in situations when this is not the case, the classroom curriculum must be judged, in part, to the degree it provides the students with the basic, fundamental skills of reading, writing, and arithmetic. Their happiness and success as members of society are largely dependent on this.

Student Attitudes and Values.   In addition to the basic academic tools, every curriculum should provide opportunities for students to explore new ideas and to evaluate old perceptions. One of the most important things that children can be taught is a tolerance for different points of view. Discussions on controversial or sensitive subjects, such as racial prejudice, provide children with insights into the problems themselves but also illustrate and develop patterns of dialogue that may lead to greater understanding.

Relevancy.   To help students effectively attain academic or social objectives, a curriculum must be relevant. Children become excited and involved in ideas that they can apply to themselves and to their lives. According to Martinello (1973), there are three ways a teacher can accomplish this:

>   1.   Make curriculum emerge from the child's life rather than impose irrelevancies upon it.
>   2.   Integrate the child's studies by making them interdisciplinary rather than unidisciplinary.
>   3.   Focus on the development of skills, those strategies which enable people to make meaning out of their diverse experience, rather than on the accumulation of information which will be forgotten and become obsolete in time. (p. 246)

This is a vital ingredient in the learning and social environment of the classroom and is a prerequisite to both participation and achievement in school.

Patterns of Success.   In addition to the subject content of a curriculum, there are numerous other factors that either contribute to or hinder its effectiveness in the classroom. As outlined by Swassing (1974), they include task presentation, performance rates, the pace of instruction, and the motivational system employed. These and other factors determine how frequently a child will succeed or fail in school. The teacher must make every effort to structure the learning environment in such a way that success is guaranteed. This accomplishment, in itself, is one of the most significant steps a teacher can take toward establishing a healthy social climate. When children are successful in school work, they are more likely to be happy, adjusted members of the class. Failure, on the other hand, breeds frustration and disruptive behaviors that have a detrimental effect on the entire class.

Active Participation.   The final characteristic by which a curriculum should be evaluated is the degree to which the students are encouraged to participate actively. Children are naturally energetic, and active involvement in the learning process is one of the best ways to stimulate their interest. At the same time it maximizes social interaction and provides a better opportunity for social growth.

Assessment Instruments and Techniques

Before discussing the informal ways a teacher can assess the impact a particular curriculum has on the social climate of the classroom, it is necessary to conceptualize, in a general way, the rationale underlying the initial selection of a curriculum. If the match between the needs and characteristics of the student and the curriculum is fundamentally unsound, then the techniques for assessment and suggestions for change discussed in this text would be superficial and inadequate. While the selection process necessitates a thorough evaluation of the child and is far too complex to be dealt with in detail here, the following discussion should help teachers avoid basic mismatches and the devastating effects they can have on the social environment in the classroom. Additionally, it should point out the suitability of starkly contrasting curricular approaches if and when they are compatible with the functioning level of the students.

Task.   Students and curricula can be compared and matched in a general way according to where they fall along three critical dimensions of instruction. Based on Hewett's learning triangle (1968), these include task, structure, and reward and are depicted in Table 3. In terms of the first dimension, task, very obvious differences exist among students, depending on the age and ability. As indicated in Hewett's hierarchy, some function at very low levels of performance and instructional emphasis must be placed on developing attention and appropriate patterns of response. Other children who have progressed to high levels of achievement would benefit most from activities that require the integration and synthesis of their accumulated knowledge. Similarly, curricula vary in terms of the objectives that they are designed to accomplish. Some are highly sequenced and very direct, such as programmed learning materials. Others are indirect and stress such areas as creativity and originality.

Structure.   The same degree of variance is evident in the second dimension. Some children need a highly structured learning situation with a set routine and frequent one-to-one assistance from the teacher. The average child, on the other hand, can learn effectively in a group setting, like that of the traditional public school classroom. A few of the more mature children can work independently with only occasional guidance from the teacher. Quite obviously, the same curriculum would not be suitable for all of these students. A highly structured learning environment would be too rigid and restrictive for most children and probably would hinder

TABLE 3   Dimensions for student/curriculum matching

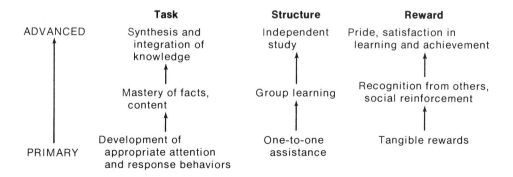

both their academic and social growth. Conversely, independent learning or even group instruction could not be handled by those who lack sufficient maturity or prerequisite social skills.

Reward.   The final dimension, reward, parallels the other two in diversity. At the lowest level of functioning are students who respond only to immediate, tangible rewards for classroom performance. By contrast, there are other students who will perform solely for pride and the satisfaction in doing a good job. Most children, however, are probably motivated by social kinds of reinforcement, whether it be recognition from the teacher, their peers, or their parents. With some curricula, tangible reinforcement can be used easily and effectively. Many other curricula, on the other hand, by their open and unstructured nature preclude any such elementary type of reward. To benefit from these approaches, the student must respond to inner or at least social, kinds of motivation.

As can be seen in Table 3, learning and school performance at the advanced level of all three dimensions are desired ultimately for every child. The ability to synthesize information, work independently, and become motivated intrinsically are all essential to a successful life. Nevertheless, because students bring to school different experiences, problems, and abilities and because they all progress at different rates, it is imperative that they be placed in facilitating environments that encourage their progress upwards in each of these important dimensions.

Given this framework, a teacher can better assess the appropriateness of various curricula for the children in the classroom. While many describe exciting ways to stimulate student thinking and enhance classroom social interaction, their successful implementation may depend on relatively high levels of student performance.

Consider, for example, the Group Investigation Model of Thelen (1960). He advocates a strategy that involves the emotions of the student and the dynamics of the learning group. Whether unplanned and spontaneous or deliberately suggested by the teacher, the group is confronted with a stimulating or puzzling problem. Based on the visual divergence of student perceptions and reactions in such situations, a problem for independent or group study is formulated. In addition to classroom dialogue and debate, various other task-related activities are initiated and pursued by the students. Their investigation of the subject may include interviews with adults, guest speakers, or trips to concerned areas. Subsequently, the group analyzes and evaluates the results. Throughout the process, the teacher acts only to facilitate the process by helping the students focus their attention on important variables, clarifying terms, insuring access to needed materials and resources, and stimulating exchange if the group bogs down. For the most part, the students themselves direct their study through a democratic, give and take of ideas and feelings.

As summarized by Joyce and Weil (1972), this approach is highly versatile and can be used in a wide range of subject areas and with children of many age levels. It can serve to develop disciplined academic inquiry in the students. Simultaneously, it can nurture tolerance for divergent points of view, independence in the learning process, and healthy interpersonal relationships. Nevertheless, its suitability to the classroom is totally dependent on the level of the students. Referring back to

Table 3, it is clear that they should probably be functioning at the highest levels of all three learning dimensions. Quite obviously, children who need frequent teacher instructions, encouragement, and tangible reinforcement would be unable to benefit from Thelen's approach.

From this discussion it should be clear that the first step in the assessment of the curriculum, in terms of its impact on the social environment of the classroom, is to make certain that, in general, it corresponds to the needs and abilities of the students. This is of fundamental importance and supercedes everything that follows. Once an adequate or near match can be assumed, however, the assessment checklist can be used to identify curricular strengths and weaknesses and to thereby modify and enhance its role in the learning process.

ASSESSMENT CHECKLIST: SOCIAL ENVIRONMENT

Components	Question	Yes	No	Undecided

A. Teacher's Behavior

1. Direct Influence

1. Can the teacher specifically state both appropriate and inappropriate student classroom behaviors he/she would like to increase or decrease? _____ _____ _____

2. Does the teacher frequently follow appropriate behavior with encouragement and praise? _____ _____ _____

3. Does the teacher refrain from punishing and criticizing students and rather consistently withdraw his/her attention following inappropriate behaviors? _____ _____ _____

4. Does the teacher objectively record (tally, tape record, use counter) and evaluate the frequency and consequences of his/her behaviors to document the effects they have on student behavior? _____ _____ _____

5. Does the teacher clearly specify the classroom guidelines, responsibilities, and limitations for the students? _____ _____ _____

6. Are the classroom rules consistently enforced? _____ _____ _____

ENTER NUMBER OF QUESTIONS ANSWERED YES

Components	Question	Yes	No	Undecided
2. Indirect Influence	7. Has the teacher continued to grow by adapting teaching plans to meet the needs of each group of students?	_____	_____	_____
	8. Is the teacher aware of any personal, social, racial, or mental prejudices and does he/she attempt to overcome these through objective teaching and evaluation methods?	_____	_____	_____
	9. Has the teacher devised a method of getting the students' perceptions and a feedback on the teacher and the class? (questionnaire, suggestion box)	_____	_____	_____
	10. Does the teacher encourage and reinforce self-expression and participation from all the members of the class?	_____	_____	_____
	11. Does the teacher attempt to vary teaching methods by using both teacher-directed and student-directed activities?	_____	_____	_____
	12. Does the teacher use new and creative outside resources (other teachers, journals, resource personnel, community events) to add interest to the class activities?	_____	_____	_____
	ENTER NUMBER OF QUESTIONS ANSWERED YES			

Components	Question	Yes	No	Undecided
B. Peer Behavior				
	13. Can the teacher identify the classroom leaders, followers, and isolates?	___	___	___
	14. Can the teacher identify the peer-group norms base and stereotypes that are held by the class?	___	___	___
	15. Can the teacher identify the patterns of friendships/ relationships that each student has in the class?	___	___	___
	16. Can the teacher identify and redirect inappropriate peer attention (laughing at a class clown, picking on a handicapped child) to promote more constructive activities?	___	___	___
	17. Does the teacher attend to the problems of the quiet, withdrawn children as much as to the acting-out problem children?	___	___	___
	18. Does the teacher use concrete activities and arrangements to maximize the social acceptance and participation of all the children?	___	___	___
	19. Do the classroom physical arrangements (seating plan) and group activities consider both the elimination of behavior problems and enhancement of social relationships?	___	___	___

Components	Question	Yes	No	Undecided
	ENTER NUMBER OF QUES-TIONS ANSWERED YES			

C. Curriculum

20. Does the curriculum encourage high levels of student independence and initiative? _____ _____ _____

21. Does the curriculum present a balanced emphasis upon students' personal social development and academic skill development? _____ _____ _____

22. Does the curriculum provide challenging new ideas that require students to develop skills in analytic and evaluative thinking? _____ _____ _____

23. Is the curriculum enhanced with a motivational system that guarantees that each child will have a successful learning experience? _____ _____ _____

24. Does the curriculum require participation and interactions both from the teacher and students? _____ _____ _____

25. Does the curriculum encourage interaction and cooperation among the students? _____ _____ _____

26. Is the subject content relevant to the interests and backgrounds of the students? _____ _____ _____

Components	Question	Yes	No	Undecided
	27. Is an effort made to mean-ingfully relate the concepts covered in class to everyday experiences?	____	____	____
	28. Does the curriculum provide ample opportunity for student enrichment by frequently introducing new and different ideas and problems?	____	____	____
	29. Are subjects presented and assignments made in a man-ner that encourages and facilitates the integration of knowledge and concepts?	____	____	____
	30. Does each child have the prerequisite skills necessary to successfully complete assigned tasks?	____	____	____
	31. Can students move at their own pace?	____	____	____
	32. Is motivation enhanced through liberal use of teacher praise and encour-agement?	____	____	____
	33. Are opportunities provided for independent study?	____	____	____
	34. Are students with special skills allowed or encouraged to share their expertise with their classmates?	____	____	____
	35. Do the students feel free to express their opinions on			

Components	Question	Yes	No	Undecided
	classroom procedures and to suggest changes in content or routine?	———	———	———
	36. Is an attempt made to incorporate student ideas and suggestions into the instructional program?	———	———	———
	37. Is meaningful feedback on homework, projects, and examinations provided to the students as quickly as possible?	———	———	———
	38. Are there outside sources of information which can be used to stimulate student thinking (guest speakers, field trips, etc.)?	———	———	———
	ENTER NUMBER OF QUES-TIONS ANSWERED YES	☐		

Summary Section

A. Teacher's Behavior (questions 1-12)

1. Direct influence (questions 1-6)   ———

2. Indirect influence (questions 7-12)   ———

Subtotal: Teacher's Behavior   ———

B. Peer Behavior (questions 13-19)   ———

C. Curriculum (questions 20-38)   ———

TOTAL INSTRUCTIONAL ENVIRONMENT SCORE   ———

ENVIRONMENTAL PROFILE: SOCIAL ENVIRONMENT

Components   *Scores: Number of Questions Answered Yes*

                                                    1 2 3 4 5 6 7 8 9 10 11 12 13 14 15 16 17 18

A. Teacher
   Behavior: Direct Influence

                    Indirect Influence

B. Peer
   Behavior:

C. Curriculum:

5

Evaluating the Physical Environment

Behavior does not occur in abstract space; it occurs *somewhere*. Each specific act of behavior takes place in a specific environmental setting; each of these settings has its own properties or attributes that may influence what sorts of behavior occur there. This is not to claim that environments singularly determine behavior, but only that knowledge of a setting's properties will improve our ability to predict the behaviors which will occur there. Any given person at any given moment may, of course, behave quite differently from the typical user of that setting. The case where the environment is the necessary *and* sufficient condition for a specified behavior will be extremely rare, human nature being what it is. Fortunately for teachers and architects, however, the behavior of most people is predictable when we know something about the environment in which the behavior is occurring.

In previous chapters, this text has examined the relationship between behavior and various social properties of school environments; this chapter will focus on the physical properties of environments and how they influence behavior, either directly or through their effect on social interaction. In doing so, we will be looking at three separate areas:

1. Environmental attributes, that is, size, quantity, temperature, color, and so forth.

2.   The actors, that is, teachers and students.

3.   Behavior, that is, what the actors do, such as lecture, recite, and compute.

The attributes of environments are related to the behavior of actors through various explanatory theories, constructs, or processes. These will be alluded to at the proper time but a general warning is called for at the outset. The study of people interacting with their environment is quite new and its rather meager base of observation supports a heavy load of theorizing (a situation that may not be totally unfamiliar to educators). In this chapter, every effort will be made to avoid overloading the data with suppositions that it cannot carry. While we will introduce teachers to some interesting and useful theories about people and their environment, we urge them not to accept uncritically anything that they are not able to verify in their own practice.

Direct Effects of Physical Properties

The physical properties of environments can influence behavior through direct physical effects and/or through psychological or sociological effects within and among people. Certain behaviors require specific environmental conditions. For example, a smooth and skid-free floor is required for basketball, and it is prohibited when the gymnasium floor is covered with chairs for a PTA meeting or with dance wax for the senior prom. The environment thus prohibits basketball at some times and allows (but does not compel) it at others.

A less precise example of a direct effect would be extended conversation, that occurs almost anywhere but is more likely to occur where comfortable seating has been provided. Architects, by the way they design, equip, and furnish rooms, are trying to insure that behavior will occur where it is supposed to and not where it should not; Barker (1968) has called this fit between the physical environment and the behavior *synomorphy*. A lecture room, for example, will have a large number of fixed seats oriented toward a central position containing various display surfaces and a lectern of some sort. (Any teacher who has tried to hold small-group discussion in such a lecture room knows what synomorphy is and isn't!) Another illustration of synomorphy is in the school cafeteria, where the positions and roles of customer and attendant are defined and supported by such environmental features as the serving counter with its tray rail and glass-display shelves.

Environments, then, can affect behavior directly by the facilities they provide and by the way these facilities are arranged. A variant of this is the location of rooms relative to each other. For example, if the physical education staff is also expected to monitor the locker rooms, its offices will often be placed next to the locker-room area with a vision panel on the appropriate wall. If administrators want to be shielded from the public, most likely a secretary's or receptionist's office will be located between their offices and the public corridor. Attaining social objectives may be attempted through the use of location; for example, more rapport between faculty and students may be sought by having their dining rooms in the same area. Conversely, rooms may be separated where minimal interaction is desired, as might be the case with band practice and the library. Better separation of student movement was recommended in a high school where assaults were more frequent in locations with conflicting cross-traffic (Crowe et al., 1976).

This list of direct effects (provision of facilities, proximity, access control, and separation) may strike the reader as not very impressive, but those who have sat on building committees will recognize that it encompasses much of what they and the architect talked about, simply because much of architectural design consists of providing properly sized and equipped rooms, which are properly located with respect to one another.

Reinforcement Properties

A slightly more subtle example of direct environmental effects on behavior comes from an analysis of the reinforcement properties of environments. That is, the manner in which environments influence behavior by rewarding some responses and not rewarding or even punishing others. The most controlled example of this reinforcement is the so-called Skinner Box in which a hungry pigeon is automatically provided with food after pecking a key under the prescribed conditions, or in which a rat can turn off a mild shock by pressing a lever. We do not normally think of human environments in such mechanistic terms, but the same principles often apply. Take the choice of a place to sit. If we choose to sit on the floor of a busy corridor, we will be punished by the cold hard surface and by the angry stares and "accidental" kicks of people trying to get by. On the other hand, if we sit in the lounge we will be rewarded with a comfortable chair and a quiet place to talk. (The fact that some people *do* sit in corridors only serves to indicate the superior intelligence of pigeons.)

The reinforcement properties of environments have been considered theoretically (Studer, 1970; Wicker, 1972), but the actual number of applications is small. It appears that there are two main approaches. In the first approach the environment is used as a reinforcer as in Cohen et al. (1970) where inmates at a boys' training school could "earn" nicer living quarters, more furniture, and so on, by performing acceptable amounts of academic work. Another example common to preschools is when going outdoors is made contingent on the child's first successfully completing some task such as putting on a coat or helping straighten up the room. In the second approach, the environment is designed to deliver consequences directly. For example, Sommer (1969) tells of a chair carefully shaped so that it becomes uncomfortable after fifteen to twenty minutes; its use in coffee shops and fast-food restaurants obviously is to encourage patron turnover. A preschool example is provided by Titus (1975). Children evaluated as isolate in their outdoor play, when presented with amusement devices and food dispensers requiring two-children operation, were much more cooperative in that environment, though not in any other.

All the preceding examples somewhat oversimplify reality, since the more usual case is that, within the same environment, different behaviors are appropriate at different times. The environment should indicate this in some fashion (the technical term is *stimulus control*). For example, turning the lights off at nap time indicates that loud talking and boisterous activity will be scolded; decorating the classroom festively indicates that much less academic work will be required than is customary; arranging chairs in a circle indicates discussion rather than lecture; displaying examples of good handwriting on the wall indicates the standard by which praise and reward will be allocated.

To summarize: the reinforcement properties of environments can in some cases be arranged so that by their immediate consequences, they influence behavior in the desired directions. You can think of this as a sort of *environmental feedback*. Access to desired features in the environment can also be bestowed as a reward for some specified behavior in the same way as praise, recognition, candy, and any other types of reinforcers are dispensed. (Later, in dealing with environments for exceptional children, this approach will be described in more detail.) Lastly, stimulus control can be utilized to support teachers' verbal instructions to the class. If they are consistent, these environmental reminders may come to exercise considerable control over behavior and thus prove to be valuable aids in the instructional program. This general line of thought is not new to teachers, though in their use of it they may not be as deliberate and consistent as they should be for maximum effectiveness.

Lest the preceding discussion of reinforcement seem too one-sided, we readily acknowledge that cognitive activity, learning, and satisfaction of curiosity can in themselves be reinforcing and need not always be supported by candy, trinkets, and access to the playground. Not all children at all times are equally eager to work at all subjects, however, so that there is a definite place for a more consciously applied program for environmental support and reinforcement of desired behavior.

Room Furnishings

The last example of a direct environmental effect on behavior concerns the room furnishings, both in terms of what is available and how it is used. We are concerned with how particular types and layouts of furnishing affect interaction and with how people use furnishings to structure interaction in the light of their expectations. An important fact to note at the outset is that although furnishings are movable, they are seldom treated as if they are. Sommer (1969) has noted the timidity of institutionalized populations toward moving even a chair into a position more comfortable for conversation. He further noted that on those occasions when the environment has been tampered with, staff are generally quick to "straighten it up" again. In a study of an experimental classroom environment in which 75 percent of the pieces could be moved in less than two minutes, Sanders (1958) found that the layout was seldom changed by any teacher. This reflects a pattern that will be familiar to many readers. The classroom will be rearranged in late August or early September and likely will remain that way at least throughout the term and perhaps throughout the year. It is as if the teacher shapes the environment and then adapts to it rather than continuously evaluating its performance and making necessary changes and improvements.

We said earlier that furnishings can affect human interaction, and now it might be best to provide an example. If a table is round, all positions are equal; in a long rectangular table, however, the occupants of the end positions are much better able to see and be seen than those along the sides. We might then expect that occupants of end positions would be more likely to take influential roles, and in fact Strodtbeck and Hook (1961) found this to be so. In a study of mock juries the occupant of an end position was more likely to be voted foreman. We also said earlier that people use furnishings to structure their interactions with others. We might then expect end positions of jury tables to be selected by more prestigious or assertive persons, and in fact this also was observed by Sommer (1961) and by Strodtbeck and Hook (1961). In general, it can be said that locations that enable persons to have better visual access to the group and/or to be central to the communication flows throughout the group (Leavitt, 1951) will enable their occupants to take a more active role in the proceedings.

Teachers can make use of this concept and vary their own location depending on what role they want to play. They may also place a somewhat retiring child in a more central position in hopes of getting him/her to be more forthcoming. Since it is known that those located either close together or opposite each other are more likely to interact (Russo, 1967; Steinzor, 1950), teachers can also attempt to draw a specific student out by varying their own positions in relation to that student, though the close-together position should be used cautiously lest the student direct himself/herself only to the teacher and not to the entire group. These considerations would seem to argue against the traditional classroom layout in which neither the teacher nor the students change their locations throughout the class session. Recall also the study cited earlier (Koneya, 1976) that found in such a classroom there was considerably lower participation by students seated in the back and sides of the room.

Sommer (1969) has studied people's seating patterns when they are engaged in conversation. Using parallel sofas he found that when the sofas were 12 inches to 36 inches apart, people sat facing each other on opposite sofas; when the sofas were positioned farther than 36 inches apart, people were more likely to sit on the same sofa. Since the actual head-to-head distance of these subjects was greater than the distance between the sofas, the range Sommer found is in general agreement with what Hall (1966) called *personal distance* (18 inches to 48 inches) and considered to be the usual conversational spacing. If a more businesslike or formal interaction is desired, furnishings can be arranged to keep people at a greater distance. For example, Haase and DiMattia (1970) found that administrators preferred layouts that interposed a desk or table between them and a visitor, whereas teachers and counselors did not.

Sommer (1969) also found that people who are talking while seated at a table are most likely to take corner-to-corner or facing positions. Facing positions are most common if they are competing; side-by-side positions are chosen for working together and sharing materials; and if they are working separately, they are likely to take up positions at opposite ends and on opposite sides of the table. (Teachers should be easily able to verify this for themselves at the library or cafeteria.) What appears to influence these decisions is the amount of proximity and eye contact that is desired. Those in conversation desire both closeness and eye contact so the corner or facing positions are the best compromises; competitors want to watch each other so facing positions are chosen. Those working together find the sharing of materials to be most important and sit side-by-side, and those working separately wish to avoid both closeness and eye contact that is best approximated by the opposite-end, opposite-side locations. An exception to the last rule is the person working separately who wishes to keep the entire table to himself/herself. He/she is likely to sit in the center facing the incoming stream of traffic and perhaps to spread books and clothing around him/her as well. It is clear from these examples that people use furnishings in a way that helps them meet their needs at the time. It follows that a good learning environment is one that allows them to do this. This argues for easily moved chairs and tables of a variety of sizes and shapes.

Since children can easily become habit-bound, this concept also suggests that the teacher should get them accustomed to changing their places for different types of tasks and to rearranging the furnishings when it is appropriate. If children can be brought to doing this rather routinely, the teacher may well see that they are able to organize the environment and themselves for academic work as effectively as they already do during their play activities.

One special case of furnishing concerns the open-plan school. Surprisingly, a recent review (Ittelson et al., 1974) finds few studies to report that have an environmental focus. Durlak (1972) compared traditional and open-plan elementary schools on a number of measures of teacher and pupil behavior. Open-plan schools that were not part of a special school board program were by most measures little different from traditional schools. What appeared to be critical was not so much the structure of the environment itself as how the teacher chose to operate within it. Whether any of this made a difference in learning is not known because academic comparisons were not made.

The research reviewed in this chapter thusfar suggests that the teacher and students should have the option of a variety of seating arrangements and work groupings for different learning tasks. On the face of it this would argue against the traditional classroom with desks all facing forward and bolted to the floor. In the absence of findings to the contrary, this appears to be the best recommendation. Moreover, the teachers can always line up the chairs and tables facing forward if they so choose!

Physiological Effects of Physical Properties

We would expect that such factors as comfortable temperature, required illumination, and tolerable noise would be solidly founded in human physiology and not susceptible to variation. In fact, Rapoport and Watson (1967) in examining the standards published by the cognizant engineering societies of several Western nations, found wide variability not only among nations but within the same nation over a period of time. Britons will accept an indoor winter temperature that is five or more degrees cooler than will Americans. And while the eyes of the American people presumably have not changed in the last generation, the standards for required illumination at the reading surface have doubled in that time. Bennett (1974) sees some evidence of a convergence of American and European standards at the higher American levels.

Illumination

Other aspects of illumination are more pragmatic. Light sources should be designed and located in a manner that eliminates glare, defined as a brightness contrast ratio between the object and the surroundings of greater than 3:1 (Haywood, 1974), or situations where the light source is behind the focus of attention, for example, when the teacher stands in front of the window. When the room permits it, light levels and types should be varied, for example, with brighter lighting at reading areas and softer lighting in areas used primarily for discussion. This makes the room look less institutional and also clearly defines different areas for different activities, which may also be defined by furniture arrangements. It appears that noise levels may be lower in less brightly lighted corridors, and some controversial evidence has been presented linking standard florescent lighting with hyperactivity in children (Arehart-Treichel, 1975).

Temperature

Some limited experimental evidence is available linking temperature with various indices of aggressiveness. Subjects in a hot room were more likely to copy a modelled aggressive response than those in a cool room (Baron & Lawton, 1972), but the hot room was very hot indeed—almost 100° F! In a less straightforward design (Griffitt & Veitch, 1971), it was found that if many additional people are put into the same room where the temperature is high, they will, by a variety of measures, show themselves to be in less friendly moods when compared to other people in a cooler and less crowded room. Once again, however, the hot room temperature was 93.5° F. These two studies, while no more than suggestive, do indicate that in oppressively hot conditions teachers would do well to consider scheduling activities that are not especially frustrating or potentially conflict-producing; they might also consider scheduling activities that involve little movement since movement may raise body temperature and also may produce situations which lead to arguments. Temperature may also be a problem during the heating season. Too much heat is the typical case, and a croopy, listless class of students is often the result. To the extent that rooms are individually controlled, the teacher may want to experiment with somewhat lower temperatures; this should be done gradually, however, so that the children have the opportunity to modify their clothing habits.

Noise

The problems with noise that would concern the teacher arise when it is either a distraction or when it directly interferes with student comprehension. An example of a distraction is a group discussion taking place alongside another group doing a math problem; an example of interference is a jet aircraft overhead with high sound levels in the speech frequencies that effectively jam student comprehension of the teacher's words. Experimental evidence (Glass & Singer, 1972) indicates that task performance need not deteriorate under exposure to intermittent and unpredictable noise, but that performance on a *subsequent* task does; thus it appears that we adapt, but at a price. Two field studies showed lower reading performance for children living on the noisier floors of an apartment building (Cohen, Glass, & Singer, 1973) or having class on the noisier side of a school building (Bronzaft & McCarthy, 1975); the reasons for these effects are not clear, however. It may be that families in the noisier apartments simply talked less, which would have lowered the child's reading readiness. In the classroom study, an elevated train passed every 4½ minutes disrupting class for 30 seconds. If we assume another 30-second refractory period (which does not seem unreasonable), this distraction results in a 22 percent reduction of available teaching time.

A third field study (Brunetti, 1972) compared traditional program (grades four to six) taught in conventional versus open classrooms and surprisingly found fewer complaints about noise in the open classrooms than in conventional classrooms; this was not true, however, for individualized programs in open classrooms. This study suggests that two groups engaging in the same activity at the same time (for example, discussion) may be highly compatible from a noise standpoint. It also suggests that teachers and students sharing common space in an open classroom may coordinate their noisy activities better than when occupying individual classrooms. The study does not argue for the inherent superiority of either open or conventional architecture from a noise-control standpoint but rather serves to indicate the need for proper coordination between teachers to make either type of classroom operate in an optimal manner. This interdependence is further highlighted in a study of schools in Jamaica (Stebbins, 1973) that are open to the outside on the ground floor; failure of one teacher to control a class wandering off resulted in distractions (whistles, comments, loitering) to many other classes. Few school buildings are so well designed acoustically that teachers do not have to be considerate of each other in their scheduling and use of movies, TV, play time, music, and discussion.

Color

Color is an area in which there is a great deal of opinion but little established fact that would be useful to the teacher. Reviews of the literature (Bayes, 1967; Drew, 1971; Heimstra & McFarling, 1974) provide numerous examples of conflicting findings (for example, color and blood pressure), no effect (for example, warm and cool colors do not influence surrounding temperature), and influence of cognitive factors (for example, judged room size and color effects disappeared when subjects knew they were in some sort of an experiment, even though they did not know what the topic was). Nevertheless, some observations can be made on the subject. Walls that are very dark or brilliantly colored make the reading task more difficult. Dark hues make light adaptation by the eye more difficult (this also applies to the surface of tables and desks), and brilliant hues color the light through reflection. Walls of brilliant colors also generally are said to make a room appear to be smaller; they also tend to dominate any display materials placed on them or in front of them (highly patterned surfaces can have this effect also). Wall surfaces should be light in tone and subdued though not drab in hue, so that they can better function as a pleasant background for whatever is placed on them or occurs in front of them.

Intense color in furnishings should be used sparingly since otherwise the environment may become overstimulating and confusing. It also should be used functionally, that is, to call attention to an object or display that is of educational importance. Whatever colors the teacher selects should be chosen when viewed in florescent lighting, since much of the year such lighting will illuminate them. If teachers fail to observe this precaution, they may find that the colors that delighted them in the showroom leave them cold in the classroom. It is important that teachers use classroom colors that are pleasant and cheerful. Depressing colors are likely to affect their teaching adversely and thus depress the students indirectly if not directly.

Spatial Behavior Effects

The preceding section looked at some physiological factors (illumination, temperature, noise, color) that may affect teacher and student mood and performance in the classroom. In this section we will examine some rather fundamental spatial aspects of people interacting with their environment. One fascinating but not too well researched area concerns use of the environment to meet security and arousal reduction needs. In naturalistic observations of monkeys and chimps, it has been noted that in the presence of an unfamiliar object or environment, periods of exploration and investigation are generally alternated with periods of retreat to corners, overhangs, edges, and large objects; mutual clinging is also frequent during these retreats. An apparently similar tendency to avoid the centers of rooms in favor of walls and corners appears in the exploratory patterns of autistic versus normal children in a novel environment (Hutt & Hutt, 1970a). Studies of the location patterns of humans on beaches and other recreational settings (deJonge, 1967) and around campus buildings (Preiser, 1972) show, at a larger scale, a preference for proximity to space-defining elements in the environment. Finally, in a finding that may relate to this topic, it has been observed that students in the rear and side seats of a classroom are less likely to participate in the discussion (Koneya, 1976; Sommer, 1969). This effect occurs whether seating is assigned or self-chosen. Students in peripheral seats are, of course, less likely to be drawn into the discussion by the teacher, but it may also be that such locations are defined by the students as more appropriate for withdrawal and observation rather than for active participation. The suggestion (and it is no more than that) from this literature is that we all need time out once in awhile to recoup; this will be discussed again when territoriality and privacy needs are presented.

Personal Space

One topic that has received considerable attention from researchers is *"personal space"*; this term describes the amounts of separation that people keep between themselves in various social situations. A recent review of this literature can be found in Altman (1975); valuable earlier contributions are those of Hall (1966) and Sommer (1969). Spatial separation appears to be a basic human way of dealing with the uncertainty or anxiety associated with another human who is unfamiliar, different, or threatening; the phenomenon is also quite common among animals, which have elaborate rituals of appeasement and reassurance that are employed in any approach situation (Eebl-Eibesfeldt, 1975). Research into personal space behavior in humans has used observation of actual distance in uncontrived field settings and contrived field and laboratory settings. It has also relied on various forms of simulation, for example, subjects are asked to place doll figures as close as they think is appropriate for different relationships and situations. The findings of the more contrived studies may or may not be accurate reflections of the way children behave in real situations. The studies conducted with children are, in general, quite consistent with similar adult studies, so only the child literature will be cited here.

Children's personal space behavior appears to have a developmental aspect, with younger children requiring less separation from each other and older children's requirements approximating adult norms. Whether maturation or experience is primarily involved is not clear, but certainly Mallenby (1974) found an experiential factor in that interpersonal distances (measured experimentally) of institutionalized hearing-impaired sixth-graders were greater than those of another group from the same institution who spent part of their day with normal children. Distances for the latter group approximated those of normal sixth-graders after a year of association with them.

Another developmental factor appears to be sex. Younger children keep greatest separation from those of the opposite sex whereas by adolescence the greatest separation is between male-male pairs, the least between male-female pairs, with female-female pairs exhibiting an intermediate separation. This general pattern appears to show some variation along cultural and subcultural lines, once again suggesting an experiential component.

A number of attributes of the other person have been noted that increase separation. These include being a stranger rather than an acquaintance, being obese, being known as an unfriendly child, and being of a different race. There are also a number of aspects of the situation that affect separation. Children sit closer together when cooperating than when competing; they also sit together when ghost stories are being told. They stand closer to their mothers in unfamiliar environments, and they place figures farther apart in formal scenes (principal's office) than in informal scenes (living room). Lastly, there are attributes of the person himself/herself that influence separation. Disturbed children appear to be less tolerant of approach and to show more variability than do normal children.

Concerning these research findings, observant teachers may discover much that is already familiar to them. They also may note that if an ideal school environment is one that allows the children to space themselves as their needs at the moment dictate, then preschoolers and children in the lower grades are much better provided for than children in the higher grades; whereas the research would suggest that if anything, the opposite ought to be true. Older children would appear to want to make more use of spatial separation in coping with a variety of interpersonal situations. However, the school environment, both in its physical dimensions and in its procedures, actually provides them with limited opportunity to communicate spatially, when their separation is compared to what is available to children in lower grades. Whether or not this is a matter of more than passing concern can only be guessed at; the research that would resolve the question is not available.

Another issue raised by the personal-space literature relates to the current emphasis on racial integration and on mainstreaming of exceptional children. *Mainstreaming* is the process of integrating as many exceptional children into regular classrooms as much of the time as possible. Both children and adults prefer to keep greater distance from another person who is different, stigmatized, unfamiliar, or feared. This suggests that the best school environment would be one that allowed individuals and groups to keep their distance from each other while they are in the process of getting accustomed to each other.

Crowding

While the personal-space literature focuses on the separation between two individuals, a related *crowding* literature examines how the functioning of individuals within groups is affected by the amount of space available to them. In an ideal crowding experiment, equal-sized groups will be placed in unequal-sized rooms and performance, attitudinal, or effective measures will be taken and compared. In a naturalistic study, some measure of social interaction will be compared between equal-sized groups with varying amounts of available space. Unfortunately, in a typical study—as compared to an ideal crowding study—group size may vary as well as crowding; conditions between rooms may not be identical in all aspects save size, and so on. Another difficulty with this literature is one shared by much research of an ecological nature: a correlation is found between some environmental variable (in this case available space) and some behavioral outcome (for example, aggression). However, the context in which the correlation is discovered gives little or no insight into what is causing it.

In the crowding literature, many hypotheses are available (Altman, 1975; Fischer et al., 1975; Stokols, 1976). None has been thoroughly tested and some of them (for example, cognitive overload) may be untestable. We can summarize the major theories by stating that when numbers of people are brought together in limited space, they may be compelled to interact in ways that cause them to interfere with each other's activities, and/or to experience an unwanted level of social stimulation. The teacher and educational administrator would want to know which, or in what combination, these two factors are operating. They would also want to know which levels of crowding are educationally acceptable and which are not, but the literature will not be too instructive on these matters.

The original interest in crowding probably stems from Calhoun's (1962) laboratory studies of the social behavior of Norway rats under a variety of environmental arrangements. It appeared that profound behavioral and physiological pathologies developed as animal density increased. Since other laboratory and field studies of animals showed similar results, it was assumed that the processes involved might also apply to humans. An overview of approximately ten years of human research would be that crowding per se cannot be unequivocally associated with pathology in real life. In experimental settings crowding makes people uncomfortable and may induce some withdrawal but does not appear to cause behavior disorders or performance decrements (Fischer et al., 1975). Moreover, in some studies, especially involving women, crowding may have caused increased performance or social interaction, recalling an earlier literature on social facilitation (Zajonc, 1965), which found that increased numbers led to improved performance on some types of tasks and cooperation (Allee, 1938; Wilson, 1975).

As to studies of children, the patterns are not clear. If the same sized group is given less space to play in, there can be either more or less interaction, withdrawal, or aggression (Hutt & McGrew, 1967; Loo, 1972; McGrew, 1970). In order for this research to be more useful, more attention will have to be placed on the interaction of such parameters as absolute amount of space per person, absolute size of group, specific furnishings of the room, and the nature of the situation. For example, McGrew (1970) found most withdrawal with the largest sized group in the smallest room, and Robe and Patterson (1974) found that reduced room size and fewer toys resulted in more antisocial play, but reduced room size by itself did not. What is not clear from either of these two studies, however, is whether these relationships would hold for other ranges of group size, other situations than free play. Richer definitions of the problem will take us rather far from the basic crowding model, but they will provide data and insights that will be more useful to the teacher, as will be seen when group size and behavior setting are discussed.

Territoriality

Still another aspect of human spatial behavior, once again using concepts derived from the study of animal behavior, is called *territoriality*. This term can be defined most simply as possession of a specific location, with continued possession sometimes but not always involving active defense against would-be usurpers (Edney, 1976). A person may become attached to or claim a particular location for a variety of reasons: simple habit; it is familiar and reassuring; it possesses certain advantages relative to other locations; it is assigned by role or status or by some investment of effort in obtaining or improving it. Much of the emotional involvement in, for example, home ownership can be explained along these dimensions. Note that none of these has the quality of inmateness associated with territoriality in, for example, birds (Wynne-Edwards, 1972).

Studies of territoriality in humans have most often involved controlled or confined populations such as mental patients, the military, school children, retardates, and the elderly. These studies require the recording of the locations of people over extended time periods to determine their locational preferences. Such studies may also seek to determine whether people of certain characteristics (for example, high status) appear to frequent certain types of locations (for example, better seats in TV lounge). A person's behavior on, as compared to off, his/her territory may also be of interest. A major line of research has been conducted by Esser and his associates on boys institutionalized because of mental retardation or psychiatric disorders (Esser, 1968; Esser, 1973; O'Neill & Paluck, 1973; Paluck & Esser, 1971). One finding—that withdrawn children frequented out-of-the-way locations—is not surprising. High social influence among peers was not a sure predictor of possession and use of a territory. Retarded boys in one case immediately took up their own special areas in a playroom, and in another case became less aggressive after individual territories were introduced. These latter findings are consistent with those of Sundstrom and Altman (1974) in a boy's rehabilitation center in that stable dominance relationships in a cottage were reflected in a clearly defined system of locational privilege and in a low level of disciplinary problems. Finally, in a study of normal children, Patterson et al. (1962) found that of all forms of peer aggression, the one most likely to be successfully resisted was invasion of another's play area, suggesting the importance to the children of this particular resource.

In summary: a limited body of research on territoriality in children, conducted primarily on institutionalized populations, is nonetheless consistent with a larger body of work on adult subjects (Altman, 1975) in finding that children tend to become attached to certain locations. They use these locations to manage interpersonal relationships and other sources of external stimulation, and their attachments are likely to be respected by their peers so long as they claim a location that is consistent with their prestige in the group. Apparently subordinate children select a territory that no one else wants before they decide to possess and defend it. The issues in this literature that should concern the teacher are:

- The environment should provide places for children to withdraw to for those times when they require them.

- No child should be allowed to withdraw permanently or for excessive periods of time.

- Environmental arrangements should be sought that naturally draw the retiring child into the stream of activity.

- No child or group of children should be allowed to monopolize prime locations or features because of greater aggressiveness or social influence.

Privacy

Consideration of human territoriality leads easily into the topic of privacy. The core of the theoretical definition of *privacy* appears to contain the notions of withdrawal from interactions with others and of control of disclosure of information about oneself (Altman, 1976). In a survey of children aged five to seventeen, Wolfe and Laufer (1974) discovered that the four main concepts, in order of frequency of mention, were (1) controlling information, (2) being alone, (3) no one bothering me, and (4) controlling spaces. The relative importance of these four did not change greatly with age, though the overall concept became more differentiated with age. Privacy allows people to pursue their own interests without interruption, to obtain emotional release and self-knowledge, and to relax (compare Ittelson et al., 1974).

Research on privacy dimensions and outcomes is very limited and present efforts are along the lines of definition and theory building (Altman, 1975). This is unfortunate, since privacy appears to be a construct that could unify the now disorganized efforts on personal space, crowding, and territoriality. It appears that the reason for the late start in privacy research is that it is a uniquely human and cognitive construct that links complex outcomes with environmental variables. Researchers in personal space, crowding, and territoriality, by contrast, were able to build upon advanced work on animal populations and moreover could relate simple overt behaviors to readily measured physical and social dimensions. When more research on privacy is available, it seems likely that its message for teachers will be consistent with recommendations made earlier in this chapter: the school environment ought to provide some places where children can withdraw from social and sensory stimulation as needed, and other places where the facilities and surrounding conditions (noise, illumination, temperature) allow them to pursue independent interests. This would be especially true for children from poorer families, since their home environments are least likely to provide these needed environmental resources. The teacher should also be on guard against the possibility that those with less privacy may, initially at least, be less able to make constructive use of it when it is made available to them. The effect of privacy experiences on privacy preferences is not significant (Marshall, 1972; Wolfe & Laufer, 1974), but its effect on behavior remains to be researched.

Behavior Settings

There is nothing inevitable in the fact that tomorrow morning the drugstore will be open, the fire station will be manned, the PTA will meet, and the Golden Age group will hold its monthly dance. Any of these expected happenings might not take place but in fact probably will. Roger Barker (1968) is convinced that these routine, recurring, unexceptional occurrences provide the basic patterning of our lives, structure the greatest part of our behavior, and merit much more attention than they have received. His name for them is the *behavior setting*; each setting consists of a number of tasks to be done, people to do these tasks, and the required material equipment or facilities. For example, the police precinct headquarters has a desk sergeant with a desk, a telephone operator with a switchboard, and the customary people with a bench. Note that all the people in a setting are not equally important to its continued functioning. In general the more essential the task, the fewer the people performing it until at the highest level there are but one or two. For example, at a concert there is one conductor, fewer than a hundred musicians with perhaps an equal number of ushers and other functionaries, and perhaps thousands of spectators. From these elementary considerations, the work of Barker and his associates (Barker, 1968; Barker & Gump, 1964; Barker & Schoggen, 1973; Wicker, 1973; Willems, 1967; Wright, 1967) shows that the behavior setting can have important effects on the life experiences and development of individuals in either of two ways: by the kinds of behavior that they permit and support and by the degree of participation that they allow. Let us examine each of these processes in turn.

Environmental Influences

In dealing with the first topic—environmental influences on behavior—Barker (1968) begins with the observation that human behavior is not randomly or homogenously distributed over space and time but is, on the contrary, highly patterned. Behavior tends to occur in softball games, banks, factories, clubs, and offices; the behavior that occurs in each of these settings does so at specific times, in specific manners, and in association with specific environmental objects. Since Barker defines behavior settings in part by the recurring and patterned types of behavior that occur in each, he can then make the circular but nonetheless useful observation that the best predictor of a person's behavior is not personality, attitudes, or motivations, but rather the behavior setting he/she chooses to occupy at the time. Sigmund Freud deals with people's fantasies and finds human nature to be highly exotic and unpredictable. Roger Barker deals with their behavior and finds quite the opposite.

Apparently if people are going to do something bizarre, they most often do it away from a behavior setting. Why is this so? By what mechanisms do settings influence behavior? They do so, first, by providing the necessary environmental facilities; for example, if there is to be a behavior setting "summer-camp swim class," there will need to be water in reasonable quantities and depths. If the school gym is to be used for the homecoming banquet, there will need to be tables and chairs, catering facilities, and a public address system. The availability of facilities does not force behavior to occur, but it does insure that it will occur, if at all, where those facilities are available. An interesting illustration is provided by Quilitch and Risley (1976). In a study of seven year olds in a playground they found that whether the children engaged in *isolate* or in *social* play depended on whether the play materials provided that day were isolate (for example, clay, puzzles) or social (for example, pick-up-stix, checkers). One cannot *be* a checkers player if the environment provides only puzzles.

Human Influences

Behavior settings are more than their environmental facilities, and the second way that they influence behavior concerns the other occupants of the setting. They come there with some rather definite expectations about what is to occur and will individually and collectively exert pressures on anyone whose behavior is not supportive. Employees of a pizza parlor who neglect their duties to socialize with friends are likely to hear about it from fellow employees, from customers, and from the manager. If they persist and if replacements are plentiful, they will be fired rather quickly. If replacements are not plentiful, coworkers, customers, and the manager will attempt to cajole and shame them into an acceptable level of performance. (Whether a substandard performer is ejected or is counseled is an important issue that we will return to later.)

Evidence of the actual effect of settings on behavior has been presented for a variety of settings, based on intensive observation of actual behavior in real settings. For example, Gump et al. (1963) found the same boy to be more active and adventuresome at camp than he was at home; contrarily, Tars and Appleby (1973) found a child would explore more at home than at an institution for children. Raush et al. (1959) found that institutionalized hyperaggressive children's hostility toward adults was not constant throughout the day but varied from setting to setting. Gump et al. (1957) found that boys at a summer camp showed more aggressive behavior toward peers during swimming and more helping behavior in crafts sessions. The importance of these findings to teachers is twofold: (1) behavior does not reside totally in a given person's personality or other traits, and (2) the most efficient way to change a person's behavior may be to change the present setting or place that person in a different setting, rather than trying to change the *person* (whatever that means). As a practical matter, this would probably require facilities and scheduling that would permit simultaneous operation of more than one setting so that children who were disruptive or inattentive on one setting could go to another more appropriate one. This sort of recommendation has implications for educational policy that cannot be resolved here. About all that can be said is that the various coercive forces available in behavior settings may be helpful to teachers if they can find ways to make use of them.

Participation

Another major effect that settings have on behavior stems from the degree of participation which they allow and encourage. Recall that not all positions in a setting are of equal importance; some are spectators and some are performers. A study of various-sized high schools in eastern Kansas (Barker & Gump, 1964) found that students in the smaller schools were much more likely to take active and significant roles in the extracurricular settings than those in the larger schools where they were more likely to be spectators or simple members, if they participated at all. Each school—regardless of its size—has only one football team; the smaller the school, the greater the likelihood that the student will be on the field instead of in the stands. The actual numbers from this study are impressive: the largest school had sixty-five times more students than the smallest school, only eight times as *many* settings and only twice the *variety* of settings; each setting had three times as many inhabitants. The consequences of these simple numbers are considerable:

1.   The criteria for acceptance are likely to be more relevant. If a student plays the clarinet, he/she can probably get in the band of a small school, but a larger school may also require that the student be attractive and popular.

2.   A student is more likely to be recruited actively to join a group in the small school since its problem is getting enough people while the big school's problem is to deal with an excess of applicants.

3.   A student's role is likely to be more demanding in the small school; the student is more likely to have an important function in the setting.

4.   In the smaller schools deviations from standard performance are more likely to be met with tolerance and patient instruction; the student is not so readily replaced as in the larger school. Even the most marginal student gets to participate in the smaller school (Williams, 1967).

The consequences for students are close to what we would expect from such findings. Small-school students reported more satisfactions such as being valued, mastering competencies, and achieving through effort. Large-school students reported more satisfactions of a vicarious nature (being part of a bigger entity, seeing a good performance, and knowing the latest inside gossip). These findings are consistent with an extensive literature from social and industrial psychology (reviewed in Barker & Gump, 1964) showing, for example, that workers in smaller factories and offices exhibit less absenteeism, better performance, more job satisfaction, and greater loyalty. Moos (1974) in a similar review draws similar conclusions. Sommer and Becker (1971), in studying a college classroom, found more complaints and less satisfaction with the room from students in large classes than those in small classes. Lastly, there are a number of putative crowding studies in which the really significant experimenter variable was probably group size (for example, Hutt & Vaisey, 1966; McGrew, 1970); for normal and exceptional children larger group sizes are associated with increases in aggression and/or withdrawal.

A setting can be said to be *undercommitted* if there is no large excess of people wanting to participate relative to the number of positions to be filled; as this excess increases, the setting is *overcommitted*. It appears from the review just cited (see also Wicker, 1973) that if the goal is participation and commitment by as many people as possible, the undercommitted setting is superior. Nonetheless, *all* indicators do not favor the undercommitted setting. For example, the football team at the small high school may be inferior precisely because the coach cannot be too selective.

The Barker and Gump study (1964) referred to earlier raises another issue in that students at the smaller high schools also reported more insecurity. Their insecurity appears to derive from the challenge of performing responsibly in a number of varied settings. Secord and Backman (1961) would hypothesize that these students remained in the settings and did not withdraw because of an ability to manage various stresses. Stern (1970) calls this sort of environmental pressure *anabolic* since it leads to growth and development. The reverse, *catabolic* pressure, is aimed at organizational stability and bureaucratic self-maintenance. Such pressure is more likely to be found in larger schools that have an excess of personnel and a shortage of essential positions.

Teachers, however, even assuming they are convinced of the superiority of undermanned settings, do not have the option of reducing the size of their schools or their classes. If anything, recent trends have been in the opposite direction. Recall, however, that the Barker and Gump (1964) research found that the largest school, compared to the smallest, added students at eight times the rate at which it added settings. Could the larger schools create more settings? In the sports area this has already happened; many schools now have teams in soccer, lacrosse, and volleyball that they did not have ten years ago. Can this happen in other areas besides athletics? Can teachers create more than one behavior setting within the classroom area itself?

The definition of behavior settings requires that each setting have a time and a place to occur on a periodic and sustained basis, and that the necessary physical facilities and supports must be available while it is in session. The setting should have a variety of responsible positions that support the goal or purpose of the setting. What might such a classroom look like? Perhaps in the front a small group is gathered around the teacher in blackboard instruction. Off to one side the Helper's Club is giving its regular Tuesday morning tutoring session in mathematics. At the rear the Evil Geniuses are in session designing apparatus to determine whether Skinnerian learning principles work with hamsters. The Ancient Sages are meeting in the corridor to decide how to make the scenery for its enactment of the purchase of Alaska. And in the center of the classroom the Spoken Word Club is having its monthly spelling bee. All of the settings are small; few have more than ten members. Each child is a member of several groups, and most children are officers in at least one of them. Each setting has an assigned time and place to occur and a limited amount of appropriate equipment and supplies. Since the activity of each one is directly tied to the academic work of the team, children are pressured to take active parts in them; and each setting periodically makes presentations to its own class and perhaps to other classes. While Barker (1968) tends to slip into biological metaphors and imply that settings are similar to organisms and have a sort of will-to-live and to survive, it is more probable that periodic reviews of some sort (including the presentations,) would be required to keep the settings functioning and task-related and their members involved and contributing.

Requirements of Exceptional Children

Recent years have seen increasing attention being given by educators to *mainstreaming*, integrating as many exceptional children as possible into the regular classroom as much of the time as possible. This means that teachers must examine classrooms and other parts of the school to determine whether these environments can meet the requirements of the exceptional child. These requirements may vary as broadly as the types of children who are included in this catchall category. However, some rather simple principles will help the teacher meet some of the basic needs of exceptional children and at the same time not interfere with the needs of normal or usual children.

Normal in a statistical sense describes variation about the mean or average. The exceptional child then is one whose deviation from the average falls outside some commonly accepted range on one or more dimensions. On this point, it is important to recognize the existence of continuity along any dimension. The limits of normal deviation are established consensually and somewhat arbitrarily within a given culture. All children differ widely from each other in sensory, cognitive, physical, and emotional functioning; the exceptional child simply differs a little more. This difference may be due to genetic or environmental factors or, more probably, to the interaction between these factors, with the greatest damage being wrought when a genetic deficit is compounded by environmental deficits (Smith, 1974).

Categories of Exceptionality

Types of exceptionality fall into specific categories, each with specific environmental requirements. First are children who have sensory impairments which may be partial or total; most commonly these involve sight, hearing, or speech. Second are children who have cognitive disabilities such as brain injury, mental retardation, and a variety of generalized or specific learning problems (some include the mentally gifted in this category also). Third are other children who have gross or fine motor deficiencies, including missing or impaired members; children with especially poor health may be included in this category also. And fourth are children who may have emotional difficulties such as poor impulse control, social maladjustment, hyperactivity, or depression. While these are presented as four discrete categories of exceptionality, unfortunately handicaps often come in clusters. For example, a crippled child may also have a hearing problem (Birch & Johnstone, 1975). The child with multiple handicaps may therefore be thought of as a fifth and fairly common category.

With such a diverse group it makes no sense to talk about *the* exceptional child; the only characteristic these children have in common is that they require special education of some sort. Mainstreaming assumes that these children will spend part of the day in special settings receiving special attention directed to their specific disability and that the rest of the day can and should be with the normal children. Wolfensberger (1972) presents a *funnel model* showing graphically the relationship between extent of exceptionality and proportion of time spent in special programs and settings. The objective is to reduce progressively the time spent in special settings. The lower limit will be set for each child by the nature and extent of the exceptionality as indicated by the funnel model. To summarize: exceptional children are a diverse group with diverse needs. Some proportion of their needs can be met within normal school settings. Ideally, this proportion will increase for most children, over time.

It is difficult to speak of *absolute* disabilities or handicaps. It is more realistic and useful to speak of handicaps as they relate to a specific task in a specific environment. This enables us to shift the emphasis away from handicapped people and on to handicapping environments. An elderly person in reasonable health may have an accident on a stair with poorly designed treads and no handrail, but the source of the handicap in such a case was in the environment and not in the person. A highly distractable child may be unable to perform academic work in a customary classroom environment but may perform quite well in another environment where the level of stimulation is lower and all stimuli are related to the learning task. Someone in a wheelchair may be very good in mathematics but is handicapped if the class is on the third floor and there are no elevators. A child who is unruly in a traditional classroom may do well in another class where positive learning principles are employed. There are, of course, innumerable tests for assessing and labeling children (Smith, 1974), but such tests and labels should be used sparingly since far too often their effect is to shift the burden from the environment onto the child. The focus in this section will be to evaluate environments instead of children since this would appear to be more educationally relevant.

In discussing the topic of school environments for exceptional children, it is well to consider Lindsley's (1964) distinction between *prosthetic* and *therapeutic*. A prosthetic device must operate continuously to compensate for a permanent deficit (for example, seeing-eye dog), whereas a therapeutic device can eventually be dispensed with (for example, a crutch for a broken leg). Recall Stern's (1970) characterization of environmental pressure as either *anabolic* (growth-enhancing) or catabolic (growth-inhibiting); it becomes clear that the environment which is too successfully prosthetic may at the same time be catabolic. For example, in institutions the staff may find it less disruptive to perform tasks for the patients rather than to help the patients learn to do the tasks for themselves. Somewhat paradoxically a review in Moos (1974) finds this to be even more the case as the patient-staff ratio increases. We do not want to oversimplify the matter here; some people's deficits are permanent and prosthetic devices and environments are required (for example, wheelchairs and ramps for crippled children). Remember, however, that a prosthetic, catabolic, custodial environment can all too quickly turn a temporary deficit into a permanent one. It is these considerations that lead Wolfensberger (1972) to argue for *normalization,* the process by which through successive approximations environments for exceptional children are brought closer and closer to normal environments. In this process the various therapeutic supports that the child initially requires are gradually withdrawn as the child progresses. How much support can eventually be withdrawn is something we cannot know at the outset, but what we can know is that normalization will almost certainly *not* occur unless it is attempted. More of the right kinds of attention early in the child's life is the best guarantee of less need for it later.

Design for Special Education

Architectural considerations for the education of exceptional children will mostly come into play when a facility is being designed or remodeled. These are well presented in, for example, Abeson and Blacklow (1971), Birch and Johnstone (1975), and Nellist (1970) and will be reviewed here only insofar as they deal with elements more directly under the teacher's control. As noted earlier, in a school where mainstreaming is in force, exceptional children will still be spending part of their days in separate classes for special training. Functional efficiency may suggest placing these facilities together but separate from the regular classrooms. Exceptional children may need special doors to the outside, special play facilities, or special eating facilities. Since they have to take special instruction away from their classmates, there will be scheduling problems and administratively it may be simpler to have them arrive, depart, play, and eat at separate times from the other children and perhaps in separate places. Such administration pressures will become greater at times when school budgets and teacher time are being stretched tight. It should be clear, however, that these efficiency and convenience considerations all work against the aim of mainstreaming, which is the spatial and temporal integration of exceptional children with their peers (Abeson & Blacklow, 1971). These pressures will have to be resisted if there is to be real, as opposed to token, mainstreaming.

Various aspects of classroom layout need to be considered. Exceptional children may not be able to persevere at a learning task so long as normal children can, either because of greater effort required or shorter attention span. In addition, their work with the teacher may involve special treatment better done in private. All these considerations suggest a need for alcoves or parts of the room where they can go to escape distractions, to calm down, to recoup their interest and energy, and to receive separate instruction. With some help from the teacher, the exceptional children should be able to withdraw themselves from the other children and the classroom activity, so that they go when they need to but return as quickly as possible. Unlimited withdrawal would, of course, defeat the purposes of mainstreaming.

There is another reason the environment should not force continued close association between exceptional children and normal children. Recall that in discussing personal space, studies were cited showing that both children and adults prefer to sit or stand farther from different people (amputees, those who are obese, hearing-impaired). A child's initial reaction to a crippled, blind, or malformed peer may well be avoidance and it would be a mistake to force the issue. Recall also the studies cited with monkeys and chimps, showing that the initial response to a novel stimulus was increased arousal and withdrawal, but that approach and exploration (often interspersed with further bouts of overexcitement and withdrawal) generally followed. It seems reasonable to assume that a similar sequence would occur when a normal child is confronted with an extraordinary peer. The implication is that the classroom environment, both in its furnishings and in its program, should allow self-regulated approach between the two groups of children, on the assumption that with time, occupying the same classroom plus natural curiosity will overcome initial avoidance.

Classroom housekeeping becomes an issue with exceptional children as well. They may have poor vision or poor balance, or may be easily distracted so that a classroom that presents no danger to a normal child might be hazardous to them. Some examples would be toys or books on the floor, small changes in floor level, or other objects—including low furniture—that present a tripping danger. The consequences of a fall are, of course, made worse if furniture, toys, and books also make navigation difficult or impossible for a child on crutches or in a wheelchair.

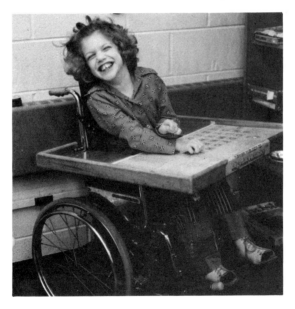

Certain types of disabilities require adaptation to
the physical environment of a regular classroom.

ASSESSMENT CHECKLIST: PHYSICAL ENVIRONMENT

Components	Questions	Yes	No	Undecided
A. School Environment				
	1. Is the school adequate in these areas?			
	a) air quality	____	____	____
	b) noise control	____	____	____
	c) traffic safety	____	____	____
	d) accessibility	____	____	____
	e) outdoor play areas	____	____	____
	f) crime safety	____	____	____
	g) attractiveness	____	____	____
	h) safety standards	____	____	____
	2. Have physical and personal safety hazards in the following areas been eliminated or controlled so that frequent injuries or assaults to students/teachers are not a problem?			
	a) classrooms	____	____	____
	b) halls	____	____	____
	c) stairs	____	____	____
	d) grounds	____	____	____
	e) lockers	____	____	____
	f) gym	____	____	____
	g) toilets	____	____	____
	h) cafeteria	____	____	____
	i) parking lots	____	____	____
	3. Does the architectural layout of the school reflect the relationship among activities? Are related, compatible activities grouped together and unrelated, incompatible activities grouped separately?	____	____	____

ENTER NUMBER OF QUESTIONS ANSWERED YES   ☐

Components	Question	Yes	No	Undecided

B. Classroom Environment

1. Physiological Effects (Illumination)

4. Are there at least 100 A-candles of light at the surface for reading and other demanding visual tasks?

5. Is the lighting throughout the classroom varied and home-like?

6. Is lighting used to help define the different activities areas of the room?

7. Is the lighting warm yet not glaring?

(Temperature)

8. Can adequate air movement be obtained when needed?

9. Is there an adequate supply of fresh air?

10. Are temperatures controlled within a comfortable range (68°-74°)? Are children assisted in making necessary clothing adjustments for the room temperature?

11. Is humidity adequate year round?

Components	Question	Yes	No	Undecided
(Noise)	12. Can windows be opened without interference from outside noise?	___	___	___
	13. Is the noise level of each classroom controlled so that the activities of the other classrooms are not disturbed?	___	___	___
	14. Is the teacher rarely asked to repeat what he/she has said?	___	___	___
(Color)	15. Are the colors in the classroom pleasantly varied?	___	___	___
	16. Is color used to define areas of the room and to attract attention to important educational displays?	___	___	___
	17. Are the colors in the room subdued, mellow, and pleasing?	___	___	___
(Materials)	18. Does the classroom contain furnishings, materials, and displays in addition to typical institutional furnishings?	___	___	___
	19. Do teachers and students bring in a variety of materials and displays related to current assignments?	___	___	___
	20. Are learning materials and displays well organized by topics or learning area?	___	___	___

Components	Question	Yes	No	Undecided
	21. Have excessive, unorganized materials been removed to eliminate confusion or distraction?	_____	_____	_____
	ENTER NUMBER OF QUESTIONS ANSWERED YES	☐		
2. Spatial effects	22. Are related compatible activities arranged together and unrelated, incompatible activities separated within the classroom?	_____	_____	_____
	23. Have an appropriate time and place been designated and assigned for all activities?	_____	_____	_____
	24. Is there a variety of places where different sized groups can meet and work?	_____	_____	_____
	25. Are there special places that individual children can go: a) for isolation b) for rest and quiet c) to let off steam d) to reward themselves e) for private instruction f) to work independently g) to be disciplined privately	_____	_____	_____
	26. Can children enter, leave, clean up, and dress, etc. without disturbing others?	_____	_____	_____
	27. Can children space themselves as they need or desire?	_____	_____	_____

Components	Question	Yes	No	Undecided
	28. Do the relative amounts of space allocated to various activities reflect their importance in the teaching program?	____	____	____
	ENTER NUMBER OF QUESTIONS ANSWERED YES	[ ]		
3. Physical Effects	29. Is the environment kept clean?	____	____	____
	30. Are the furnishings (desks, displays, etc.) moveable to provide a variety of groupings and areas within the room for different learning tasks?	____	____	____
	31. Can the teacher control visual distractions between groups of children (by separating groups, rising room dividers, etc.)?	____	____	____
	32. Does the environment provide feedback (mirrors for grooming and posture) and exemplars (handwriting samples) where they will catch the children's attention?	____	____	____
	33. Are storage facilities accessible to the students for getting out and putting away materials which they are allowed access to?	____	____	____

Components	Question	Yes	No	Undecided
	34. Have high physical barriers been eliminated so that the teacher has visual access to the entire room?	____	____	____
	ENTER NUMBER OF QUES-TIONS ANSWERED YES	☐		
4. Setting Effects	35. Is there a variety of places, materials, methods, and equipment for reaching different learners in different ways?	____	____	____
	36. Are there adequate numbers of materials and activities to engage all the children without disputes over property rights?	____	____	____
	37. Can the teacher identify an "overcommitted" setting (one in which most children are observers rather than performers and leaders) and then attempt to create new, smaller work or activity groups?	____	____	____
	38. Have physical barriers to handicapped children been removed?	____	____	____
	39. Is the environment and its use specifically referred to in the teacher's lesson plan?	____	____	____

Components	Question	Yes	No	Undecided
	40. Do the lesson plans include the use of specific parts of the environment in achieving the goals of the program?	___	___	___
	41. Does the teacher periodically change the environment to improve the teaching program?	___	___	___
	42. Does the teacher systematically observe and evaluate the effects of the environment and the social behaviors and learning of the class?	___	___	___
	ENTER NUMBER OF QUESTIONS ANSWERED YES			

Summary Section

A. School Environment (questions 1–3)   _____

B. Classroom Environment

   1. Physiological effects (questions 4–21)   _____

   2. Spatial effects (questions 22–28)   _____

   3. Physical effects (questions 29–34)   _____

   4. Setting effects (questions 35–42)   _____

   Subtotal: Classroom Environment   _____

TOTAL INSTRUCTIONAL ENVIRONMENT SCORE   _____

ENVIRONMENTAL PROFILE: PHYSICAL ENVIRONMENT

Components   *Scores: Number of Questions Answered Yes*

                              1 2 3 4 5 6 7 8 9 10 11 12 13 14 15 16 17 18

A. School
   Environment:

B. Classroom   Physiological
   Environment: Effects

                 Spatial Effects

                 Physical Effects

                 Setting Effects

6

Evaluating
Community Services

Social agencies are directed, even driven, by the environment within which they function. Cities emphasize programs that local residents, state and federal governments are willing to support. To a very large extent, the focus of such programs depends on the unique and idiosyncratic characteristics of the social milieu. Some communities, for example, provide a relatively high level of support for housing with comparatively less subsidy given for transportation. Other communities emphasize preschool education or mental health services and deemphasize upgrading the physical environment. There is, then, a direct relationship between the services and programs a community provides and the values exhibited and expressed by the residents. Sweden provides a good example of this generalization at a national level. The citizens apparently value equal and full medical services for everyone, whatever their situation and, thus, are willing to be taxed at a relatively high level.

Schools are an integral part of society. As with other social agencies, educational programs that are emphasized by a school district are a direct reflection of the values, attitudes, and character of the environment in which they are situated. The nature of the curriculum, the instructional methods, the materials of instruction, and the administrative organization of the school system all depict the orientation desired by the community that has responsibility for supporting the schools. Some communities emphasize the high school football program and make much less support available for other aspects of the school, such as the foreign language or mathematics programs. Other communities value aspects of the academic areas and willingly support these values with appropriate financing. It is certainly not an overgeneralization, then, to state that the public schools provide programs and services that the community values and is willing to support with its tax dollars.

A certain number of the programs and services provided by the schools either are mandated by law or are required in order for the schools to receive accreditation by professional organizations. A certain number of mathematics courses, for example, must be available so that students who wish to continue their education may qualify for admission into institutions of higher education. Specific courses and curricula in science, English, and physical education are required by federal and state laws, and a reasonable array of elective subjects is usually provided in various majors. It is traditional for schools to provide certain clusters of services that supplement the curricular requirements. Guidance counselors are usually assigned to secondary schools but less often to elementary programs. School psychologists, speech and hearing specialists, and remedial consultants are frequently employed to provide services to an entire school system on a regularly scheduled basis. Large school districts frequently assign such ancillary personnel to a cluster of schools, and they, in turn, are totally responsible for providing appropriate services to the children in those schools.

Unfortunately, many of the services necessary to provide a comprehensive public school program are not fully realized in most communities. Financial impoverishment inevitably leads to budgeting reallocations among programs within a school district. Choices must be made, and such decisions usually result in a significant reduction in one or more of the existing programs or services. School administrators and members of school boards have the Solomon-like duty to make judgments about priorities for the allocation of existing resources. They must deal with various special interest groups and political pressures, hear from advocates for the various sides of an issue, and make the ultimate decision. Such decisions typically are based on factors such as the expressions by valued members of the community, the extent to which the various programs are required by the majority of the students, the relative visability of the different programs, and the presumed quality of the programs and services.

Ancillary Services

Under the conditions just described, then, it is not at all surprising that the ancillary services are usually among the first to be reduced or even completely eliminated when financial difficulties hit a school district. Such action is understandable in the context of our earlier discussion. First, most ancillary service programs focus on a relatively narrow spectrum of students and often are not involved in any way with the general population of youngsters. School psychologists, psychometricians, speech correctionists, and remedial specialists might deal with 15 percent of the children in a school district. This simply means that such programs and services are likely candidates for reduction because the advocacy group is so small and often relatively inarticulate. Moreover, these specialists deal with children who are in trouble, academically or otherwise. They are not high-visibility students in a positive way, for example, in a fashion that makes the parents and schools proud of a winning basketball team. Most people, including those involved in administering a school system, would prefer not to give emphasis to problems. This simply means that it is a lot easier to reduce programs and services that involve a comparatively small group of inept children than it is to eliminate major segments of other programs whose supporters are large in number and especially vocal.

There are a few scattered exceptions to this generalization. If an influential parent or a group of politically knowledgeable parents feels strongly that ancillary services or certain programs should be provided within a school district, they may be able to mobilize enough community support to prevail. For example, the Pennsylvania Association for Retarded Citizens, a parents group, was singlehandedly instrumental in stimulating the courts to require that the public schools provide free public education to all children irrespective of their degree or type of disability or handicap. Civic clubs are often motivated to encourage community agencies, such as the schools, to be responsive to the needs of all children, including those who require intensive instructional and/or therapeutic management. Community pressure, then, can be influential in strongly encouraging schools to provide services required by certain children whose problems are unique and difficult.

The overriding purpose of education is to provide an environment that will allow children to learn how to function as productive and independent people within the open community. The vast majority of youngsters is able to realize this basic objective. There are numerous students in every school system, however, who require certain unique programs and services in order to develop the fundamental skills expected of most people. Such students' characteristics and needs differ widely. They are complex and are manifested in different ways according to the peculiarities of the youngsters themselves and the uniquenesses of their environment. Just as we should not expect the children in a class or school to exhibit a relatively homogeneous pattern of weaknesses or needs, it is equally improbable that the program and service needs of a youngster will remain the same over a period of time. The fact is, then, that children need multiple services, not just those that are related to education, to develop skills that will allow them to become functionally competent adults. For some children this will mean long-term speech therapy; other children will require frequent psychological evaluations by competent psychometricians. Some youngsters will need intensive mental health counseling over a period of time, and, still others will need vocational or rehabilitation counseling.

Professional educators and school boards have acknowledged their moral obligation to provide a total educational program for children. Their idealism has often been compromised as a result of inadequate funds, and the special services are the most frequent sufferers. This compromise is no longer possible because new legislation at state and federal levels requires that comprehensive educational and ancillary services be made available to all children. This means that the community must provide the full range of multiple services that are needed by every youngster. This legislation fully recognizes that educational services must be buttressed by a variety of other unique services in order for children to become reasonably functional adults. There is, then, legislative and judicial weight behind the oft-repeated moral pronouncements of educators and community leaders to the effect that every child should "be provided an optimum educational experience."

Resource Services

Obviously the schools cannot provide in-house services of the range and magnitude expected by the legislators and courts. As a consequence, there has been a standing-together of small- and intermediate-sized school districts into larger units for the singular purpose of providing unique services to special groups of children. Each school system provides some financial support to the unit and in return receives services from the specialists who are employed by this collective resource unit. In this way, services that are reasonably unique can be provided and the financial responsibilities can be distributed among the school districts. In fact, numerous states have adopted the intermediate or resource unit concept as the most reasonable way to provide special programs. Such units frequently are able to develop an adequate expertise to allow for the receipt of special federal or state grants and contracts that allow for an impressive comprehensive program of resources. The special libraries are often developed, braille reading and writing services are provided, and itinerant consultants are employed to assist regular-class teachers in providing for unique forms of exceptionalities within a classroom. Instructional materials centers are often located in these resource units, and consultants are provided to the contributing school districts to assist in developing and writing research and training proposals. The range of services provided by many of the resource units is quite impressive, and properly applied, will result in the contributing school districts' becoming more efficient and effective instructional centers. The concept of a resource unit is much like that evidenced in most medical centers. Physicians have available the services of various clinical laboratories and specialists who serve as consultants when the originating physician determines what services are desirable or necessary. This frees the physician to spend more time dealing directly with the patient; at the same time, the expertise of specialists is available when needed.

Community Services

Someone or some agency must assume responsibility for assuring that children who need special services receive them promptly, efficiently, and effectively. Parents who suspect or know that their child is having difficulty often turn to the family physician or to the child's teacher for counsel and direct assistance. Both of these professionals should be prepared to accept the responsibility of properly referring the parents to an appropriate service agency. Parents of handicapped children, particularly, are prone to clinic hop to an extent that is debilitating. Obviously, it is wise to secure a second opinion where appropriate. However, when school and community services are poorly articulated, an excessive amount of changing from one professional to another can be expected. It is then an important duty of teachers to assist parents in locating services in the schools and within the community from which their child could benefit. In addition, teachers should follow-up after the initial contact with the service agency has occurred. This will foster a sense of confidence by the parents in the teacher and in the service agency. Follow-up also allows the teacher to better appraise whether the child should be referred to other possible service agencies and to coordinate and articulate more effectively recommendations concerning therapy and treatment.

Accountability

The entire responsibility for assuring that services are provided within and outside of the schools should not fall to the teachers alone. Although the teacher is closest to the consumers of such services and has more opportunity to appraise the types of specific services a child might need, it is incumbent on the school administration to monitor carefully the range of services provided within and outside of the school. Administrators should serve as advocates for those children who need such help. Moreover, school administrators are responsible for providing comprehensive assistance to teachers as they endeavor to provide assistance to parents and children. This support can take the form of providing additional aides, secretarial assistance, summer supplemental employment, tuition assistance for postbaccalaureate work, and assistance in securing relevant professional literature. By far, however, the best type of support administrators can provide teachers in this regard is a positive and supportive attitude toward the teacher's role in coordinating and articulating school and community services on behalf of children. Administrators should serve as advocates for those teachers who are involved in service-oriented behavior on the part of youngsters. In addition, community leaders, school board members, and other influential citizens have an important responsibility to take whatever political action is necessary to convince the community of the need to provide and support a wide spectrum of services for children. Some community leaders have become so convinced that psychological, social, and medical services should become an intimate and integrated part of the entire fabric of the community that they have supported a centralized service unit within the community to coordinate and administer disparate services as a total entity. The base service-center concept emerged as a result of frustration that people experienced over the lack of proper referral and comprehensive articulation among service units. People in communities who have initiated such coordinating units are finding the concept is readily implementable and using it can effect efficiencies that theretofore had not been possible.

Throughout this chapter the term *services* has been used in a generic way. Among the specific services offered within many school districts, under the auspices of the schools themselves, are speech and hearing evaluation and therapy, psychological and educational testing, counseling and guidance services of a personal and vocational nature, school nursing services, and remedial programming for children who have fallen behind in certain subject areas. Quite naturally, the larger the school district and the more varied the populations served by the schools, the greater will be the scope and depth of in-school service programs available to children. The range and nature of the services provided by the community, outside of the overall jurisdiction of the school district, are also dictated by the community's interests, needs, and willingness to provide the necessary support. Most typically, however, a range of health-care services is available including nursing services, consultation services with various types of medical specialists, occupational and physical therapy, family counseling, vocational rehabilitation, psychological and psychiatric examination and treatment, and child-care services. Once again, the extent to which full range of services is available within the community is in large measure dictated by the size of the community, the priorities established by its people, and the extent to which the area can attract competent professional personnel in the various specialty areas.

In a previous section a number of general comments were made concerning the basis on which communities determine to provide key services to parents and children. As a teacher or administrator, people in the community will look to you for leadership in mobilizing an effort to convince others on the desirability of establishing and maintaining specific types of services. The following outlines, in very brief form, a checklist which you may find helpful in systematically mobilizing such an effort.

1. Evaluate the Need.   Of utmost, fundamental importance is the need for you to assess the extent and type of services required within the community. Anecdotal information and subjective viewpoints should not be used as the major bases for justifying a proposal that the community provide certain services to its people. Instead, the need for such services should be assessed together with relevant data that have been systematically gathered and interrelated in a reasonably sophisticated way. You might establish an empirical profile of the community which describes income levels, the manner in which its resources are being expended, the characteristics of people within the community, the primary needs of the community and its people and the manner in which these needs are being satisfied, the existing interrelationships among service agencies within and outside of the schools, and the role the proposed service agency would play in concert with existing agencies.

2. Specify the Consequences of Not Providing Proposed Services.   This section of your proposal might use the data expressed in the earlier section and particularly emphasize the presumed pros and cons of not providing the service. Some emphasis should be given to the long-term consequences of children's not receiving certain services and the possible negative effects this might have on the community as well as the child's family.

3. Propose a Plan.   Using information summarized in the preceding sections, you are now prepared to develop a coordinated plan to establish the proposed service. Your plan should identify the major dimensions required to provide the service and should include:

■   The manner in which the service would be administrated.

- The types and characteristics of professional personnel involved.

- The financial requirements and proposed budget.

- The manner in which the service would be phased in (perhaps over a period of several years).

- The requirements of the physical plant.

- The manner in which the service would undergo continuous evaluation and modification.

- The role the community would play in monitoring the efficiency and effectiveness of the service.

- The approach used by the agency to interrelating its service with others in the community.

- The advantages and disadvantages of several possible organizational and delivery schemes.

- The manner in which clients would be served.

4. Enlist Advocates.   The extent to which a proposed plan to establish key and necessary service agencies within a community will become established is inextricably related to the strength and support of its advocates. It is of utmost importance that groups of influential people articulate strong support for any proposed plan that involves the expenditure of public resources, in spite of the fact that the plan involves a provision of services to all people within the community. Such advocates need to be identified, informed of the proposal, and organized effectively to support the plan before, during, and after the proposal has been described to and discussed with the community. The most well-written, effectively documented, and elegant proposal for the provision of community services within or outside of the school system will be doomed unless appropriate marketing techniques are used. The people must be convinced that the service is needed, the consequences grave unless it is provided, and that the proposed plan is economical and effective.

5. Provide for Continuous Evaluation.   Any proposal you develop should embody a program of continuous evaluation. Specific goals and objectives should be described within reasonable time dimensions. If, for example, a service is to be financially free-standing and dependent on fees for the services rendered after a period of three years, it would be particularly appropriate for the proposal to describe the intermediate steps and goals expected during the first three-year period. Similarly, if certain services are to be elaborated upon and extended during that same three-year period, the proposal should describe steps that will be taken to effect such elaborations and extensions. Finally, the criteria against which the services will be measured should be specified as early as possible so that the public will know the extent to which the plans are being realized.

Thus far attention has been directed to suggesting general approaches for considering how to encourage school districts or communities to recognize the need for services and then how to begin the process of establishment. Understandably, the problem involves political as well as professional considerations. The remainder of this chapter will suggest procedures that teachers and ancillary school personnel can use to evaluate the utility and quality of services that are presently available. Two factors must be considered in determining the type of in- and out-of-school services required within a community. First, it is obvious that the needs and characteristics of the children must be inventoried—especially those traits and attributes that currently are not being adequately cared for. Second, it is important for teachers, as well as an entire school district, to survey the service resources that are presently operative. But that is not enough. An analysis should be made of the additional resources the schools need in order to respond effectively to the collective needs of students. In conducting such inventories simply contrast student needs with existing services and extend the analysis by asking: What else do we need to do within the community in order to deal effectively with the problems evidenced by students and their parents? Here are several illustrations of the types of information you might want to include in inventories.

What About the Students?

1.   Of the entire school population, how many students appear to be experiencing difficulties with the school environment?

2.   What types of school problems are evident among students? Use the following categories to identify problems of specific youngsters as well as those associated with groups of children who are having difficulty in school: (a) socially related, (b) emotional problems, (c) academic disorders, (d) family, (e) physical problems, and (f) communication difficulties.

3.   Within each of the broad problem areas just specified, what specific performance inadequacies are disproportionately more frequent than others? For example, is there a higher percentage of reading problems among children who are classified as having difficulty in school than there are arithmetic problems? In addition, it will be helpful to tabulate the frequency of and types of problems evidenced among children in certain grades, in specific schools within a school district, and for children who have followed specific curricular tracks.

Programs provided by public libraries supplement regular school programs.

4. Of the children who are experiencing difficulty in school, is there a common pattern of characteristics that separates them from other children? For example, analyze if there is a tendency for one group to have come into the school system from other districts at a certain time. Determine if children who have problems have been exposed to a particular instructional approach that is different from that of other youngsters. Assess the hypothesis that one group of youngsters may have unique social or emotional traits that perhaps are not shared by other children in the school system who are not having difficulty with school.

5. To what extent has there been a history of children having difficulty with certain areas of the curriculum or program?

What Is the Status of Services for Students with Unique Needs?

1. What services are provided within the school environment to assist children in resolving their difficulties? Are there services such as personal and vocational counseling, psychological and/or educational testing, remedial instruction, resource-room assistance, speech-and-hearing evaluation and correction, adaptive physical education, nursing assistance (visual screening and dental checks), library assistance, special nutritional programs (hot breakfast or hot lunch programs) and family counseling? Are any or all of these services provided on a formal basis and are they available to any child or family in the community?

2. What services are provided out-of-school or in the local community? Are there services such as medical consultation and assistance, personal and family counseling, vocational rehabilitation, foster home placement, halfway house programs, sheltered workshops, psychological and/or psychiatric evaluation and counsel, library programs, adult education, and family planning? Are such services readily available to all members of the community?

3. Is there a central coordinating agency within the schools, within the community, and between schools and community that serves the purpose of fostering articulation among those services that are available?

4. Each of the service agencies, whether associated directly with the schools or located in the community, typically has a variety of professional personnel associated with its respective staff. It is often difficult to adequately evaluate the competence of those professionals in their areas of expertise; however, the responses to the following questions will be generally indicative of the capabilities of the professionals who are associated with the service agency.

  a. Are the professionals able to focus directly on the relevant problem? Does there seem to be an inordinate amount of delay in their grasping the key issues?

  b. Are the professionals prompt in meeting their appointments and obligations? Are they personable, able to establish rapport with clients in an easy and natural manner? Are they ethical in their interrelationships with others?

  c. Do the professionals acknowledge their limitations and refer clients to specialists when and where appropriate? Are they confident in their skills?

Is their behavior deliberate and sure? Do they demonstrate emotional maturity during difficult periods?

d.   Are the approaches of the professionals to the issues or problems reasonable, reliable, and valid or are they eclectic and experimental? If the latter, is the client informed about the experimental nature of the procedure and given a briefing on the real or possible consequences of participating?

e.   To what extent and in what manner are the observations, results, conclusions, and recommendations by the professionals communicated to clients and parents? Is there ease in communication? Do the clients have ample opportunity to express concern, ask questions, or make their own observations? Are the professionals willing to take whatever time is necessary to satisfy the needs of the clients? Is the language used in communicating results easily understood by the client?

ASSESSMENT CHECKLIST: COMMUNITY SERVICES

Components	Question	Yes	No	Undecided
A. Students	1. Can the teacher identify students in the school currently who are experiencing difficulties due to:			
	a. socially related problems	_____	_____	_____
	b. emotional problems	_____	_____	_____
	c. academic delays	_____	_____	_____
	d. physical problems	_____	_____	_____
	e. family factors	_____	_____	_____
	f. communication difficulties?	_____	_____	_____
	2. Can the teacher identify students in the school's history who were experiencing difficulties?	_____	_____	_____
	3. Can the teacher document the extent and need for special services by recording the number of children, past and present, and the types of difficulties?	_____	_____	_____
	ENTER NUMBER OF QUESTIONS ANSWERED YES			
B. Services	4. Are there services or persons within the school to assist children in resolving the difficulties listed previously?			
	a. personal counseling	_____	_____	_____
	b. vocational counseling	_____	_____	_____
	c. psychological and educational testing	_____	_____	_____
	d. remedial instruction	_____	_____	_____
	e. resource-room assistance	_____	_____	_____
	f. speech and hearing evaluation and correction	_____	_____	_____
	g. adaptive physical education	_____	_____	_____

Components	Question	Yes	No	Undecided
	h. nursing assistance (visual and dental checks)	____	____	____
	i. special nutritional programs	____	____	____
	j. family counseling	____	____	____
	5. If these services are not provided within the school, are there facilities to cover these needs in the larger community?	____	____	____
	6. Is there a central agency that coordinates the services within the school and community?	____	____	____
	7. Each of the in-school and out-of-school services that is available can be evaluated as follows:			
	a. Can the service be easily located and is the entry to the service readily available?	____	____	____
	b. Are there different ways whereby a student or parent can be referred to the service?	____	____	
	c. Is the service coordinated with other services in the schools and community?	____	____	____
	d. Is the waiting list short for the services rendered?	____	____	____
	e. Does the agency evaluate the efficiency and effectiveness of its own services?	____	____	____
	f. Does the agency follow-up on its services when appropriate? Do professionals assist clients in moving among service groups?	____	____	____
	g. Are agency services comprehensive, on-target (not fragmented)?	____	____	____

Components	Question	Yes	No	Undecided
	h. Has the agency had a positive impact on clients and a history of success?	_____	_____	_____
	ENTER NUMBER OF QUESTIONS ANSWERED YES			
C. Professionals	8. Are the service professionals able to identify and focus directly on the relevant problems?	_____	_____	_____
	9. Are the professionals prompt in meeting their appointments and obligations?	_____	_____	_____
	10. Are they personable and able to establish an easy natural rapport with clients?	_____	_____	_____
	11. Are they ethical and professional in their relationships with other service agency personnel?	_____	_____	_____
	12. Do they acknowledge their limitations and refer clients to specialists when appropriate?	_____	_____	_____
	13. Are the approaches of the professionals to the issues or problems reasonable, reliable, and workable?	_____	_____	_____
	14. Do the professionals take the necessary precautions			

Components	Question	Yes	No	Undecided
	and steps to protect the individual rights and dignity of clients?	____	____	____
	15. Are the professionals' observations, results, conclusions, and recommendations communicated to client and parents?	____	____	____
	16. Are professional communications to the client in a form that can be easily understood?	____	____	____
	17. Can clients freely express their concerns, feelings, and questions to the professional?	____	____	____
	ENTER NUMBER OF QUESTIONS ANSWERED YES			

Summary Section

A. **Students (questions 1–3)**   _____

B. **Services (questions 4–7)**   _____

C. **Professionals (questions 8–17)**   _____

TOTAL INSTRUCTIONAL ENVIRONMENT SCORE   _____

ENVIRONMENTAL PROFILE: COMMUNITY SERVICES

Components   *Scores: Number of Questions Answered Yes*

1 2 3 4 5 6 7 8 9 10 11 12 13 14 15

A. **Students:**

B. **Services:**

C. **Professionals:**

7

Building an Effective Evaluation Program

Throughout this text the position has been expressed that educators traditionally have been preoccupied with evaluation of the child and have failed to give enough attention to evaluation of the instructional environment. While it is important to consider the characteristics of each youngster, through the collection of various types of test information, it is shortsighted to use those data alone in making decisions about how to proceed in the process of teaching. The teacher's major responsibility is to arrange the best possible instructional setting by manipulating the curriculum, the methods of instruction, and the instructional materials. To provide an effective instructional environment, the teacher must be able to:

1. Identify factors in the instructional environment that influence learning.

2. Determine the character of those factors and make judgments about those that negatively or positively affect the performance of each child.

3. Plan a program of environmental intervention that the data suggest will enhance learning.

4. Evaluate the child's status and the quality of the instructional environment.

At this point, we will describe the procedures and practices for integrating the various aspects of an evaluation program. In addition, we will give some attention to using evaluative information in designing programs of instruction. The first matter that will be discussed is generic in nature. General rules, principles, or admonishments that have pertinence in the evaluation of the child *and* the environment will be highlighted. Next, attention will be given to issues and procedures that have particular relevance or are unique for the evaluation of the child. Finally, the essence of the message contained in this book, evaluating the instructional environment, will be summarized. In short, this final chapter will bring together the central concerns associated with the total evaluative effort required within the classroom so that children will be taught appropriately and so that learning will occur efficiently and effectively.

General Concepts of Evaluation

Adopt a Positive Approach

Our personal beliefs, philosophy, and attitudes have fundamental influence over the entire spectrum of evaluative procedures and practices. This is true in the evaluation of the child as well as the environment. It is of utmost importance that the evaluator be accepting. It is vital that the child be viewed in a positive way. The literature is replete with evidence documenting the adverse effects of a child's appearance, body odor, unclean clothes, and negative information in school records on the attitudes of others, especially teachers. Such youngsters are devalued by other people. They are not expected to do well in school, and they are treated less well by virtually every segment of the hierarchy within the schools. The upshot of such unfortunate attitudes is that these children actually do perform poorly. There is a clear cause-and-effect linkage among (1) a poor attitude toward a child because of homely appearance, which leads to (2) a developing perception that not much can be expected of the child in school, which leads to (3) less enthusiasm by the teacher in providing a high-level instructional program (because what is the use if the kid is not "capable"), which leads to (4) the child's actually doing poorly in school.

Clearly, anyone who has responsibility for evaluating a child must approach the task with a positive attitude toward the youngster; otherwise, the child will not receive an adequate, accomplished evaluation and diagnostic review.

Evaluators also must be understanding and accepting of the child. The fact that a child comes from a neighborhood different from that of the evaluator could bias the collection and interpretation of diagnostic data. Similarly, if the evaluator makes unwarranted assumptions or conclusions about the child or the environment before all the data are collected, errors of omission or commission are likely to occur; the ultimate disservice will be to the child. The major precept to keep in mind throughout the evaluation process is: *remain neutral and objective at all stages and make no preconceived conclusions in the absence of definitive evidence. Do not condemn a child because of his/her past or appearance.*

It is also important that evaluators, whether teachers or psychometricians, have positive attitudes toward themselves. This factor is related to their ability to conduct an appropriate and thorough evaluation, and to their confidence in their skills and potential to identify the relevant problems. They must assume an attitude of openness concerning circumstances that may warrant consulting another person or testing specialist. In short, the degree to which evaluators view themselves as competent professionals, within realistic limitations, greatly influences the reliability and validity of the evaluation process and information that is collected.

Fundamental to the accuracy and appropriateness of all types of evaluative practices is an accepting and positive attitude by educational personnel toward the child, situation, prognosis for improvement, and toward themselves. Indeed, such an attitude will have a direct bearing on the child's performance and on the accuracy of the evaluator's assessment of the environment.

Employ a Clinical-Statistical Approach

Teachers have been challenged over the years to base their educational decisions on hard data. The incidence of college courses on statistics, measurement, and educational diagnosis has increased dramatically since the 1960s. Again, however, the focus of this effort has been on evaluating the *child* and not his/her educational environment. Nonetheless, one orientation for making judgments about a child's instructional needs is statistical, that is, dependence is placed on the use of quantitatively oriented techniques. This approach includes formal or informal tests, computer diagnostic protocols, actuarial-type tables, statistical probabilities, decision rules based on empirical research, flow charts, decision trees, and functional-analysis techniques. These examples illustrate the data-based quantitative approach used in making decisions to ameliorate educational difficulties of children.

Ideally, implementation of a purely statistical approach in decision making requires that a direct translation occur between data about a child (and/or his/her environment) and the preferred instructional program. The linkage between the data and the educational program must be direct; a statistical approach does not allow for multiple interpretations or alternatives. While there are obviously various differences among advocates of the quantitative methods, basically the approach is almost "cookbook like". For example, if x, y, and z are present in a, b, and c environments, then "program 642 is *the* one to use for a specific child or group of children."

Recognizing that such precision is virtually impossible to achieve and, in fact, may not be desirable, educators have chosen to adopt a more clinical approach in decision making. This strategy is relatively more artlike than strictly data-based and does not depend so much on quantitative techniques. A major argument advanced to justify the clinical approach is that it effectively identifies the subtle characteristics and patterns expressed by children. The conflicting evidences can be weighed with more sensitivity, than is possible with a strictly statistical or actuarial approach. The clinical approach strives to provide what is best for the individual child. In that no two children or settings are identical, those who subscribe to a clinical approach express the view that describing characteristics of populations has relatively little applicability for dealing with the day-to-day educational problems of children. Advocates of a clinical process emphasize that judgments concerning a child or a situation are difficult to quantify since they involve identifying subtle patterns, weighing conflicting evidence, analyzing complex interrelationships among a variety of factors, and dealing with situations that are anything but static.

In reality, most skillful teachers use a combination of the statistical and clinical approaches in identifying, describing, and remediating educational problems. Usually data on student performance are gathered from tests, hypotheses are generated from this information, and a final judgment eventually is made about the most appropriate instructional procedure. Too little or too much test data can have an adverse effect on the diagnostic interpretations and judgments made in a clinical context. It is just as difficult to arrive at reasonable conclusions and solutions in instances when an abundance of information is presented as when inadequate information is presented. In addition, of course, the wrong kinds of information, as well as erroneous data, can be equally debilitating and lead to highly inappropriate generalizations and solutions. As mentioned earlier, computer experts have said, "garbage in—garbage out," to emphasize that the output from a computer is only as good as the quality of the information that was programmed into the computer. This generalization is equally true with regard to the diagnosis and remediation of educational disorders in children.

Teachers, then, are faced with the problem of striking a reasonable compromise between a highly statistical approach to decision making and a heavily clinical orientation. Some reasonable intermediate position between these two extremes seems most appropriate. Teachers must decide which kinds of data are absolutely necessary to formulate hypotheses concerning the character of the child's educational needs and subsequently verify the validity of these hypotheses. Data are interrelated in various ways to discern the nature of complex interactions that may be operating and to discern what types of possible problems should be given first consideration in remediation.

In addition to resolving the statistical versus clinical approaches in decision making, teachers must also discern what kinds of information are required to characterize each child's educational performance. This is no small task. All too often mountains of information from batteries of tests are presented to teachers in an effort to describe the child from all angles. Although we certainly subscribe to the need for collecting diagnostic data about a child's performance, the primary focus of this text has been on developing information concerning each child's environment. This is a problem for teachers because until now very little has been done to develop evaluative instruments to assess the instructional environment. However, in evaluation teachers must use both types of data, that is, information collected about the child and information illustrative of the child's instructional environment. Clinical skills become predominant when teachers are required to analyze both types of data and decide how best to arrange the instructional environment to assist the child. The remainder of this chapter will be devoted to summarizing the specific steps that teachers can take in translating educationally relevant information and data into an individually appropriate educational program for each child.

Identify Problems and Monitor Changes

First, it is important for teachers to be aware that a problem exists, whether with respect to the environment or to the child. A general guideline to use in assessing a possible problem is to note changes that have occurred in the child and/or environment over a period of time. If the child's behavior or performance shows marked depressions that stand out from the usual achievement record on a specific task, the teacher might suspect that a problem exists. Similarly, if the instructional environment has changed from its usual character, difficulties may result. So, comparisons of the same phenomenon over a period of time will help the teacher become aware of a possible problem.

Another way to become alert to a possibility of a problem is by comparing one child with another child (or group of children) and another environment. Ideally, of course, the teacher would want to make such comparisons against other children and other environments that are reasonably alike in their major characteristics. For example, it would be incongruous to compare a fourth grader's arithmetic performance with that of a ninth grader or to judge an instructional environment designed for teaching reading with that typical of an art classroom. There has to be some commonality between the areas being compared in order for the information obtained to be meaningful.

Second, it is important for the evaluator to be aware of the educational objectives against which the child and/or the environment are assessed. If the teacher develops a series of educational objectives for a reading group that are related to increasing word-attack skills, then the evaluation procedures used to assess the performance of each child in that reading group should reflect that curricular orientation. Likewise, the teacher decides that teaching word-attack skills will include using the Distar Reading Program. Evaluation of the environment, therefore, should be focused on observing and measuring the extent to which the Distar Reading Program is properly presented and satisfies all of the required procedures demanded by that system. Certain standards of presentation, student response, teacher reaction, and physical arrangement are necessary, indeed required, by the Distar Reading Program and other similar devices, to maximize the probability that each child satisfactorily will accomplish the tasks. If the teacher is unclear about the behavior objectives and has no firm concept about the character of the instructional environment that is predicted, it will be most difficult to focus the evaluative process and procedures precisely. Indeed, such vagueness inevitably will result in the evaluator's conducting an inefficient and ineffective assessment.

Structure Ongoing Evaluation

It is important that the process of evaluation be continuous and longitudinal. The observation and collection of data related to student performance and environment should be indebted within the total instructional program. This is not optional and, therefore, teachers must be careful not to avoid, ignore, or procrastinate collecting the appropriate educational data on the child and the environment. One way to avoid such delays is to incorporate the procedures into the routine daily activities. Do not put it off. Teachers should set up an appropriate system of evaluation that will force them to avoid deferring this important activity until later.

There are several other substantive considerations, which are somewhat technical, that evaluators should consider prior to entering the process. For the most part these pertain to the collection of data on the child as well as on the environment.

1. Be precise and specific in establishing the goals, objectives, and procedures of the evaluation program. Know with certainty the steps that should be taken in evaluating a child and the environment. Have definite plans and procedures outlined before the evaluation takes place. This will avoid inefficiently using an approach that might not be productive. A helpful guideline is to write out in specific, measurable terms what you are seeking to determine.

2. Be able to generalize your observations about a child or the child's environment beyond a certain evaluative event. You want any conclusions that you may draw to be reasonably accurate reflections of what is typically the case. You can increase the generalization of information by employing these guidelines:

a. Collect data consistently over a period of time. Do not be satisfied with gathering information on a single occasion and then assuming that the information collected reflects the typical or usual situation for either the child or the environment.

b. Collect data within the context of the child's usual or natural environment. This will involve your judging *usualness* by constantly observing the prominent characteristics of the environment with which the child interacts and then taking note of any particular deviations either in the youngster's behavior or in his/her environment.

c. Use a variety of procedures or evaluative devices to collect and assess information about the child and the environment. It is often desirable to ask another person to make a second evaluation simply to check on the reliability of your own observations.

d. Ignore information, whether about the child or the environment, that is retrospective or primarily impressionistic. Certainly it is appropriate and important to construct hypotheses about the consequences of certain environmental characteristics on the child's behavior. However, be sure that such information is clearly labeled as hypothetical and not viewed as "truth" until objective verification has been developed and presented. There are always hazards involved in using information that is accumulated by asking people to recall a certain situation. Such material inevitably is inaccurate. Do not depend on your own recollections; do not ask someone to comment on a child's behavior or the characteristics of an environment that demand information that is derived from subjective hindsight.

e. Secure data in a direct and objective way. It is often tempting to talk about a "socially permissive classroom" or to characterize a child as "psychologically distressed." In each instance the description defies direct observation until such time as the evaluator clearly describes what exactly constitutes a permissive environment and what variables are descriptive of psychological distress. For example, if a "socially permissive classroom" is one characterized by children's being able to speak without raising their hands, leaving their desks whenever they wish without permission, and doing whatever work they desire for a portion of the day, then all these behaviors can be observed and measured through direct observation. "Psychological distress" could be characterized by lack of spontaneous language by the child, an unwillingness to interact with peers of same sex or excessive absenteeism from school. While we might quarrel with those three factors as being a manifestation of psychological distress, we cannot legitimately take exception to the view that each can be observed directly and appropriately quantified. Evaluators should overcome the temptation to use vague and ill-defined terms; they should focus exclusively on dimensions that can be observed and measured directly. Another helpful guideline is to ask, "How much agreement can I expect if someone else were observing the child or the environment at the same time I am conducting the evaluation?"

    f.   Simplicity should be a foundation on which all evaluative policies and procedures are founded. Try as much as possible to avoid developing a complicated plan for observing, collecting, and interpreting information about the child and the environment. Be direct, precise, and efficient in all of the procedures used during the evaluative phase.

Child Evaluation

The major purpose for evaluating children is to learn how to manipulate their environment so that their individual behaviors can be managed effectively and efficiently. This book has focused on one of the important segments involved in this process, the assessment of the educational environments. Although this has constituted the major focus of this text, it is equally necessary for evaluators systematically and appropriately to collect relevant data on youngsters. They must relate those data to information collected about the environment within which the behavior occurred. This section will reiterate some of the major concepts required to accurately assess the child.

Recognize Individual and Group Variability

People perform in ways that may be very similar but often they do so for reasons that are significantly different. We cannot legitimately assume that identical values, attitudes, or performances of children have a similar origin, cause, or characteristics. Just as it is obviously inappropriate to treat all infections with the same type of medication, it is equally unacceptable to consider providing an identical curriculum, methodology, or instructional media for children who may have similar characteristics. Difficulties in learning—whether they are mainly social, intellectual, personal, communicative, or otherwise—should be treated individually, according to each youngster's unique profile of characteristics. This means, we believe, that the teacher must become skilled in continuously evaluating and assessing signs of strengths and weaknesses within the classroom setting.

One matter on which most teachers would agree is that substantial variation usually exists on most all dimensions within a group of children. Let's assume that we are concerned about studying arithmetic computation achievement of children who are in the fourth grade in a large school system. We might administer a standardized battery of achievement tests in arithmetic and calculate the overall arithmetic computation achievement score for each child. On the basis of these data, it would be possible to construct a curve of achievement for the entire group of students. If we had enough subjects, we would expect to see a relatively normal distribution of scores, much like the theoretical curve of intelligence with which teachers are all too familiar. This curve would show that certain children perform arithmetic computations much above the general average for the total group; other children from the same population perform relatively lower than the group average.

It really makes no difference what school variable we select. We would receive the same type of distribution of scores if we had decided to study achievement in reading, comprehension, motor performance, penmanship, broad jumping, or repeating digits. It is a simple fact that we all vary in performance to different degrees when we are compared with other people who are members of the population of which we are a representative.

We could further separate the population of children tested on whatever variable desired, say, by sex. All of the males that were tested could be grouped and their performance on the arithmetic computation test could be compared with that of a group of females. There may or may not be distinguishing characteristics between these two groups in arithmetic computation achievement.

Recapitulate for a moment. When we tested all of the fourth grade children, differences in their performance were manifest; this might be termed *inter-individual variability*. When the entire group was separated according to certain criteria, another type of variability was manifest, *inter-population variability*. In the second case we may have observed that the males as a group did relatively better in arithmetic computation than the females as a group. A third type of variability is one which Kirk (1972) has termed *intra-individual variability*. This is exhibited by way of analyzing the performance of individual children on the subtasks that are contained within a larger area such as arithmetic computation.

We could select two youngsters both of whom are performing in arithmetic at the same general level, but each of whom has a different cluster of strengths and weaknesses among the subtasks in the larger area, arithmetic computation. For example, one child may have difficulty in organizing the problems so that the columns are in proper form and the answers are recorded accurately. Another child may have relative weaknesses in carrying addition or borrowing in subtraction or in understanding the general concepts of place value. While the two boys may be underachieving in arithmetic at exactly the same general level, it is patently clear that the focus for the remedial program would differ greatly between the boys. These are intra-individual differences, and they have significant meaning for the focus of instructional programs.

If a teacher is not aware of the different reasons for each youngster's problem, there will be a tendency to provide the same instructional program for all youngsters. For example, the familiar technique for dealing with children who have serious achievement problems is to offer some sort of individual tutoring as remediation. This focus, unfortunately, is misplaced, for the best tutor in the world can provide the most inappropriate remedial instruction if the child's relative strengths and weaknesses within the area needing the remediation have not been developed and identified. Remediation in and of itself is inappropriate unless it considers the individual weaknesses of each child. If the wrong approach is offered to the wrong child, the entire tutorial experience is destined to fail. It is our opinion that the field of education is aggressively moving toward the viewpoint that all teachers need to be able to observe and collect appropriate data within the confines of the classroom in order to formulate an appropriate instructional program. Teachers need to examine both the child's behavior and their own behavior in an effort to identify possible reasons for and potential contributors to the limited performance of the child in some particular area. Having done this, the teacher must then appropriately deal with the environment to increase the potential for the child to learn within a reasonable period of time and at a satisfactory level of performance. Children vary a great deal within themselves, not only among subject areas but also at various times during their development. Appropriate teaching requires that subject matter, instructional methodology, and materials or media of instruction be designed to meet each child's particular needs after consideration of what are realistic educational objectives for the youngster.

Use a Systematic Process

A number of models have been developed to provide some structure for collecting appropriate data on a child in a rationally sequenced fashion. The general view of most of the models is that the initial level of assessment should be relatively broad

Careful evaluation of the child and environment provides direct evidence for building a sound educational program.

and as informal as possible. As information is collected at a more general level, hypotheses concerning the types of weaknesses in performance by a given child are developed, and further more penetrating evaluative procedures are developed at a relatively more formal level. In this latter case, the evaluation usually makes use of formal diagnostic instruments. Smith (1971) has described a simple flow chart which delineates various stages in the evaluative process (see Figure 18). Suppose we elaborate briefly on each of the various stages in this flow chart.

Level I.   At Level I the child should be observed by teachers, parents, and others for relatively obvious disorders that could subsequently influence the child's performance socially, emotionally, intellectually, linguistically, or in terms of speech development. Problems that could be identified at this level of review include turned-in eyes, serious delays in language development, unintelligible speech, hearing problems, significant lags in physical development, unexplainable lethargy, continuous anger or hostility, self-destructive behavior, and other forms of maladaptive behavior.

It is virtually impossible to be specific about what constitutes "gross disorders" in any of these areas; however, as a guide, simply note the frequency of the occurrence of the behavior in question over a period of time. Then compare this frequency with that of other children in the classroom. If the frequency is inordinately high or low (in the case of desired behaviors), it may be advisable to refer the youngster to the proper specialist as early as possible. At this level of evaluation it is always better to err on the side of overreferral to a specialist than to allow a significant problem to prevail. Conditions that are relatively serious and that go unattended will inevitably generate a whole galaxy of related problems that will only further complicate the child's educational future.

Level II.   On the assumption that the problems identified at Level I receive proper attention, at Level II a determination is made of the existence of possible problems in learning. Most commonly, this determination is based on the youngster's achievement test scores. This procedure for most teachers, simply involves profiling the achievement test scores of individual children in a number of educational areas. Once the profile has been completed, it is a simple matter to identify areas in which a youngster seems to be relatively weak and those in which he/she may be relatively strong. In fact, most standardized achievement tests that are used by school systems provide a mechanism for teachers to record achievement test scores for individual children using a profiling format.

Level III.   At Level III a teacher moves from a relatively broad evaluative style to an investigation of the particular and specific characteristics of the learning problems that have been identified at the preceding levels. This more penetrating analysis could involve the administration of specific formal diagnostic tests that have been developed to probe into precise skill areas. For example, the Diagnostic Chart for Fundamental Processes of Arithmetic, the Gray Oral Reading Tests, and the Spache Diagnostic Reading Skills are illustrative of such formal diagnostic approaches.

It is at this level that teachers may require the advice and assistance of a trained school psychologist or educational diagnostician. Many of the diagnostic

FIGURE 18   Flow chart for diagnostic-remedial process

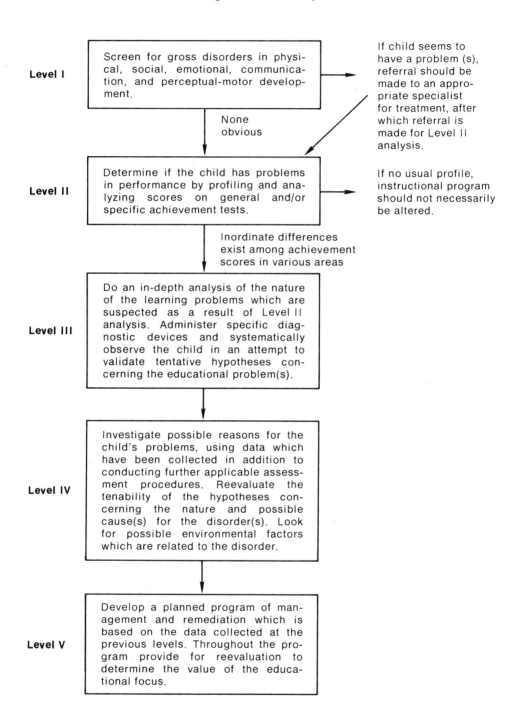

Source: From *"An Introduction to Mental Retardation"* by R.M. Smith, p. 38. Copyright 1971 by McGraw-Hill. Reprinted by permission.

tests that have been developed require a level of supervised clinical experience by the administrator which often surpasses the training and background of teachers. This is not to suggest, however, that the teacher should automatically turn over responsibilities for investigating performance weaknesses through the use of formal diagnostic devices. We feel that a teacher should be alert to the knowledge requirements and the clinical experience demanded of the recommended evaluative instruments. Teachers should not use formal diagnostic instruments if the administration and interpretation of these devices assumes that the test administrator has had special training. At Level III in the flow chart a teacher may wish to consult other school personnel while conducting an in-depth analysis of the character of the child's learning problems.

From the diagnostic clues obtained, the teacher can decide in which direction to move for purposes of obtaining even more information. For example, the teacher might be suspicious about a test for auditory or visual memory problems or difficulty in discrimination, sound blending, left to right progression, and/or reversals. Problems in any of these specific areas could, indeed, influence a child's performance in more general aspects of various subject areas, and the teacher will want to determine whether it is advisable to proceed with more intensive evaluation of any of these problems.

Level IV.   An attempt should be made to identify the possible causes for the educational disorder at Level IV. In the preceding three levels some effort was made to identify characteristics of the difficulty. Observation of a child's behavior might reveal that the youngster's difficulties are caused by problems such as

1.   Exposure to an instructional program that is inconsistent or ambiguous.
2.   Association with an improperly sequenced course of study.
3.   An inability to work under conditions of speed.
4.   Too much pressure to achieve from the parents or the teachers.
5.   Difficulty in following directions, or
6.   Unpleasant behavior which was rewarded.

Such factors might be possible causes for educational difficulties, and the teacher or parent might well want to collect data that will serve to verify one or more of these hypotheses. Levels I, II, and III in this proposed evaluative process focus primarily on assessing the child's performance. The focus in Level IV reflects the importance of assessing the characteristics of the environment that may either foster or hinder the child's learning.

Level V.   From the previous data, then, core areas of difficulty can be delineated and hypotheses generated concerning possible reasons for a youngster's doing poorly in certain subject areas. Evidence collected from the student and from the student's instructional environment can be used to plan an appropriate program of placement and remediation. Such a plan is based on evidence and not on impulsive or random selection of any instructional technique that might seem appropriate. Fundamentally, teachers have available the child's curriculum, the methods of instruction, materials used for teaching, and the physical setting. These may be manipulated to determine how best to work with each youngster's educational needs.

Some Additional Thoughts

We urge that each teacher consider the advantages in making use of informal evaluative strategies on a day-to-day and week-by-week basis within the classroom. There are a multitude of advantages in using information that has been collected informally as a basis for the design of an appropriate instructional environment. First, the teacher is in the best position to assess educational problems of the child because the rapport between teacher and student typically is stronger than between the child and other adults. Second, the teacher has more opportunity to observe the characteristic behavior of a child than, in many instances, even the parents have. Third, the classroom environment provides a setting in which the child's performance can be observed in a realistic and not contrived circumstance.

The types of activities that the teacher can use informally to observe and diagnose school-related disorders are important. Smith (1969) has suggested that teachers who are disposed toward using informal diagnostic observations consider the following criteria in selecting activities:

1.   The activities used for the purposes of evaluating a skill should be part of the ongoing program and should not be used in a contrived environment. The informal diagnostic activity should be incorporated into the daily classroom routine.

2.   Activities in which the child is engaged should be interesting so that attitudinal or motivational difficulties do not complicate the child's performance. Select the content of each activity so that it is compatible with the ongoing instructional sequences and inherently interesting to the child. A necessary prelude to evaluation using informal devices is to determine the types of activities that are going to interest each youngster.

3.   Diagnosing activities should be selected to measure specific educational dimensions. It is essential for the teacher to have a clear picture of the educational dimensions to be measured. After the behavior to be evaluated has been identified, the activities should be chosen.

4.   Activities should be presented so that each youngster's performance can be measured directly in specific skill areas. Do not select tasks that require inordinate assumptions, extrapolations, or generalizations that exceed the data. For example, just because a child does poorly in arithmetic computation, do not assume that the same child necessarily will show faulty arithmetic reasoning skills. Determination of this specific issue can only be made after asking the youngster to perform certain arithmetic reasoning activities that are designed specifically to check on reasoning skills.

5.   Every diagnostic activity should be selected for objectivity, and every attempt should be made to control possible sources of bias in the collection, interpretation, and translation of the data. To reemphasize the point: remember to

report observations only and do not succumb to the temptation of overclassifying or overinterpreting behavior.

6.   Activities should be varied enough so that the child does not become too familiar with the tasks.

7.   Children should be tested on more than one occasion in order to gain reliable evaluation of performance. Observations and other assessment devices are unreliable to some extent, and it is important to make sure that ample data on numerous occasions are gathered.

In summary: it is important to recognize that child assessment is not the sole responsibility of the school psychologist or educational diagnostician. Indeed, an assessment of the child should involve everyone who has some responsibility for the youngster's management. This could include the teacher, speech therapist, parents, physician, and others with whom the child has contact. The important fact is that each person understand the basic requirements related to observing behavior systematically and maintaining accurate records over time. Pertinent data can and should be collected through both formal and informal approaches; however, the types of information needed and the means by which the data are collected depend on the goals that the teacher has described for the child. Obviously, children with very profound disorders require more intensive diagnostic efforts than youngsters who are more mildly affected.

As data are collected systematically, patterns begin to emerge that allow for the development of hypotheses concerning the direction an educational program should take. As the program is implemented, it is important to continue reevaluating the child's performance in order to validate the appropriateness of the conclusions reached during the earlier evaluative stages. The ultimate check on whether the evaluation and remediation have been appropriate and effective is the extent to which performance changes occur in the individual child as a result of altering the environment.

Environmental Evaluation

Evaluation of the environment can occur either routinely, after an environmental change has been introduced, or in response to the appearance of problems believed to be environmentally caused. In an evaluation, existing environment-behavior conditions are compared either to criterion conditions, to conditions in a comparable environment, or to conditions as they were at some earlier time. These comparisons show whether the environment is performing as well as it should, as well as some similar environment, or as well as it has. Any of these comparisons can be used either to evaluate the effect of some change that has been introduced or simply as part of a periodic assessment. Using the assessment checklists at the end of the chapters will prove helpful in conducting this evaluation.

Sources of Error

Evaluations that attempt to "prove" that a change has worked introduce a number of problems concerning what constitutes acceptable evidence in the social sciences.

Good summary treatments of this issue are available with special emphasis on education (Campbell & Stanley, 1963; Kerlinger, 1973), environmental design (Heimstra & McFarling, 1974; Ittelson et al., 1974), and behavior change (Kazdin, 1975). Teachers are not held to the same standards of scientific rigor that apply to experimentalists. At the same time, however, they should be aware of some obvious traps. By being wary of these, teachers may avoid claiming success when the observed results actually could have been caused by something other than the environmental change being evaluated. The observed effect may have been caused by events outside the classroom. For example, less disruptive behavior in class may be the result of easing of racial tensions in the community rather than the teacher's new furniture arrangement. If the innovation was introduced in the fall, the true cause of the decrease in disruptive behavior may have been the usual settling down that occurs at the time. The behavior of the class may change simply because they know they are being observed, because discussions about the change have made them more aware of their own behavior, or because the children know what the teacher hopes to prove and are being cooperative subjects. If teachers are collecting the data, they may unwittingly shift criteria over time due to fatigue or a desire to see hypothesis confirmed. (*See* Rosenthal & Rosnow, 1969, for a discussion of other sources of subject and experimenter bias.)

A teacher may rearrange the classroom over the summer or employ new instructional materials and find that the children in the new school year are much more attentive and studious. The true explanation, however, may lie in the fact that a new class happens to be considerably above average in its studiousness. A particular class may be unique in a variety of ways, so that a treatment which is effective for it may not be effective for classes in general. A change in class composition during the evaluation, such as an extended illness of a leading troublemaker, may be the true cause of any effects noted rather than the environmental change under study. Lastly, there is the possibility of the famous *Hawthorne effect*, that is, the case where almost any change would have caused the same effect.

All these threats to validity can be reduced to three main types of potential error:

1.   Claiming change that did not actually occur.

2.   Giving the wrong reasons for a change that did occur.

3.   Believing (erroneously) that what was successful with one particular class will be successful in general.

Any of these errors can lead to a situation where what works for one teacher is a failure for another, or even where what works for a given teacher at one time does not do so later on. These are analogous to Type I Errors (accepting what should have been rejected). The reverse or Type II Error can also occur, for example, in a *delayed-reaction effect* that was *not* observed because the evaluation was terminated too soon.

It goes without saying that teachers do not have available to them all the paraphenalia for conducting evaluations which will help them totally avoid all sources of error. These include: elimination of change in all but the independent variable(s), quantification and controlled delivery of the independent variable(s), precise specification and measurement of the dependent variable(s), divorce of experimenter from the measurement process, random assignment of subjects to conditions, and hoaxing of subjects. However, let us examine some of the things teachers *can* do to avoid false evaluations.

Feasible Control of Sources of Error

As a first step to control errors, *explicitly state* which specific environmental changes are to have what effects on which behaviors. In other words, you must first state the hypothesis to be tested. If there is loose thinking at this stage, precision in the subsequent stages cannot atone for it. The original idea for the undertaking may derive from a fleeting observation, a casual remark, or a chance occurrence; all sorts of blue-sky brainstorming may follow. This is an expected and enjoyable part of the creative process. However, before the idea is ready to be *tested,* environmental elements, behaviors, and the relationships assumed to operate between them must be specified.

1.   Be sure to specify the *independent variable* (IV) of interest. State explicitly what circumstance (material, method, arrangement) you are evaluating.

2.   Likewise, specify the *dependent variables* (DV) of concern. State explicitly the events (child behaviors, assignments done, amount of noise) you expect to be influenced by the independent variable. For example, if you state that use of red chalk will increase attention, you have indicated an IV (use of red chalk) and a DV (increased attention).

3.   Verify the *delivery* of the new arrangement. You must be certain that the change you introduce is actually encountered by your students. Records need to be kept on individuals even if a group research design is being used; attendance records will suffice in some cases but not in all. If some children are not to be exposed to the change, they become the *control group,* and separation must be provided either through scheduling or through physical arrangements.

4.   Keep a record or diary of outside significant events that may have an influence on the new treatment. An example might be an extended run of poor weather that keeps children indoors more than usual and thus perhaps defeats an environmental modification to reduce aggression (compare to, Patterson et al., 1962).

5.   In considering when to begin and end a study, guard against the alternative explanation that the effects actually resulted from predictable events of the school year. Examples of these events include the settling-down in the fall, being confined indoors during the winter, and receiving college acceptance letters in the spring.

6.   Define the types of cases in which a procedure successful in one instance will be successful again *(maintenance).* Good descriptive records of students need to be kept on such dimensions as family background, aptitude, and achievement. Avoid selecting subjects for treatment on the basis of extreme scores. Children most in need (low achievement) or most likely to benefit (high aptitude) may at

first appear to be ideal candidates for treatment. Actually, in these cases effects that appear or fail to appear as a result of treatment may just as easily be explained as the statistical regression of extreme scores (Campbell & Stanley, 1966), and good results with able students do not guarantee comparable results with more typical students.

7.   Standardize and dimensionalize the new materials, social arrangement, or physical circumstances of the effects being evaluated so that you can determine and record with precision how many units were actually delivered to each subject. How many minutes on how many days did Sally spend in the new learning center? How many times was Mike's wrist slapped?

8.   The introduction and termination of treatment should be clearly defined and abrupt. For example, it would be very difficult to determine effects associated with the onset of treatment in the case of a new room arrangement that took a week to complete during which time class was meeting as usual.

9.   The shorter the experimental period, the better, since the effects of outside events are easier to control. Treatment obviously has to be administered enough times to allow an effect to occur, but no longer. This judgment is based partially on the logic of the research and partially on statistical analysis. For statistics, you should rely on the school system's research department for guidance. Expert statistical opinion should also be sought on the question of how many subjects will be required to allow for interpretable results. Of course, in many if not most instances, you will not be concerned with any real statistical descriptions of results.

10.   If you are evaluating more than one condition, assignment of students to conditions should be done by randomization as much as possible.

11. In the *ideal* case, neither the children nor the teacher would know that something new was being evaluated and that they were being observed. In addition, observers would not know what the changes were or what results were expected. The real situation at times may be almost the opposite. However, the potentially biassing effects can be minimized. Avoiding questionnaires or other pretests that may sensitize the children to the dependent measure of the research, delivering treatment in ways that do not highlight when and under what conditions treatment is being received and by whom, and avoiding distracting observation or recording techniques may lessen the biassing effect. If teachers are going to collect their own data, use of categories not subject to interpretation is preferable; for example, a count of "time away from desk" instead of "teacher evaluation of class attentiveness." Measures that reflect or suggest an evaluative component should also be avoided so that neither teachers nor students feel that their standing or prestige is linked to the success of the new circumstances. This could have a powerful biassing effect.

The procedures just described will not guarantee valid and generalizable research results. However, they will at least help insure that the basic premises or hypotheses have been stated clearly, that the independent and dependent variables have been defined in measurable terms, that some gross student subject and teacher bias has been minimized, and that major influences outside the classroom setting have been considered and their effects kept to a minimum. Using these procedures can help the teacher attain the objective of good research design, which is to reduce the persuasiveness of plausible alternative hypotheses, so that the most convincing explanation for the observed results is that the environmental manipulation had or did not have the desired effect. As long as one or more competing explanations of the observed results are possible, the hypothesis has not been properly tested.

A number of reasonably simple experimental designs is presented in Bechtel (1974), Campbell (1969), Campbell and Stanley (1966), and Kazdin (1975). Some of these appear to be appropriate for teacher evaluation of the effect of environmental changes. Selection of which design to use would depend on the nature of the hypothesis, limitations of the classroom situation, and statistical considerations. These will be discussed in terms of group design. If data are kept on individuals within groups as well, however, more compelling evidence may be available since effects on individuals are not brought together into a group mean.

Reversal Design.   The teacher may well find a class that cannot be divided into an experimental and a control group. One option would be the *reversal design* in which measures are taken continuously and the treatment is presented and removed a number of times. If behavior shows a change during each treatment and returns to pretreatment levels at other times, a convincing demonstration has been made. For example, the hypothesis of greater student attentiveness in windowless classrooms might be tested in regular classrooms by drawing the blinds on randomly selected days while continuously measuring attentiveness. A design similar to the reversal design can be used if the behavior change has a tendancy to endure and stabilize at some new level. If it does so with each reintroduction of treatment, the demonstration is highly convincing. This raises an important point: one properly designed and conducted experiment may show that a treatment is having an effect, but a whole series of studies may be required to show precisely *why* it is doing so. For teachers, however, sure knowledge that it works may be enough, leaving it to theorists to discover why.

Multiple Baseline.   Before leaving the subject of research designs dealing with the class as a whole, another useful type is the *multiple baseline* in which the effect of treatment on behavior is demonstrated by the sequential introduction of treatment to settings or individuals. For example, to test a hypothesis that student aggression varies inversely with lighting levels, every week or so the lights could be turned down in an additional part of the room while disputes, fights, and other hostile behaviors are continuously recorded. Behavior in a given part of the room should be unchanged until the illumination is lowered there, at which time it should show a decrease. Note that this design is not appropriate if behavior change in one part of the room will cause changes elsewhere in either direction.

Group Designs.   Turning to group designs, one which is frequently used attempts to use one class as a control group for another. True control groups are, of course, formed by random assignment and all circumstances are identical for both groups except receipt or nonreceipt of treatment. This will seldom be the case in schools. The more these requirements are approximated, however, the more convincing the demonstration will be. Persuasiveness will also be increased if the treatment is introduced sequentially in a number of classrooms (multiple baseline, discussed earlier). In this instance each classroom is compared to itself for the effect of treatment and to others for effects other than treatment. The simplest design with just two classrooms, one the control group and the other the experimental group, would involve pretest in both classrooms, introduction of treatment in one of the classrooms, and a posttest in both of them. In a variant of this test repeated measures are taken in both classrooms before and after the introduction of treatment in one of them. We would hope to see a shift in the experimental group but none in the control group. Compared to a single pretest and posttest, the *repeated-measures group design* presents more compelling evidence that effects should be attributed to treatment rather than to some external factor(s).

It would be very unsatisfying for a teacher to go to a great deal of effort in testing an idea, only to be shown at the end that the results can be explained in at least one other way, thus invalidating the whole demonstration. The simple designs discussed here can reduce that possibility. Bear in mind, though, that just as no amount of statistical sophistication can compensate for poor experimental design, so no amount of design sophistication can compensate for a poorly conceptualized and implemented hypothesis. Exotic experiments to test ideas that were never well formulated in the first place are all too common in contemporary research, and education is no exception. Teachers who are well grounded in the reality of the classroom have a real contribution to make in increasing the quality and relevance of educational research. A good teacher is constantly running mini-experiments and evaluating their success. The results help the teacher to adjust and to change aspects of the instructional setting.

The Dimensions of Environments and Behavior

Educational research often deals with measures such as improvement in achievement scores over one or more school terms. However, in assessing the effect of environmental changes on student behavior, much more direct and immediate measures are required. This section will discuss some appropriate measures and measurement methods. Since we will be studying the effect of environment on behavior, we must be able to dimensionalize accurately and to measure both environments of interest and behaviors of interest.

Environmental dimensions you may wish to measure include those variables discussed earlier in each chapter on the several aspects of the instructional environment. The Assessment Checklists specify the many concerns that may suggest changes in materials, methods, social arrangements, and physical settings. When you make changes, you will then want to evaluate the effect these changes have on student performance.

Evaluation of changes in student performance as a direct result of changes in the instructional environment must be carried out with more precision and immediacy than is typically the case in assessing student achievement. It may be useful to obtain general measures of general student progress, but such measures do not reflect on the specific new practices or arrangements you may wish to evaluate.

While the ultimate goal of schooling may be to increase the child's cognitive capacity, social empathy, and so forth, these are poor dimensions for our purposes. Both in terms of latencies and measurement of change they are unsatisfactory. What we require are behavior dimensions that are educationally relevant, environmentally influenced, subject to change within a reasonably short time span, high in rate, subject to repeated measurement, reliably measurable, and easily recorded. If possible, they should also be *nonreactive* (the process of measurement does not influence the measurement obtained), and *unobtrusive* (subjects are not aware that their behavior is measured or observed). If behavior changes are being measured on several dimensions, they should be unambiguous, mutually exclusive, and exhaustive, so that relevant behavior is neither overlooked nor overcounted. The behavior dimensions should be appropriate to the sampling method being used. Some environmentally influenced behavior that teachers would have an interest in are these:

1. **Academic:** in-seat and working, responding, facing teacher, disrupting, reading, unattentive, investigating, and doodling.

2. **Social:** helping, annoying, destructive, isolated, fighting, interrupting or hindering, comforting, watching, conversing, or sharing.

3. **Self-care:** dressing, washing, and toileting.

4. **Spatial:** distance from other children, number in group, location in room, and seating preferences.

The teacher can add to this list in these areas and in other areas such as nonacademic cognitive activity, play, participation in organized games, and artistic expression. As will be discussed, teacher behavior as well as student behavior can be recorded; for example, proportion of day the teacher spends maintaining order and enforcing rules.

The Measurement of Behavior

Once the specific behaviors of interest have been selected, it is necessary to select a method of measuring them. The method chosen will be governed by the purpose of the research, the nature of the behavior, the equipment and/or personnel available for the research, the nature of the place and situation in which the observation is occurring, and the statistical analysis proposed. These five considerations are highly interrelated. If the behavior is low in frequency, it must be recorded every time it occurs so that the difference in frequencies before and after treatment will be of sufficient magnitude for tests of statistical significance. This is especially true of behaviors that are both low in frequency and short in duration (fights).

Behavior Sampling.   Other behaviors that occur more frequently and/or are of longer duration allow the use of the *behavior sampling*. In its most common form the first subject is observed for about two minutes and his/her predominant behavior, location, associates, and/or stimulus materials are recorded every ten to fifteen seconds. The next student then will be observed, and then the next, until the first subject's turn comes again. The total length of observation will be determined by length of class, play period, or whatever situation the behavior is occurring in.

When sampling, it is important to guard against time bias. For example, children might very well be found to be more hyperactive if only the last class period in the day or only the last fifteen minutes of a class were observed. For other types of behavior the appropriate measure would be elapsed or total time. Teachers might record the time from the bell signaling beginning of class until 90–100 percent of the students are at work. Teachers interested in the efficiency of different classroom layouts might record the time it takes to set up for a movie or to clean up after arts and crafts.

Trace Measures.   Finally, for some behaviors it will be more efficient to record the number of students exhibiting the behavior at a given time, for example, number of children in-seat and at work, the number choosing the science and mathematics areas. At times it will be preferable to count not the behavior itself but some *trace measure* of it (Webb et al., 1966). Examples would include pieces of litter, number of paintings produced, items reported stolen or broken, number of rewards or prizes won, and number of toys not put away. The advantage of these trace measures of behavior is their unobtrusive and nonreactive quality. The disadvantage is that they do not tie behavior to persons and situations. Therefore, the prescription of treatment and analysis of results can never be so precise as with direct observation.

Observer-Recorded Behavior.   Of the various means available for recording behavior, the most commonly used system includes a set of well-defined behavior categories, an observer trained to use these categories, a stopwatch, and a sheet with the rows and columns labeled so that the observer with symbols can identify quickly the subject, the behavior, and various aspects of the environmental situation in which the behavior occurred. The on-site observer may be replaced by film or TV, and the pad may be replaced by tape recorder or event recorder, as described in Ittelson et al. (1974) and in Hutt and Hutt (1970a); the core of the system is still a set of well-defined categories and an observer to assign actual or reproduced behavior to those categories. Cartwright and Cartwright (1974) provide a useful guide to simple observational techniques for educators.

Self-Recorded Behavior.   In addition to observer-recorded behavior, there is self-recorded behavior. The simplest version of this employs a counter such as shoppers use in supermarkets. The count is increased by one each time the target behavior occurs. For example, you might record each time you say "now children." With two counters, you could also record each instance of using positive or negative reinforcement. Children could be asked to record each time they were interrupted in their study, or each time their work was delayed because of a lack of available space or equipment. If the children are capable of a more demanding task, they may be asked to self-record their behavior in a small diary. This would include the time each activity began and ended, the nature of the activity, the location, others present, and what caused the activity to terminate. In general, this form of self-recording is not appropriate for children except perhaps for major events of the day; for these a retrospective interview, as described in Michelson (1973), may do just as well. You may find the diary method useful in recording their own behavior, however. It provides much of the information of time-lapsed photography, without the need for special camera and projectors.

Only the simplest types of observation systems have been discussed, since these are the ones that teachers are most likely to have available. Fully automated systems have been used to monitor the movements of a laboratory rat colony (Olson, 1972), telemetry and brain implants have been used to control the behavior of a free-ranging baboon (Van Clitter & Franklin, 1975), and the EEG's of preschool children at play were monitored through the use of "spaceman helmets" (Hutt & Hutt, 1970b). (The interested reader can find a good summary of sophisticated applications in Mackay, 1968.) The approach and equipment used must help the teacher get accurate records of behavior without influencing that behavior. A human observer, showing obvious interest in what a particular child just did and quite obviously making some notation about it, is *not* unobtrusive. This would be especially true if the word had leaked out to the class that the study was about, "exploratory behaviors in femininized males." On the other hand, an observer sitting in some inconspicuous location in the room, paying attention to no particular child or type of behavior and giving no clues as to what and when was recorded would, in all probability, quickly fade into the background for the children. These same strictures and guidelines apply when the teacher is doing the recording. If equipment is being used, it should be silent, otherwise children will be reminded of its presence and—even worse—of what behavior is being recorded.

A school librarian is said to have ordered the book *Penguins of Antarctica* thinking children would enjoy it. When the first child returned it, the librarian began flipping through it and found on the last page in small handwriting the following: "This book told me more about penguins than I really wanted to know." Many people have probably said the same about their behavior inventories when they were completed. The disciplined observation of behavior is a challenging and fascinating activity, and there is the danger of overenthusiasm, of obtaining too much data rather than too little, of obtaining data that simply are not useful. Moreover, data that were truly essential may still have been ignored. The best protection is to state the hypothesis in terms that describe a relationship between specific behaviors and specific aspects of the environment, and then to set up an observation system to gather data about *those* environmental aspects.

Instruments for Evaluation.   If properly used, the Assessment Checklists and Environmental Profiles will highlight areas of deficiency and suggest effective changes to make. While an assessment can be made subjectively, it will be of more value if carried out in a structured manner while using objective instruments. The latter approach allows better comparisons to be made, either before and after for the same environment, between different environments, or between different raters. Moreover, merely dealing with a standardized instrument insures that questions are raised which might otherwise have been overlooked. This gives a more complete picture of how the environment supports the teaching program and what parts of it ought to be changed. This is why we urge you frequently to use the assessment checklists and profiles for each dimension of the instructional environment.

Through the Assessment Checklists a broad spectrum of affective, attitudinal, behavioral, and environmental data can be obtained. The checklists provide data that allow comparison with norms, other groups, or the same group at other time periods. They enable you to evaluate the environment as well as the effect of changes in the environment. These changes must be introduced in a quasi-experimental format, as explained earlier. The checklists are no substitute for the teacher's judgment based on a working familiarity with the class in its environment, but they will be a valuable aid in systematically monitoring and estimating the quality of the instructional environment.

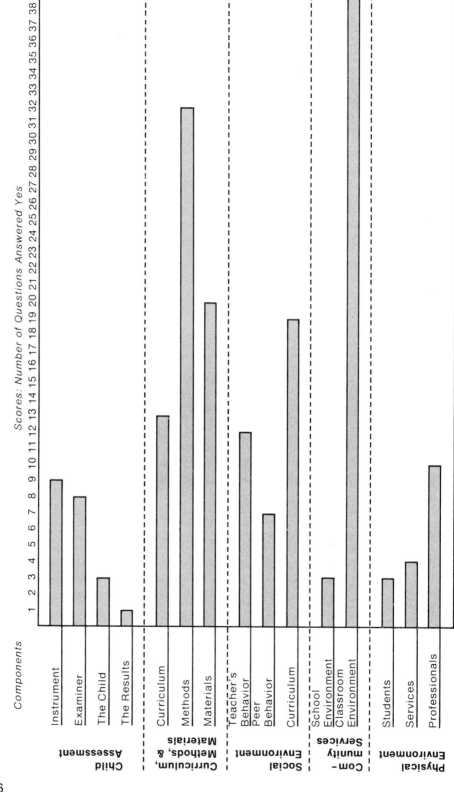

COMPREHENSIVE ENVIRONMENTAL PROFILE

Scores: Number of Questions Answered Yes

Components

196

References

Abeson, A., & Blacklow, J. Findings and recommendations. In A. Abeson & J. Blacklow (Eds.), *Environmental design; new relevance for special education.* Arlington, Va.: Council for Exceptional Children, 1971.

Adams, G. S. *Measurement in education, psychology and guidance.* New York: Holt, Rinehart, and Winston, 1964.

Adams, R. S., & Biddle, B. J. *Realities of teaching.* New York: Holt, Rinehart, and Winston, 1970.

Allee, W. C. *The social life of animals.* New York: Norton, 1938.

Allman-Snyder, A., May, L., and Garcia, M. Classroom structure and children's perceptions of authority. *Urban Educations,* 1975, *10,* 131–149.

Altman, I. *The environment and social behavior.* Monterey, Calif.: Brooks/Cole, 1975.

Altman, I. Privacy: A conceptual analysis. *Environment and Behavior,* 1976, *8*(1), 7–29.

American Psychological Association. *Standards for educational and psychological tests.* Washington, D.C.: APA, Inc., 1974.

Arehart-Treichel, J. The good, healthy shining light. *Human Behavior,* 1975, *4*(1), 16–23.

Arthur, R. J. Success is predictable. *Military Medicine,* 1971, *136,* 539–545.

Bandura, A. Psychotherapy based on modeling principles. In A. Bergin & S. L. Garfield (Eds.), *Handbook of psychotherapy and behavior change: An empirical analysis.* New York: John Wiley & Sons, 1971.

197

Bandura, A., & Kupers, C. J. Transmission of patterns of self-reinforcement through modeling. *Journal of Abnormal and Social Psychology*, 1964, *69*, 1–9.

Barker, R. G. *Ecological psychology*. Stanford: Stanford University Press, 1968.

Barker, R. G., & Gump, P. V. *Big school, small school*. Stanford: Stanford University Press, 1964.

Barker, R. G., & Schoggen, P. *Qualities of Community Life*. San Francisco: Josey-Bass, 1973.

Baron, R. A., & Lawton, S. F. Environmental influences on aggression: The facilitation of modeling effects by high ambient temperatures. *Psychonomic Science*, 1972, *26*, 80–82.

Barrish, H., Saunders, M., & Wolf, M. M. Good behavior game: Effects of individual contingencies for group consequences on disruptive behavior in a classroom. *Journal of Applied Behavior Analysis*, 1969, *2*, 79–84.

Battle, E. S., & Lacey, B. A context for hyperactivity in children, over time. *Child Development*, 1972, *43*, 757–773.

Bayes, K. *The therapeutic effect of environment on emotionally disturbed and mentally subnormal children*. London: Gresham Press, 1967.

Bechtel, R. B. Experimental methods in environmental design research. In J. Lang, C. Burnette, W. Moleski, & D. Vackon (Eds.), *Designing for human behavior*. Stroudsberg, Pa.: Dowden, Hutchinson, and Ross, 1974.

Becker, W., Engelmann, S., & Thomas, D. *Teaching: A course in applied psychology*. Chicago: Science Research Associates, 1971.

Bennett, C. A. Let's shed a little light. In D. H. Carson (Ed.), *EDRA five*. Milwaukee: Environmental Design Research Association, 1974.

Birch, J. W., & Johnstone, K. *Designing schools and schooling for the handicapped*. Springfield, Ill.: Charles C Thomas, 1975.

Bloom, B. C. *Stability and change in human characteristics*. New York: John Wiley & Sons, 1964.

Bloom, B. S. (Ed.). *Taxonomy of educational objectives, handbook I: Cognitive domain*. New York: David McKay, 1956.

Boocock, S. The school as a social environment. *Sociology of Education*, 1973, *46*, 15–50.

Braun, S. H. Ethical issues in behavior modification. *Behavior Therapy*, 1975, *6*, 51–62.

Bronfenbrenner, V. The graphic presentation of sociometric data. *Sociometry*, 1944, *7*, 283–289.

Bronzaft, A. L., & McCarthy, D. P. The effect of elevated train noise on reading ability. *Environment and Behavior*, 1975, *7*(4), 517–528.

Brown, E. C., & L'Abate, L. An appraisal of teaching machines and programmed instruction with special reference to the modification of deviant behavior. In C. M. Franks (Ed.), *Behavior therapy: Appraisal and status*. New York: McGraw-Hill, 1969.

Brown, L., Fenrick, R., & Klemme, H. Trainable pupils learn to teach each other. *Teaching Exceptional Children*, 1971, *4*, 18–21.

Bruner, Jerome S. The process of education revisited. *Phi Delta Kappan*, September 1971, *53*, 18–21.

Brunetti, F. A. Noise, distraction, and privacy in conventional and open school environments. In W. J. Mitchell (Ed.), *Environmental design: Research and practice.* Los Angeles: University of California, 1972.

Calhoun, J. B. A "behavioral sink." In E. L. Bliss (Ed.), *The roots of behavior.* New York: Harper, 1962.

Calvert, B. *The role of the student.* London: Rutledge and Kegan Paul, 1975.

Campbell, D. T. Reforms as experiments. *American Psychologist,* 1969, *24*(4), 409–429.

Campbell, D. T., & Stanley, J. C. *Experimental and quasi-experimental designs for research.* Chicago: Rand McNally, 1966.

Cartwright, C. A., & Cartwright, G. P. *Developing observation skills.* New York: McGraw-Hill, 1974.

Chenault, J. *Mental retardation as a function of race, sex, and socioeconomic status.* Unpublished doctoral dissertation, Michigan State University, 1970.

Cohen, H. L., Filipczak, J. A., Goldiamond, L., & Pooley, R. C. *Training professionals in procedures for the establishment of educational environments.* Silver Spring, Md.: Educational Facility Press, 1970.

Cohen, S., Glass, D. C., & Singer, J. E. Apartment noise, auditory discrimination, and reading ability in children. *Journal of Experimental Social Psychology,* 1973, *9,* 407–422.

Crowe, T. D., Pesce, E. J., Riemer, A., & Hanes, L. F. *Crime prevention through environmental design schools demonstration plan: Broward County, Florida.* Arlington, Va.: Westinghouse Electric Corporation, 1976.

Dawe, H. C. The influence of size of kindergarten group upon performance. *Child Development,* 1934, *5, 295–303.*

Deutsch, M., Fishman, J. A., Kogan, L. S., North, R. D., & Whitman, M. Guidelines for testing minority children. In D. Payne & R. McMorris (Eds.), *Educational and psychological measurement.* Waltham, Mass.: Blaisdell, 1967.

Dewey, J. *Experience and education.* New York: Macmillan, 1938.

Drew, C. Selected research: Effects of environmental manipulation. In A. Abeson & J. Blacklow (Eds.), *Environmental design: New relevance for special education.* Arlington, Va.: Council for Exceptional Children, 1971.

Durlak, J. T., Beardsley, B. E., & Murray, J. S. Observation of user activity patterns in open and traditional plan school environments. In W. J. Mitchell (Ed.), *Environmental design: Research and practice.* Los Angeles: University of California, 1972.

Edney, J. J. Human territories: Comment on functional properties. *Environment and Behavior,* 1976, *8*(1), 31–48.

Eebl-Eibesfeldt, E. *Ethology: The biology of behavior.* New York: Holt, Rinehart, and Winston, 1975.

Ekehammar, B. Interactivism in personality from a historical perspective. *Psychological Bulletin,* 1974, *81,* 1026–1048.

Esser, A. H. Dominance hierarchy and clinical course of psychiatrically hospitalized boys. *Child Development,* 1968, *39*(1), 147–157.

Esser, A. H. Cottage fourteen: Dominance and territoriality in a group of institutionalized boys. *Small Group Behavior,* 1973, *4,* 131–146.

Fischer, C. S., Baldassare, M., & Ofshe, R. J. Crowding studies and urban life: A critical review. *Journal of the American Institute of Planners,* 1975, *41*(6), 406–418.

Fishe, D. W., & Cox, J. A., Jr. The consistency of rating by peers. *Journal of Applied Psychology,* 1960, *44,* 11–17.

Flanders, N. A. *The role of the teacher in the classroom.* Minneapolis: Amiden and Associates, 1963.

Flanders, N. A. *Interaction analysis in the classroom: A manual for observers.* Ann Arbor, Mich.: University of Michigan School of Education, 1964.

Flanders, N. A. Interaction analysis: A technique for quantifying teacher influence. In H. G. Clarizio, R. C. Craig, & W. A. Mehrens, *Contemporary issues in educational psychology* (2d ed.). Boston: Allyn & Bacon, 1974.

Fox R., Luszhi, M. B., & Schmuch, R. *Diagnosing classroom learning environments.* Chicago: Science Research Associates, 1966.

Gardner, W. I. *Children with learning and behavior problems: A behavior management approach.* Boston: Allyn & Bacon, 1974.

Garner, G. Modifying pupil self-concept and behavior. *Today's Education,* 1974, pp. 26–28.

Gilbert, H. B. On the IQ ban. *Teachers College Record,* 1966, *67,* 282–285.

Glass, D. C., & Singer, J. E. *Urban stress: Experiments on noise and social stressors.* New York: Academic Press, 1972.

Gold, M. Factors affecting production by the retarded: Base rate. *Mental Retardation,* December 1973, pp. 41–45.

Goldenson, R. M. *The encyclopedia of human behavior.* Garden City, N.J.: Doubleday and Company, 1970.

Goodman, P. *New reformation.* New York: Random House, 1970.

Green, R. L. Tips on educational testing: What teachers and parents should know. *Phi Delta Kappan,* 1975, *57,* 89–93.

Griffitt, W., & Veitch, R. Hot and crowded: Influences of population density and temperature on interpersonal affective behavior. *Journal of Personality and Social Psychology,* 1971, *17*(1), 92–98.

Gump, P. V., Schoggen, P., & Redl, F. The camp mileu and its immediate effects. *Journal of Social Issues,* 1957, *13*(1), 40–46.

Gump, P. V., Schoggen, P., & Redl, F. The behavior of the same child in different milieus. In R. G. Barker (Ed.), *The stream of behavior.* New York: Appleton-Century-Crofts, 1963.

Haase, R. F., & DiMattia, D. J. Proxemic behavior: Counselor, administrator, and client preference for seating arrangement in dyadic interaction. *Journal of Counseling Psychology,* 1970, *17*(4), 319–325.

Hagen, J. W. The effect of distraction on selective attention. *Child Development,* 1967, *38,* 685–694.

Hall, E. T. *The hidden dimension.* New York: Doubleday, 1966.

Hall, J., & Baker, R. Token economy systems: Breakdown and control. *Behavior Research and Therapy,* 1973, *11,* 253–263.

Hall, R. V., Lund, D., & Jackson, D. Effects of teacher attention on study behavior. *Journal of Applied Behavior Analysis,* 1968, *1,* 1–12.

Hammill, D. D., & Bartel, N. R. *Teaching children with learning and behavior problems.* Boston: Allyn & Bacon, 1975.

Harrow, Anita J. *A taxonomy of the psychomotor domain.* New York: David McKay, 1972.

Hart, B. M., Allen, K. E., Buell, J. S., Harris, F. R., & Wolf, M. M. Effects of social reinforcement on operant crying. *Journal of Experimental Child Psychology,* 1964, *1,* 145–153.

Haywood, D. G. Psychological factors in the use of light and lighting in buildings. In J. Lang, C. Burnette, W. Moleski, & D. Vackon (Eds.), *Designing for human behavior.* Stroudsburg, Pa.: Dowden, Hutchinson, and Ross, 1974.

Heber, R. F., Garber, H., Harrington, S., Hoffman, C., & Falender, C. *Rehabilitation of families at risk for mental retardation: Progress report.* Madison, Wisc.: University of Wisconsin, 1972.

Heimstra, N. W., & McFarling, L. H. *Environmental psychology.* Monterey, Calif.: Brooks/Cole, 1974.

Hewett, F. M. *The emotionally disturbed child in the classroom.* Boston: Allyn & Bacon, 1968.

Hollander, E. P. Validity of peer nominations in predicting a distant performance criterion. *Journal of Applied Psychology,* 1964, *49,* 434–438.

Hutt, C., & McGrew, W. C. *Effects of group density upon social behaviors in humans.* Paper presented at the Association for the Study of Animal Behavior, Symposium on Changes in Behavior with Population Density. Oxford, England, July, 1967.

Hutt, C., & Vaizey, J. J. Differential effects of group density on social behavior. *Nature,* 1966, *209,* 1371–1372.

Hutt, S. J., & Hutt, C. *Behavior studies in psychiatry.* Elmsford, N.Y.: Pergamon, 1970a.

Hutt, S. J., & Hutt, C. *Direct observation and measurement of behavior.* Springfield, Ill.: Charles C Thomas, 1970b.

Ittelson, W. H., Proshansky, H. M., Rivlin, L. G., & Winkel, G. H. *An introduction to environmental psychology.* New York: Holt, Rinehart, and Winston, 1974.

Jensen, A. R. How much can we boost IQ and scholastic achievement? *Harvard Educational Review,* 1969, *39,* 1–123.

deJonge, D. Applied hodology. *Landscape,* 1967, *17,* 10–11.

Joyce, B. and Weil, M. *Models of teaching.* Englewood Cliffs, N.J.: Prentice-Hall, 1972.

Karnes, M. B., & Zehrbach, R. R. Curriculum and methods in early childhood special education: One approach. *Focus on Exceptional Children,* April 1973, *5,* 1–11.

Kazdin, A. E. *Behavior modification in applied settings.* Homewood, Ill.: Dorsey, 1975.

Kerlinger, F. N. *Foundations of behavioral research: Educational, psychological, and sociological inquiry.* New York: Holt, Rinehart, and Winston, 1973.

Kirk, S. A. *Educating exceptional children* (2d ed.). Boston: Houghton Mifflin, 1972.

Klienfeld, J. S. Classroom climate and participation. *Journal of Educational Research,* 1963, *67,* 50–52.

Koneya, M. Location and interaction in row-and-column seating arrangements. *Environment and Behavior,* 1976, *8*(2), 265–282.

Krathwohl, D., Bloom, B. S., & Masia, B. B. *Taxonomy of educational objectives, handbook II: Affective domain.* New York: David McKay, 1964.

Lahey, B. B. Modification of the frequency of descriptive adjectives in the speech of

Head Start children through modeling without reinforcement. *Journal of Applied Behavior Analysis,* 1971, *4,* 19–22.

Leavitt, H. J. Some effects of certain communication patterns on group performance. *Journal of Abnormal and Social Psychology,* 1951, *46,* 38–50.

Lindsley, O. R. Geriatric behavioral prosthetics. In Kastenbaum, R. (Ed.), *New thoughts on old age.* New York: Springer Publishing Company, 1964.

Loo, C. M. The effects of spatial density on the social behavior of children. *Journal of Applied Social Psychology,* 1972, *2,* 372–381.

Maccoby, E. E. Selective auditory attention in children. In L. P. Lipsitt & C. C. Spiker (Eds.), *Advances in child development and behavior* (Vol. 3). New York: Academic Press, 1967.

Mackay, R. S. *Bio-medical telemetry.* New York: John Wiley & Sons, 1968.

Madsen, C. H., Becker, W. C., & Thomas, D. R. Rules, praise, and ignoring: Elements of elementary classroom control. *Journal of Applied Behavior Analysis,* 1968, *1,* 139–150.

Mahoney, M. J. The self-management of covert behavior: A case study. *Behavior Therapy,* 1971, *2,* 575–578.

Mallenby, T. W. Personal space: Direct measurement technique with hard-of-hearing children. *Environment and Behavior,* 1974, *6*(1), 117–122.

Malott, R. W. A behavioral-systems approach to the design of human services. In D. Harshbarger & R. F. Maley (Eds.), *Behavior analysis and systems analysis: An integrative approach to mental health programs.* Kalamazoo, Mich.: Behaviordelia, 1974.

Marshall, N. J. Environmental components of orientations toward privacy. In J. Archea & C. Eastman (Eds.), *ADRA two.* Pittsburgh, Pa.: Carnegie Mellon University, 1972.

Martinello, M. L. Learning to teach from children's interests. *Educational Leadership,* 1973, *31,* 245–249.

Matczynski, T., & Rogus, J. Criteria for program analysis. *NASSP Bulletin,* 1975, *59,* 44–51.

McAllister, L. W., Stachowiak, J. G., Baer, D. M., & Canderman, L. The application of operant conditioning techniques in a secondary school classroom. *Journal of Applied Behavior Analysis,* 1969, *2,* 277–285.

McGrew, P. L. Social and spatial density effects on spacing behaviors in preschool children. *Journal of Child Psychology and Psychiatry,* 1970, *11,* 197–205.

McKenzie, H. S., Clark, M., Wolf, M. M., Kothera, R., & Benson, C. Behavior modification of children with learning disabilities using grades as tokens and allowances as back up reinforcers. *Exceptional Children,* 1968, *34,* 745–752.

Menzel, E. W., Jr. Naturalistic and experimental approaches to primate behavior. In E. P. Williams, & H. L. Raush (Eds.), *Naturalistic viewpoints in psychological research.* New York: Holt, Rinehart, and Winston, 1969.

Mercer, J. R. Sociological perspectives on mild mental retardation. In M. C. Haywood (Ed.), *Socio-cultural aspects of mental retardation.* New York: Appleton-Century-Crofts, 1970.

Meyer, J. L. How teachers can reach the disadvantaged. In J. J. Kaufman, & M. V.

Lewis, *The school environment and programs for dropouts.* University Park, Pa.: The Pennsylvania State University, 1968.

Michaelis, J. U., Grossman, R. H., & Scott, L. F. *New designs for elementary curriculum and instruction.* New York: McGraw-Hill, 1967.

Michelson, W. Time-budgets in environmental research: Some introductory considerations. In W. F. E. Preiser (Ed.), *Environmental design research* (Vol. 2). Stroudsberg, Pa.: Dowden, Hutchinson, and Ross, 1973.

Moos, R. H. *Evaluating treatment environments: A social ecological approach.* New York: John Wiley & Sons, 1974.

Moreno, J. L. *Who shall survive? Foundations of Sociometry, Group Psychology, and Sociodrams* (2d ed.). New York: Random House, 1953.

Nellist, J. *Planning buildings for handicapped children.* Springfield, Ill.: Charles C. Thomas, 1970.

Newland, T. E. Psychological assessment of exceptional children and youth. In W. Cruickshank (Ed.), *Psychology of Exceptional Children and Youth.* Englewood Cliffs, N.J.: Prentice-Hall, 1971.

O'Connor, R. Modification of social withdrawal through symbolic modeling. *Journal of Applied Behavior Analysis,* 1969, *2,* 15–22.

O'Leary, K. D., Kaufman, K. F., Kass, R. E., & Drabman, R. S. The effects of loud and soft reprimands on the behavior of disruptive students. *Exceptional Children,* 1970, *37,* 145–155.

Olson, L. E., Jr. Gross spatial motions of a social group within a complex environment. In W. J. Mitchell (Ed.), *Environmental design: Research and practice.* Los Angeles: University of California, 1972.

O'Neill, S. M., & Paluck, R. J. Altering territoriality through reinforcement. *Proceedings of the 81st Annual Convention of the American Psychological Association,* Montreal, Canada, 1973.

Paluck, R. J., & Esser, A. H. Territorial behavior as a indicator of changes in clinical behavior condition of severely retarded boys. *American Journal of Mental Deficiency,* 1971, *76*(3), 284–290.

Patterson, G. R. An application of conditioning techniques to the control of a hyperactive child. In L. P. Ulsmann & L. Krasner (Eds.), *Case studies in behavior modification.* New York: Holt, Rinehart, and Winston, 1965.

Patterson, G. R., Littman, R. A., & Bricker, W. Assertive behavior in children: A step to a theory of aggression. *Monographs of the Society for Research in Child Development,* 1962, *32*(5), 113.

Preiser, W. F. E. The use of ethological methods in environmental analysis: a case study. In W. J. Mitchell (Ed.), *Environmental design: Research and practice.* Los Angeles: University of California, 1972.

Quilitch, H. R., & Risley, T. R. Effects of play materials on social play. *Journal of Applied Behavior Analysis,* 1976, *6,* 573–578.

Rapoport, A., & Watson, N. Cultural variability in physical standards. *Transactions of the Bartlett Society,* 1967–68, *6,* 63–83.

Raush, H., Dittman, A., & Taylor, T. Person, setting, and change in social interaction. *Human Relations,* 1959, *12,* 361–378.

Reynolds, H. H. Efficacy of sociometric ratings in predicting leadership success. *Psychological Reports,* 1966, *19,* 35–40.

Rice, F. P. *The Adolescent.* Boston: Allyn & Bacon, 1975.

Robe, W., & Patterson, A. H. The effects of varied levels of resources and density on behavior in a day care center. In D. H. Carson (Ed.), *EDRA five.* Milwaukee: The Environmental Design Research Association, 1974.

Rosen, B. C., & D'Andrade, R. D. The psycho-social origins of achievement motivation. *Sociometry,* 1959, *22,* 185–195; 215–218.

Rosenthal, R., & Jacobsen, L. What teacher behavior mediates. *Psychology in the Schools,* 1975, *12,* 454–461.

Rosenthal, R., & Rosnow, R. (Eds.) *Artifact in behavioral research.* New York: Academic Press, 1969.

Ross, A. O. *Psychological aspects of learning disabilities and reading disorders.* New York: McGraw-Hill, 1976.

Russo, N. F. Connotation of seating arrangements. *The Cornell Journal of Social Relations,* 1967, *2,* 37–44.

Sameroff, A., & Chandler, M. Reproductive risk and the continuum of caretaking casualty. In F. D. Horowitz, M. Hetherington, S. Scan-Salapatek, & G. Siegel (Eds.), *Review of child development research* (Vol. 4). Chicago: University of Chicago, 1974.

Sanders, D. C. *Innovations in elementary school classroom seating.* Bureau of Laboratory Schools Publication No. 10. Austin: University of Texas, 1958.

Sarason, I. G., & Glanzer, V. J. Social influence techniques in clinical and community psychology. In C. C. Spielberger (Ed.) *Current topics in clinical and community psychology.* New York: Academic Press, 1969.

Secord, P. F., & Backman, C. B. Personality theory and the problem of stability and change in individual behavior: An interpersonal approach. *Psychological Review,* 1961, *68,* 21–32.

Shaftel, F. R., & Shaftel, G. *Role playing for social values: Decision making in the social studies.* Englewood Cliffs, N.J.: Prentice-Hall, 1967.

Sherman, A. R. *Behavior modification: Theory and practice.* Belmont, Calif.: Wadsworth Publishing Co., 1973.

Sherman, J. A., & Bushell, D. Behavior modification as an educational technique. In Horowitz, Frances Degen (Ed.), *Review of child development research* (Vol. 4). Chicago: University of Chicago, 1975.

Shinn, R. *Culture and school: Socio-cultural significances.* San Francisco: Intext Educational Publishers, 1972.

Sinclair, I. *Hostels for probationers.* London: Her Majesty's Stationery Office, 1971.

Skinner, B. F. *The technology of teaching.* New York: Appleton-Century-Crofts, 1968.

Skinner, B. F. *About behaviorism.* New York: Knopf, 1974.

Smith, R. M. *Teacher diagnosis of educational difficulties.* Columbus, Ohio: Charles E. Merrill Publishing Co., 1969.

Smith, R. M. *An introduction to mental retardation.* New York: McGraw-Hill, 1971.

Smith, R. M. *Clinical teaching: Methods of instruction for the retarded* (2nd ed.). New York: McGraw-Hill, 1974.

Smith, R. M., & Neisworth, J. T. *The exceptional child.* New York: McGraw-Hill, 1975.

Sommer, R. Leadership and group geography. *Sociometry,* 1961, *24,* 99–110.

Sommer, R. *Personal space: The behavioral basis of design.* Englewood Cliffs, N.J.: Prentice-Hall, 1969.

Sommer, R., & Becker, F. D. Room density and user satisfaction. *Environment and Behavior,* 1971, *3*(4), 412–417.

Spaulding, R. L. Personality and social development: Peer and school influences. *Review of Educational Research,* 1964, *34,* 588–589.

Starlin, C. Peers and precisim. *Teaching Exceptional Children,* 1971, *3,* 129–140.

Stebbins, R. A. Physical context influences on behavior: The case of classroom disorderliness. *Environment and Behavior,* 1973, *5*(3), 291–314.

Steinzor, B. The spatial factor in face-to-face discussion groups. *Journal of Abnormal and Social Psychology,* 1950, *45,* 552–555.

Stern, G. *People in context: Measuring person-environment congruence in education and industry.* New York: John Wiley & Sons, 1970.

Stevenson, H. W. *Children's learning.* New York: Appleton-Century-Crofts. 1972.

Stokols, D. The experience of crowding in primary and secondary environments. *Environment and Behavior,* 1976, *8*(1), 49–86.

Strauss, S. Learning theories of Gagne and Piaget: Implications for curriculum development. *Teachers College Record,* 1972, *74,* 81–102.

Strodtbeck, F. L., & Hook, L. H. Social dimensions of a twelve-man jury table. *Sociometry,* 1961, *24,* 297–415.

Studer, R. G. The dynamics of behavior-contingent physical systems. In H. M. Proshansky, W. H. Ittelson, L. G. Rivlin (Eds.), *Environmental psychology: Man and his physical setting.* New York: Holt, Rinehart, and Winston, 1970.

Sunderman, H., Hinely, R., & Simms, R. School subject matter for the inner city. *NASSP Bulletin,* 1975, *59,* 21–23.

Sundstrom, E., & Altman, I. Field Study of dominance and territorial behavior. *Journal of Personality and Social Psychology,* 1974, *30*(1), 115–125.

Surratt, P., Ulrich, R. E., & Hawkins, R. P. An elementary student as a behavioral engineer. *Journal of Applied Behavior Analysis,* 1969, *2,* 85–92.

Swassing, R. H. Parameters of classroom environment for beginning teachers. *Education and Training of the Mentally Retarded,* 1974, *9*(2), 89–92.

Sweetlove, H. W. *The concept of educational innovation as treated in selected professional journals.* Unpublished doctoral dissertation, Rutgers University, 1972.

Tannenbaum, A. J. A study of verbal stereotypes associated with brilliant and average students. Unpublished doctoral dissertation, Teachers College, Columbia University, 1959.

Tanner, O., & Tanner, L. N. *Curriculum development: Theory into practice.* New York: Macmillan, 1975.

Tarkin, R. W. Social exchange in the elementary school classroom: The problem of teacher legitimation of social power. *Sociology of Education,* 1975, *48,* 400–410.

Tars, S. E., & Appleby, A. The same child in home and institution: An observational study. *Environment and Behavior,* 1973, *5*(1), 3–28.

Tasseigne, M. W. A study of peer and adult influence on moral beliefs of adolescents. *Adolescence*, 1975, *10*, 227–230.

Thelen, H. *Education and the human quest*. New York: Harper and Row, 1960.

Thomas, D., Becker, W. & Armstrong, M. Production and elimination of disruptive classroom behavior by systematically varying teacher's behavior. *Journal of Applied Behavior Analysis*, 1968, *1*, 35–45.

Titus, R. M. *Environmental behavior modification: Responses of "isolate" preschool children to a cooperation-contingent treatment environment and associated changes in free play behavior*. Ann Arbor, Mich.: Dissertation Abstracts, 1975.

Tyler, R. W. The father of behavioral objectives criticizes them: An interview. *Phi Delta Kappan*, 1973, *55*, 57.

Van Clitters, R. L., & Franklin, D. L. *Blood pressure and flow telemetered from free ranging baboons*. Abstracts of the 23rd International Congress of Physiological Science at Tokyo, 1975.

Wagner, P. Children tutoring children. *Mental Retardation*, 1974, *12*(5), 52–55.

Watson, J. B. *Behaviorism*. New York: Norton, 1925.

Webb, E., Campbell, D., Schwartz, R., & Sechrest, L. *Unobstrusive measures*. Chicago: Rand McNally, 1966.

Weigand, D. A study of the extent to which peer group status interacts with the students perception of the classroom learning climate. *Dissertation Abstracts International*, 1973, *33*, 911.

Wexler, D. B. Token and taboo: Behavior modification, token economies and the law. *California Law Review*, 1973, *61*, 81–109.

Whaley, D. L., & Malott, R. W. *Elementary Principles of Behavior*. New York: Appleton-Century-Crofts, 1971.

Wicker, A. H. Processes which mediate behavior-environment congruence. *Behavioral Science*, 1972, *17*, 265–277.

Wicker, A. W. Undermanning theory and research. *Representative Research in Social Psychology*, 1973, *4*(1), 185–206.

Williams, E. P. Sense of obligation to high school activities as related to school size and marginality of student. *Child Development*, 1967, *38*(4), 1247–1260.

Wilson, E. O. *Sociobiology*. Cambridge, Mass.: Belknap, 1975.

Winkler, D. R. Educational achievement and school peer group composition. *Journal of Human Resources*, 1975, *10*, 189–204.

Winett, R. A., & Winkler, R. C. Current behavior modification in the classroom: Be still, be quiet, be docile. *Journal of Applied Behavior Analysis*, 1972, *5*, 499–504.

Wolfe, M. & Laufer, R. The concept of privacy in childhood: In D. H. Carson (Ed.), *EDRA five*. Milwaukee: The Environmental Design Research Association, 1974.

Wolfensberger, W. *Normalization*. Toronto: Leonard Crainford, 1972.

Wright, H. F. *Recording and analyzing child behavior*. New York: Harper and Row, 1967.

Wynne-Edwards, V. C. *Animal dispersion in relation to social behavior*. New York: Hofner, 1972.

Yarrow, M. R., & Campbell, J. D. Person perception: In children. *Merrill-Palmer Quarterly of Behavior and Development*, 1963, *9*, 57–72.

Zajonc, R. B. Social facilitation. *Science*, 1965, *149*, 269–274.

Index